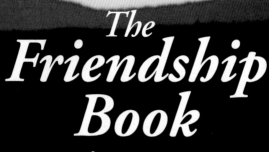

The
Friendship Book

of Francis Gay

A THOUGHT
FOR EACH DAY
IN 2010

D. C. THOMSON & CO., LTD.
London Glasgow Manchester Dundee

*Write it in your heart that every day is
the best day of the year.*

Ralph Waldo Emerson.

January

Friday — **January 1**

EVERY year the Lady of the House and I receive a card from our friend Harry wishing us a Happy New Year. One time he wrote these thought-provoking words beside a miniature drawing of a cottage, its door ajar in welcome.

Walls for the wind
And a roof for the rain,
And drinks beside the fire,
Laughter to cheer you,
And those you love near you
And all that your heart may desire.

This New Year I, in turn, wish you the same blessing for the year ahead. Happy New Year!

Saturday — **January 2**

ARE you thinking of starting a diary for this New Year? Well, did you know that at least a thousand years ago Japanese ladies would keep a Pillow Book?

Written at the end of each day, the Pillow Book was not so much an account of the day, but an account of the feelings of the day. These might best be expressed by poems, sketches, ideas, lists, memories or something that made you think.

In years to come your Pillow Book might not say much about what you did, but what better way to remember the pleasure in your heart.

Sunday — **January 3**

ONE of my favourite lines from the Lord's Prayer is: "Give us this day our daily bread."

It does not sound much to ask for and I'm sure most of us take for granted that there will be bread on the table, but we are the lucky ones. For many in the world there will be none or very little.

Perhaps we should sometimes quietly change the line to say "Thank you this day for our daily bread".

Monday — **January 4**

OUR old friend Mary has a little verse in a frame sitting on her mantelpiece. "It's always there to remind me," she says and she often recites it to visitors:

Life is an echo
That all comes back,
The good, the false
And the true.
So give to the world
The best you possess,
And the best will
Come back to you.

Wise thoughts to keep in mind at the start of this new year.

Tuesday — **January 5**

I WOULD like to share with you today these words by the sixteenth-century Italian writer Pietro Aretino :

"I keep my friends as misers do their treasure, because of all things granted us by wisdom, none is greater or better than friendship."

THE CALLING

Wednesday — **January 6**

WERNER von Braun, the father of the American space programme, met a clergyman at a fund-raising dinner. A space enthusiast, he quizzed von Braun about his work for most of the meal before the scientist had the chance to quiz him, in turn.

"Oh, my work is quite simple," the clergyman replied.

"Simple?" von Braun retorted. "I only show men the way to the moon, you show them the way to Heaven."

Thursday — **January 7**

THE clocks inside the jeweller's shop
  Were all set at ten to two,
To welcome people with a smile
  And stop them feeling blue.

But in another jeweller's shop
  On the other side of town
Twenty past seven said all the dials,
  Each clock displayed a frown.

And so it is with the face we show
  To the folk we daily meet,
And it is simply our choice
  Which face we use to greet.

So, don't be like those sad old clocks
  On the other side of town,
Just set your face at ten to two
  And banish every frown.
                    Colin Hammacott.

Friday — **January 8**

THE Lady Of The House had been visiting a dear friend who runs a playgroup. "It's so nice," she observed afterwards, "to see children learning to share. In fact, I sometimes think it's one of the most important lessons we ever learn."

Sharing is important in every aspect of our lives, and that includes knowledge, not just material things. When in the seventeenth century, the Dutch scientist Antonie van Leeuwenhoek used a home-made microscope to discover the existence of bacteria, he was just one of many of the great thinkers who have used their skills to benefit the rest of the world. He wrote:

"Whenever I found out anything remarkable, I thought it my duty to put down my discovery on paper, so that all ingenious people might be informed thereof."

Thank goodness for all those people who share so willingly — and no-one needs to make a microscope to see the sense in that!

Saturday — **January 9**

A GROUP of early explorers was pressing as fast as they could through the jungle. Day after day they urged their bearers to hurry on.

At last they had had enough. "We must rest," they said, "and let our souls catch up."

In today's busy world we can easily be in such a rush that we are often in danger of neglecting our souls, not giving them the peace they need. Those men have spoken wisely to us across the years.

THE FRIENDSHIP BOOK

OUR friend John says don't laugh at folk who keep saying, "Have a good day!" — just make up your mind to have one.

"Today is the day the Lord hath made; let us rejoice and be glad in it."   Psalms (118:24)

DASHING through a busy international airport, journalist Carl Honore caught sight of an advertisement for a collection of one-minute bedtime stories for children.

He hurried into the bookshop, thinking it would be the perfect way to make his two-year-old son's bedtime more "efficient" — then he stopped, apalled he could even think of trying to speed up such a precious time.

Looking around, he could see he wasn't the only person in a hurry. Everyone nearby was rushing around, speaking on mobile phones, while business meetings were being hastily held over cups of coffee.

Carl went home, sat quietly for a while, then began to write. His book "In Praise Of Slowness" contradicted the idea that faster is better; he urged people to slow down and enjoy the important things in life.

He described movements like the Slow Food Association, which promotes traditionally-prepared food.

Let's hope that some of the slower approaches which he recommended find their way into all our lives — and that his son enjoyed his longer storytimes.

THE VISITOR

Tuesday — **January 12**

WE all feel disheartened at times and it is easy to think that not bothering with a relatively trifling matter to help a friend or colleague — even a total stranger — is the easiest option. But take heed of these words from Aesop, author of the world-renowned fables:

"No act of kindness, no matter how small, is ever wasted."

Wednesday — **January 13**

*A HUG is a handshake that comes from
   the heart,
A welcome embrace after time spent apart,
A sweet "Good to see you", or loving "Godspeed",
Or perhaps just to comfort a friend who's in need.
For hugs have a meaning no handshake
   can hold:
To those you love best they are worth more
   than gold,
A warm, wordless gesture each human can share
That speaks your affection, and shows how
   you care.*

Margaret Ingall.

Thursday — **January 14**

THE Scottish writer Neil Gunn believed that all of us have great moments in our lives which he called "atoms of delight". He felt it was important for us to celebrate such times, to gather them up like treasure inside and remember them all our lives.

Everyone's store will be different, but each will be precious.

THE FRIENDSHIP BOOK

Friday — *January 15*

SANDRA was telling us about the course in English Literature from which she graduated as a mature student. "It's been such a fulfilling experience," she said, "and given me a whole new confidence in myself — and yet, I would never have thought of going back to full-time education if it hadn't been for a friend's suggestion.

"Thank goodness for those who open new doors for us, doors that otherwise we might never have noticed."

It's a point made clearly by writer and diarist Anais Nin in these words: "Each friend represents a world in us, a world possibly not born until they arrive, and it is only by this meeting that a new world is born."

I hope that we, too, can inspire others to create their own new worlds.

Saturday — *January 16*

SIR Edmund Hillary, who died in 2008, made history by being the first man to set foot on the summit of Mount Everest. Afterwards, in London, he was fêted and pressed for interviews.

For this most modest of men it was all too much. "I could not take it seriously," he said. "I mean, we'd only climbed a mountain!"

He used his fame and experience to set up the Everest Foundation to help the Sherpa people of the region by providing schools and other facilities. Tenzing Norgay, the Sherpa who had made it with him to the top, remained his friend for life. These two great men should never be forgotten.

*Sunday — **January 17***

SHIPWRECKED, alone and thousands of miles from home, Robinson Crusoe was a man without hope. Then he found a special book amongst his salvage.

"One morning, being very sad," he recalled, "I opened the Bible upon these words, 'I will never, never leave thee, nor forsake thee.' Immediately it occurred to me that these words were for me."

And for me. And for you . . .

*Monday — **January 18***

THE comfort of a cup of tea
 Suits any dire emergency.
It spreads its message far and wide,
 It bridges every known divide.
It seals our friendships, soothes our foes,
 Shares our gladness, mends our woes.
With cups of tea old friends are hosted,
 Weddings planned, new babies toasted.
Whether in bags or floating leaves
 This welcome beverage relieves.
To win the hearts of folk next door,
 Invite them in and say, "I'll pour!"

Joan Howes.

*Tuesday — **January 19***

ACHES and pains. Loneliness. Misunderstandings. If only there was one "cure", one single thing that could take the sting from all life's problems.

Well, Sophocles believed there was. "One word frees us from all the weight and pain in life. That word is love," he wrote.

Wednesday — **January 20**

THINK of these lines when everything outside is blanketed in snow; they were written by the Victorian poet Coventry Patmore, a librarian at the British Museum.

With the infant harvest, breathing soft below
Its eider coverlet of snow.
Nor is in field or garden anything
But, duly look'd into, contains serene
The substance of things hoped for,
in the Spring.

Let us join the poet in anticipation of the appearance of fresh, green shoots from the depths of the dark earth and the gradual unfolding of new leaves, for the earth only rests temporarily in Winter as part of the cycle of the seasons.

Thursday — **January 21**

I HAD to smile at this old Yiddish proverb. Soap and laughter aren't things I ever thought about comparing before, but it makes so much sense!

"What soap is to body," wise men of old said, "so laughter is to the soul!"

Friday — **January 22**

A CHEROKEE BLESSING

MAY the warm winds of heaven blow softly on your home,
And the Great Spirit bless all who enter there.
May your moccasins make happy tracks in many snows
And may the rainbow always touch your shoulder.

Saturday — *January 23*

I'M sure we all know the kind of person who fully intends to do this, that and the next thing — one of these days. If we're lucky we also know folk who quietly get on and do whatever they can, whenever they can.

To both sets of people I'd like to dedicate this old Chinese proverb: *Words are mere bubbles of water, but deeds are drops of gold!*

Sunday — *January 24*

THE eagle, it seems, has a unique ability. To conserve energy it can lock its wings in the outstretched position, gliding instead of flapping, waiting for the next current of air to lift it higher.

Our equivalent of that locking mechanism must surely be faith. Next time you feel yourself getting in a bit of a flap, just stop and glide a while, knowing that a wind of inspiration will be along shortly.

"Those who wait upon God get fresh strength. They spread their wings and soar like eagles."
(Isaiah 40:31)

Monday — *January 25*

YARD by yard, life is hard
Inch by inch, life's a cinch.

Just a few simple words by an anonymous writer but they add up to advice that's worth following. Don't waste time fretting about what's further down the road.

Take the situation in front of you, and just do the right thing. You'll find that many worries about the future will never come to anything, after all.

Tuesday — *January 26*

THE well-loved poet Alfred Tennyson referred to snowdrops as "the fairy firstlings of the year". They seem to spring up overnight upon the Winter scene taking us all by surprise.

It always amazes me that such dainty blooms, so delicate and fine, can meet icy winds, snow storms and harsh, freezing weather yet stand there brave and bold, quite undaunted.

Perhaps we could all learn a lesson from these fragile, little flowers with their secret inner strength.

Wednesday — *January 27*

HERE is a thought-provoking saying the Lady of the House read in a magazine:

You can make more friends in two months by becoming interested in other people than you can in two years by trying to get other people interested in you.

Thursday — *January 28*

THE story goes that Booker T. and the M.G.s recorded their classic instrumental track while waiting for a singer to turn up. Because it was a "throwaway" piece they named it after something that might be thrown away — and "Green Onions" has been evocative of the 1960s ever since.

Life is made up of lots of little moments and we might be tempted to simply throw some of them away, but remember, with a little effort and a little care each one has the potential to become a classic!

Friday — *January 29*

WE have a world wonderfully full of variety, but differences of race, culture, religion and lifestyle are, on occasion, the cause of conflict. The way forward was surely summed up perfectly by a young girl who died for these very reasons.

"We all live with the objective of being happy," Anne Frank wrote. "Our lives are different — and yet the same."

Saturday — *January 30*

THE writer J. R. Caldwell once recalled passing a Scottish croft as a woman stepped outside. She shaded her eyes and basked for a moment in the heat of the day.

"I've the whole sun all to myself," she sighed.

We are surrounded by blessings, if we only choose to see them.

Sunday — *January 31*

IN Amanda's secondary school there is a group of teenagers who meet on Wednesday mornings. Amanda brings along her guitar and they sing, pray and read the Bible.

On her guitar case is written this quote by American novelist Edith Wharton: *There are only two ways of spreading light — to be the candle or the mirror that reflects it.*

When we know God intimately His light shines through us, warming others, illuminating the way and making our steps secure.

"I love those who love me, and those who seek me diligently will find me." (Proverbs 8:17)

FROSTY FINGERS

February

A SHEPHERD recalled the time he set out to find his flock in a snowstorm, in conditions he called a "black drift". Colleagues told him it was too wild to venture outdoors but he insisted he could succeed. Hours later he was lost and cold.

Finding footprints in the snow, he followed them for a while before realising they were his own. He was walking round in circles with no idea where he was or the best way to safety.

Finally, he gave up and placed all his hope in his dog. Staying just within sight of his master, he led him unerringly to the flock and then back to the farm.

Sometimes life can be like that snowstorm and we end up lost and confused. That's when we need to put our faith in something other than ourselves and trust we'll be led safely home.

GEORGE Bernard Shaw was famous for his large output of plays and other writings. He once said, "Life is no brief candle for me. It is a sort of splendid torch which I have got hold of for the moment. I want to make it burn as brightly as possible before handing it on to future generations."

What a great aim to hold!

Wednesday — **February 3**

JOY and Sorrow were sisters. They grew up together but were very different in nature. Joy said, "I will go into homes and make people laugh and be glad."

Sorrow said, "I, too, will go into homes but bring people tears and sadness."

Joy shook her head. "Then you will never be welcome and will wander the world an outcast, while every door will be open to me and there will be a welcome on every hearth."

And so it has been ever since, for don't we all welcome Joy into our homes and hearts?

Thursday — **February 4**

A UNIVERSITY professor always started off his first lecture to new students with these words.

"It is not what you know that matters. What really matters is if you know how to learn."

It was his way of saying that he looked in his students for the enquiring mind that never shuts out but always lets in the light.

Not a bad aim for any of us.

Friday — **February 5**

A CORRESPONDENT has sent me these lines and I hope that you will enjoy sharing them today:

Time is . . .
Too slow for those who wait,
Too swift for those who fear,
Too long for those who grieve,
Too short for those who rejoice,
But for those who love —
Time is not.

Saturday — *February 6*

HOW strange, that deep in Winter's gloom
When all the world seems grey,
A sudden shaft of Winter sun
Can change the dullest day.
The buildings glow with golden light,
The pavements seem to gleam.
The puddles, just like splintered glass
Reflect each fragile beam.
The grass shines like a satin quilt
With stitches earthy brown,
Red berries glint in hedgerow's grasp
Like jewels within a crown.
And though this transformation may
Be quick to disappear
A little glimpse of Winter sun
Makes hope shine bright and clear.

Margaret Ingall.

Sunday — *February 7*

IS there a more cheerful sound than church bells ringing out on a Sunday morning?

Bells are believed to have been introduced to the Christian church around 400 AD in Campania, near Naples, and this custom spread across Europe over the centuries.

Their early purpose was to summon monks and nuns but gradually they were used to call local congregations to worship. Bells are at their most cheerful when rung for a wedding or some other happy occasion.

May our bells go on merrily ringing for many years to come!

Monday — **February 8**

THE Lady of the House went to see an amateur production of "No, No, Nannette", so I wasn't surprised to hear her humming the music the following day.

She saw me smiling. "Yes, I know it's an old-fashioned show," she said, "but I still think these words are as relevant now as they ever were. *'I want to be happy, but I can't be happy, till I make you happy too!'* is such a true sentiment. Bringing happiness to those we love is surely one of the greatest pleasures we ever experience."

She's right, of course — and I soon found that I couldn't stop humming that very tune!

Tuesday — **February 9**

WHEN Ellen was a child her grandmother said to her: "If you have the name of an early riser, you can stay in bed all day."

This is so true. We all know if you are late just twice in a row you can be labelled a "bad time-keeper" forever and if someone lets us down just once we tend to feel they are unreliable. It can take years of effort to erase these impressions.

The philosopher Socrates said: "The way to gain a good reputation is to endeavour to be what you desire to appear." If we want people to think well of us we must give them good reason to.

The best way to acquire a good reputation is simply to be true to ourselves. William Shakespeare probably expressed this best when he wrote: "This above all — to thine own self be true: and it must follow as the night the day, thou canst not then be false to any man."

Wednesday — **February 10**

AT the end of Nancy Spiegelberg's poem "Repeat Performance" are two inspirational lines that tell us all we need to know about human frailty and God's infinite love. For those of us still trying to aim as high as we can, despite a million little setbacks:

Oh, God of Second Chances and New Beginnings, Here I am again.

Thursday — **February 11**

HERE are a few encouraging thoughts to recall next time you're feeling low:

If you're at the bottom of a hole there is only one way you can go — upwards.

Think things are looking gloomy? Well, remember, the darker the night the brighter the stars to guide you.

You don't know which way to turn? Don't turn. Go right ahead.

Friday — **February 12**

MANY readers will be familiar with that well-loved book by Alexandre Dumas, "The Three Musketeers" — a stirring tale that introduced the Musketeers' famous rallying call.

How many times had I read it? How many times had I heard it shouted aloud on stage and screen? And just think how wonderful a world it would be if we could all live by their motto.

Remembering we are one big family, let's try our best to make this world, "All for one, and one for all!"

THE CAT'S WHISKERS

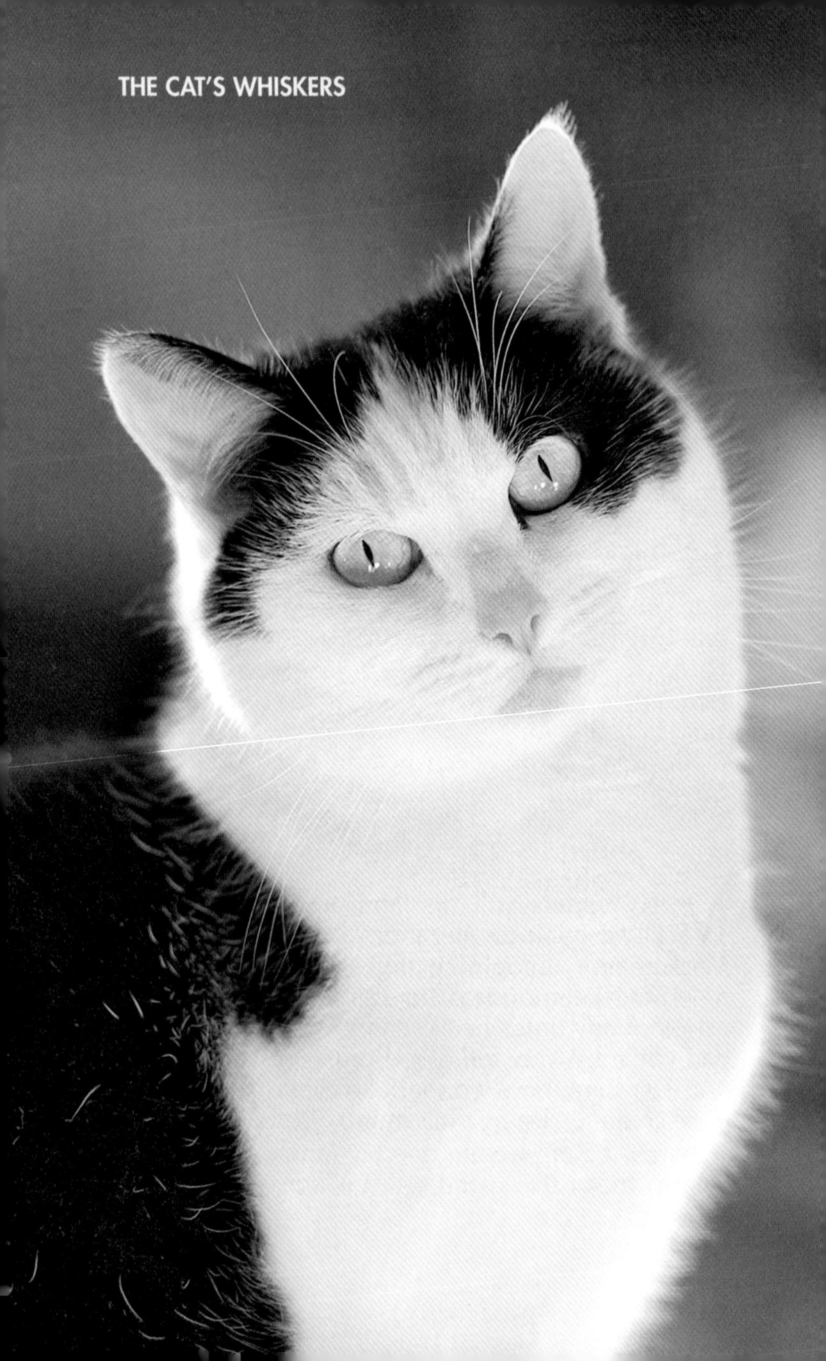

Saturday — **February 13**

TRUTH

*M*AY I speak Truth today;
*And speak it well.
May my words frame each hour of each day
    In light, clear and whole.
When I rise I will clothe myself in Truth;
    I will inhale its humility,
Exhale its honour
    And grow strong in its freedom,
I will harvest Truth from my garden,
    Pluck it from my trees,
Set my table with it
    And lay my head upon it at night.
May there be Truth above me,
    Truth below me,
Truth in me,
    And Truth around me.
May I live Truth today
    And live it well.*

Rachel Wallace-Oberle.

Sunday — **February 14**

IS our society becoming image-obsessed? It's true that some people now place great store on designer labels, the latest diet fad or even cosmetic surgery.

But if you're not one of that number don't feel left out. Perhaps you share a sense of what is important with the prophet Samuel who wrote this many centuries ago:

"Man looks at the outward appearance, but the Lord looks at the heart." (Samuel 1 16:7)

Monday — *February 15*

ED ROBERTS was the inventor of the world's first commercially viable personal computer. To help him with the business side of things, he hired a young software writer called Bill Gates. Eventually Roberts sold his company and trained to be a doctor, while Bill Gates went on to become one of the richest men in the world.

From his practice in a small town Ed Roberts had this to say, "The implication is that inventing the PC was the most important thing I ever did, and I don't think that's true. Every day I deal with things that are equally, if not more important, here with my patients."

Proof, if ever it were needed, that it's not what you get in this life that matters, but what you give!

Tuesday — *February 16*

THE teachers at Mark's primary school take their work seriously and their dedication was clearly reflected in this sign at the school entrance:

In every child is planted the seed for a great future.

I'm sure every pupil will take this inspiration and encouragement to heart, don't you agree?

Wednesday — *February 17*

IT is perhaps not great poetry but this snatch from a musical called "La Poupee" strikes the right note for me:

A contented mind is a blessing kind,
And a merry heart is a purse well lined,
So what care I? Let the world go by,
'Tis better far to laugh than cry.

Thursday — **February 18**

HAVE you heard of Gladys Aylward? She was born in 1902, the daughter of a postman. Her education was basic and her first job was as a parlour maid. Believing she had received a call to become a missionary in China, she refused to let failure at the Mission Centre examinations deter her, likewise her lack of funds.

When, after overcoming many obstacles, she eventually arrived in China, she decided that to run an inn would not just be the best way to achieve acceptance, but would also be the most effective way of sharing her faith. Her persistence, courage and practical good works became so respected that the Mandarin of Yangchen made the decision to convert to Christianity.

Perhaps her most famous achievement was to lead a hundred orphan children on a twelve-day trek to safety away from the invading Japanese armies — an astonishing achievement.

Gladys Aylward was truly a remarkable and inspiring woman. She died in 1970, in Formosa, and the story of her triumphs lives on.

Friday — **February 19**

DUBLIN-born playwright Sean O'Casey neatly summed up the essence of life when, looking back over the years, he wrote these thought-provoking words:

"I have found life an enjoyable, enchanting, and sometimes terrifying experience, and I've enjoyed it completely. A lament in one ear, maybe, but always a song in the other."

Saturday — **February 20**

HAVE you ever heard of The Yellow Book? If you're at all interested in gardening then you probably have, for this is the publication which lists all the private gardens in England open to the public in aid of charity.

The scheme has its roots in events which happened in 1859, when a Liverpool merchant called William Rathbone needed a nurse to help care for his seriously-ill wife. Realising just how valuable such professional care could be, he became determined to start a fund to ensure that this kind of aid could be available to all.

His initiative led to the start of district nursing, and eventually became known as Queen Victoria's Institute, a national voluntary organisation. It wasn't until 1926 that the idea of opening gardens to help fund-raising came to fruition, but it quickly became so popular that, under the National Garden Society, it now supports a whole variety of nursing organisations.

A sound idea can bear wonderful fruit!

Sunday — **February 21**

TEN-YEAR-OLD Amy had done her best to look good for her baptism. Commenting on how neat her hair looked, the clergyman apologised for the mess he was about to make of it with the baptismal water.

"This'll probably go everywhere," he said, raising the bowl. "But then so does the love of God!"

"May the Lord make your love increase and overflow for each other and for everyone else, just as ours does for you."   (Thessalonians I 3:12)

SPRING SERENADE

Monday — *February 22*

FLORENCE SHINN was an artist, writer and teacher in the first half of the twentieth century. She had a knack of relating great truths to everyday situations — for example, "The game of life is a game of boomerangs. Our thoughts, deeds and words return to us sooner or later, with astounding accuracy!"

So take her advice and make sure you only put into life things you would be glad to welcome back again.

Tuesday — *February 23*

LET nothing disturb you,
Let nothing dismay you,
All things pass,
God never changes.
                St Teresa of Avila.

Wednesday — *February 24*

TAKE three little words, I was once told, and you can come up with all kinds of meanings.

Consider "Rise and shine," sounding a positive note when you wake up in the morning.

Then there's "Take it easy," advice worth heeding whatever the time of day, if life is becoming too demanding.

Of course, there's "I love you," a message for all age groups, one that will never die.

But I think that one of the best and most practical three-word combinations must be the one that I recently saw on a fridge magnet: *Do it now . . . !*

Thursday — **February 25**

HE who has conquered his anger has conquered an enemy.

German Proverb.

Friday — **February 26**

FROM north and south, from east and west
I hear the four winds blow,
I watch the clouds dance on the hills
    Or feel the threat of snow.
Anticipation stirs the heart
    As winds blow from the north,
For though they have a chilling breath
    The Spring will soon come forth.

The south wind moves the plants and ferns
    And sings of Summer days,
Reviving happy memories
    In many different ways.
And from the east come icy blasts
    As sharp as any knife,
And I give thanks for home and warmth
    And comfort in my life.

The west wind has a gentle touch
    Caressing field and tree,
It whispers through the waving grass
    Of things that are to be.
On moorland track or busy street,
    Or where tides ebb and flow,
Through all the seasons of my life
    I hear the four winds blow.

Iris Hesselden.

Saturday — **February 27**

PETER was enjoying a rest after a day spent hill-walking. "It's strange, isn't it," he observed. "Although most of the time I really enjoy exploring the outdoors with friends, now and then it's great to be all by myself."

I know what he meant, for sometimes a little solitude is exactly what we all need. I think it's well summed up by writer and teacher Gladys Taber, who said:

"Perhaps, after all, our best thoughts come when we are alone. It is good to listen, not to voices but to the wind blowing, to the brook running cool over polished stones, to bees drowsy with the weight of pollen.

"If we attend to the music of the earth, we reach serenity. And then, in some unexplained way, we share it with others."

Now that, I think, is the voice of someone who really did know what she was talking about.

Sunday — **February 28**

ARE you feeling rather lost and alone? There can be few people who have never experienced these emotions, and if you are feeling particularly vulnerable today, let me offer a few words from Psalm 139 to give courage and comfort:

If I ascend to heaven, You are there;
If I spread out my wings towards the morning
Or dwell in the uttermost parts of the sea,
Even there Your hand shall lead me
And Your right hand shall hold me.
Beautiful words to sustain us all.

March

Monday — **March 1**

ISAAC ASIMOV was talking about the "real" world when he said, "No sensible decision can be made any longer without taking into account not only the world as it is, but the world as it will be."

In the film "Gladiator" General Maximus had a different world in mind when he tells his men, "What we do in life, echoes in eternity."

Wise words to keep in mind — always.

Tuesday — **March 2**

I WAS reading a farmer's account of clearing the rocks from a ploughed field. It's a chore that has to be done every year to keep his ground green and productive. Often as he removes these objects it becomes obvious that the stones are scarred from many contacts with the plough blade.

How like the petty dislikes and prejudices that many of us carry, just under the surface. These hidden "rocks" will bear scars from contact with people or places that might have improved us — if we hadn't knocked them aside.

A farmer might dread the job of clearing away the stones but he knows that the end result will be worth the effort. Likewise, if we could carry a few of our own personal "rocks" to his trailer for disposal, we too could look forward to the green shoots of new growth.

Wednesday — **March 3**

A NEWSPAPER once ran an unusual competition. For a large cash prize a question asked, "Which is the shortest way to London?" It didn't say where from, but didn't have to.

As every seasoned traveller knows, "The shortest way to London (or anywhere) is good company."

Thursday — **March 4**

I DON'T know who thought of this take on the "glass half full" idea, but how true it is!
The Pessimist sees the glass as half empty.
The Optimist sees the glass as half full.
The Giver sees a glass of water — and looks for someone thirsty!

Friday — **March 5**

G EORGE HERBERT, dressed in his finery, was on his way to play the violin with friends. On the way he met a carter whose wagon had fallen over, tipping all his goods into the ditch.

Now, as a seventeenth-century man of the cloth, George Herbert would not have been expected to get his hands dirty, so his friends were taken aback when he arrived, late and dishevelled.

"If I am bound to pray for those in distress," Herbert replied, "I must practise what I preach. I would not willingly pass a day without comforting a sad soul, or showing mercy, and I praise God for this occasion. Now let us tune our instruments."

Kind hearts, like fine violins, should always be kept in tune.

Saturday — *March 6*

A YOUNG child doesn't have much chance in life if his mother's an alcoholic and his father a violent bully. By the time he was five years old, John Bird's family was on the streets. Taken into orphanages and raised in care, like many youngsters in his situation he slowly drifted into a life of petty crime.

Yet deep down John managed to hold on to the belief that he was worth more than the dead-end life he was experiencing. Eventually he managed to start up a small printing press, but even as it grew ever more profitable, he never forgot his harsh beginnings.

In his mid-forties he launched "The Big Issue", a magazine to be sold by the homeless with the aim of helping them escape from life on the streets. It was to transform many lives for, from an original print run of under a hundred, and with a team of only ten vendors, its sales are now worldwide.

In 1995 John Bird received a well-deserved MBE for services to homeless people — but perhaps even more importantly, he has shown that even the harshest circumstances can still be overcome.

Sunday — *March 7*

COUNTLESS writers and poets have urged us not to fret about what might happen in the future, but has it ever been put more eloquently than in the King James Version:

"Take, therefore, no thought for the morrow; for the morrow shall take thought for the things of itself. Sufficient unto the day is the evil thereof."

(Matthew 6:34)

Monday — **March 8**

INTERNATIONAL Women's Day on 8th March is a national holiday in many countries. Women on all continents come together, a time to celebrate ordinary women as makers of history in the struggle for equality, justice and peace.

Share this message that has been circulating on the Internet and think about each kind of strength:

A strong woman exercises daily to keep her body in shape. A woman of strength kneels in prayer every day to keep her soul in shape.

A strong woman isn't afraid of anything, but a woman of strength shows courage in the midst of fear.

A strong woman tries to avoid repeating the same mistakes, but a woman of strength realises life's mistakes can be God's blessings.

A strong woman walks with confidence, but a woman of strength knows God will catch her when she falls.

A strong woman believes she is able to make the journey. A woman of strength believes the journey will make her able.

Tuesday — **March 9**

QUARRELS — does any good ever come of them? Well, each time two people fall out and later make up, one heart, even to the tiniest degree, forgives and the other heart appreciates this.

St Francis de Sales put it well when he said, "A quarrel between friends, when made up, adds a new tie of friendship."

Wednesday — **March 10**

OF four couples whom our friends Jack and Meg met on holiday, three of the men happened to be called David.

"I've always found the Davids of this world to be very nice chaps," John remarked, a comment greeted by smiles all round, because these Davids were indeed ideal companions.

Then one stroked his chin thoughtfully, and observed quietly, "I doubt if Goliath thought so!"

Thursday — **March 11**

LIFE is a series of if, but and maybe,
Of doubt and misgiving and fear,
Of wondering where the road may be leading
And wondering why we are here.

A series of problems, of puzzles and tests,
And lessons we all have to learn,
With so many questions, and very few answers
And wondering which way to turn.

Yet there in the midst of the ifs and the doubts
A light seems to show us the way,
Love lifts the spirit as hope wakes anew,
And life is a gift every day!

Iris Hesselden.

Friday — **March 12**

EVERY baby is a fresh chance for mankind. But so is every old person, for in him or her lies the knowledge and the wisdom of experience.

Maurice Fleming.

*Saturday — **March 13***

PAUL is an engineer. His job is demanding and often takes him to the other side of the world for weeks at a time. He was offered — and accepted — promotion which meant more travel, increased responsibility and longer hours, often working at weekends.

When I asked him how he deals with the challenges of his position, he showed me a little card with these inspiring words that he carries in his wallet:

> *Meditate.*
> *Live purely. Be quiet.*
> *Do your work with mastery.*
> *Like the moon, come out*
>   *from behind the clouds!*
>   *Shine.*
>   Buddha.

*Sunday — **March 14***

EVEN on a Sunday, in the hectic scramble that is so often modern life, a little peace and quiet can be hard to find, but Charles Markham had an idea worth keeping in mind:

> *At the heart of the cyclone tearing the sky*
> *And flinging the clouds in the towers by*
> *Is a place of central calm.*
> *So here in the roar of mortal things*
> *I have a place where my spirit sings*
> *In the hollow of God's palm.*

"I will grant peace in the land, and you will lie down and no one will make you afraid."

(Leviticus 26:6)

Monday — **March 15**

IF there's a project that needs a helping hand or a good cause in need of support, then Stella's enthusiasm will get things going.

"You see," she says, "I always remember the days when I was a student teacher and my headmistress wanted to set up a school library. It wasn't the best time, for money wasn't plentiful, but nevertheless, she refused to be intimidated by the size of the task and, amazingly enough, we had our new library within a couple of years.

"It reinforced the truth of some words of the Russian author, Ivan Turgenev: 'If we wait for the moment everything, absolutely everything is ready, we shall never begin.' And personally," she added with a twinkle, "I like to think the sooner we start working towards any goal, then the sooner we achieve it!"

Tuesday — **March 16**

WHY do golf balls have dimples? Why does the manufacturer go to all that effort and expense? Surely it would be easier and cheaper to mass produce perfect spheres?

Well, yes, but it's been scientifically proven that a "perfect" ball travels only half as far as one covered with what some might see as "imperfections". Dimples reduce air drag and let the golf ball really fly along.

So, next time you think of some characteristic or physical "imperfection" you'd like to change, think of the golf ball, and be sure the Manufacturer had a reason in mind.

Wednesday — **March 17**

MODESTY is a precious quality which is often underrated. I have never forgotten the piece of advice a teacher once gave our class:

"If at first you do succeed, don't look smug about it!"

Thursday — **March 18**

WE often hear of wealthy, apparently successful people who still find themselves lonely and unfulfilled, yet I have met folk who are not well off financially, but live happy, contented lives. What makes the difference?

Pierre Teilhard put it this way: "Love alone is capable of uniting living beings in such a way as to complete and fulfil them, for it alone joins them by what is deepest in themselves."

Friday — **March 19**

FORGET-me-nots and columbines,
  Convolvulus the fence entwines,
Sweet crocus drifts of vivid hue,
  With buttercups and feverfew,
White daisies dappled in the lawn,
  And poppies nodding by the corn,
The willows wear a hint of green,
  With golden daffodils serene,
Fresh dew-hazed meadows in the sun,
  Just make the whole world feel at one,
Such simple signs that come to say,
  Spring, once more, is on its way.

Brian H. Gent.

Saturday — **March 20**

I ONCE heard someone say that life is like a bicycle. You won't fall off as long as you keep pedalling. Other people may pass you by, but you may well catch up with them at the next traffic lights.

Sunday — **March 21**

THERE are many types of cross, with many different meanings. The Lindau Cross represents beauty, the Cross of Bethlehem symbolises family unity, the Cross of St Margaret is a blessing of love and the Flower Cross is said to bring the gift of happiness.

Wonderful creations, but we mustn't lose track of the plain wood and rusty nails which, by Grace, became all of those things and so much more. Think of these well-loved words by George Bennard:

"So I'll cherish the Old Rugged Cross, till my trophies at last I lay down. I will cling to the old rugged cross, and exchange it some day for a crown."

Monday — **March 22**

A FRIEND once handed me a piece of a wasps' nest. Now I have always had a struggle with wasps; to my mind they sound like angry little warplanes and like most people I've only ever wanted to avoid them.

However, that section of wasps' nest taught me a lesson. It was so intricate, so beautiful — amazing things can come from unexpected sources.

BUILDING FOR
THE FUTURE

Tuesday — *March 23*

THERE was an unexpected late snowfall one year. Our friend Ian was clearing his garden path not long afterwards and I remarked to him how bitterly cold it was.

"Yes, it certainly is," he replied. "You know, this is the kind of day when I remember the poet James Thomson's words: 'Come, gentle Spring, ethereal mildness, come!' and echo them with enthusiasm."

I nodded, looking forward to tea and toast beside the warmth of the fire.

Wednesday — *March 24*

OUR old friend Mary read this delightful quote about laughter in a magazine:

"It is like physical exercise — jogging on the inside."

Truly, laughter is still the best medicine.

Thursday — *March 25*

MANY of us will have given up something for Lent, but there's another side of the coin. We look, not only to give something up, but to improve ourselves spiritually and when better to move towards a new kind of life than during Lent which originally meant Spring.

Such changes can't be made quickly, but all the same forty days can seem a long time, until we remember these insightful words from the Methodist preacher George Whitefield: "The renewal of our natures is not done in a day. We have not only an old house to pull down, but a new one to build up."

Friday — *March 26*

*M*ANY people, when in bed,
    Find worries chasing round their head.
Much more use, it must be said
To count the day's triumphs instead.

There's a lot of truth in this little ditty. It's all too easy to dwell on the day's frustrations and concerns about the future, but it's a rare day that doesn't contain a chink of light or a small success.

So next time your thoughts keep you awake, find the day's high point. Congratulate yourself on the cake you made; remember the smallest step you took towards a distant goal; relive a welcome phone conversation with a friend.

This is the stuff of everyday life, but it's worth more than we sometimes realise — and we can make it all the more meaningful by choosing to dwell on the positive.

Saturday — *March 27*

I READ these thought-provoking words one day: *Sometimes you just have to take the leap and build your wings on the way down!*

Sunday — *March 28*

*H*ERE is a reflective prayer written in the nineteenth century by John Henry Newman:

May he support us all the day long, till the shades lengthen and the evening comes, and the busy world is hushed and the fever of life is over and our work is done. Then in his mercy may he give us a safe lodging and a holy rest and peace at last.

Monday — **March 29**

HERE are some thoughtful words to consider today: "When you were born, you cried and the world rejoiced. Live your life in such a manner that when you die the world cries and you rejoice."

Tuesday — **March 30**

EACH life holds sun and shadows,
Each life holds joy and tears,
Sweet days of warmth and laughter,
Bleak days of pain and fears.
But sometimes, in our sadness,
It's easy then to feel
That gladness is illusion,
And only gloom is real.
But oh, take heart, take courage,
For sad times too slip past,
And though each day brings challenge,
Soon joy will come at last.
So trust, in course, that sunshine
Will always follow shade,
And one day we'll awaken
To Light that will not fade.

Margaret Ingall.

Wednesday — **March 31**

SOMETIMES it's not easy to count your blessings. Well, here's a tip from Robert Louis Stevenson:

"The best things are the nearest; breath in your nostrils, light in your eyes, flowers at your feet, duties at your hand and the path of God just before you."

April

Thursday — *April 1*

CAN there be anything more delightful in this world than making a new friend? Edward Ford was a philanthropist with a special interest in education, who also appreciated the value of friendship.

"Meeting someone for the first time," he said, "is like going on a treasure hunt. What wonderful worlds we can find in each other!"

Friday — *April 2*

A BRIGHT April morning,
A brisk April breeze,
It hops through the hedgerows,
It tickles the trees.
It dusts down the alleys,
Through houses in rows.
It whispers, it teases
Wherever it goes.
And folk in the city
Lift hopeful heads high
To breathe in its freshness
To feel it dance by.
They hear its glad message,
The promise that's clear:
The blue skies are coming,
Springtime is here!

Margaret Ingall.

Saturday — **April 3**

HAVE you heard of Robert Foulis? You may not know his name, but I'm sure you'll have heard of his most famous invention.

Born in Scotland, Robert emigrated to Canada in 1818, where he worked as a portrait painter, an engineer, a teacher and a chemistry lecturer. He opened an iron foundry and a school of art, and also surveyed the upper reaches of the St John River.

In short, there was very little Robert Foulis couldn't do, but his greatest achievement was to make a device that worked by piping high-pressure steam through a nozzle, making a noise loud enough to be heard for miles. Are you still puzzled?

You'll probably recall visiting the coast on a foggy night and hearing a foghorn, Robert Foulis' simple yet brilliant idea to warn mariners away from danger. No-one can guess just how many lives it must have saved, but one thing is certain — it's an invention everyone should hear about!

Sunday — **April 4**

DEATH is as much a part of the grand scheme of things as anything else. The well-known parliamentarian and speaker Tony Benn once talked about this subject in a lecture.

Death, his mother had told him, was God's last and greatest gift to each of us. And his grandmother had laughingly told a much younger Tony that the best thing about death was that at last there was a trip you didn't have to pack for!

"Where, O death, is your victory? Where, O death, is your sting?" (Corinthians 1 15:55)

Monday — *April 5*

PASQUE is an old word for Easter, and a flower for this time of year is the aptly-named Pasque flower. This beautiful anemone has bell-shaped, purple flowers and golden yellow stamens; its leaves were once used to colour Easter eggs.

In our old friend Mary's garden at this time each year the Pasque flower blooms, a reminder of the joy and rejoicing of the season.

Tuesday — *April 6*

IT seems, at times, as if the world is becoming smaller. Suzanne's aunt made a long trip to the Bahamas, her cousin lived in Australia for six months on a student exchange programme and a neighbour's son spent his Summer holiday in Florida.

While I was mulling over how accessible these far-flung places have become, I came across this quote by St. Augustine:

"People travel to wonder at the height of the mountains, at the huge waves of the seas, at the long course of the rivers, at the vast compass of the ocean, at the circular motion of the stars, and yet they pass by themselves without wondering."

Wednesday — *April 7*

AUTHOR Richard Bach wrote these memorable words: "There are no mistakes. The events we bring upon ourselves, no matter how unpleasant, are necessary in order to learn what we need to learn: whatever steps we take, they're necessary to reach the places we've chosen to go."

THE FRIENDSHIP BOOK

Thursday — **April 8**

HARRIET Beecher Stowe thought that in each lifetime we probably only come across, "a dozen faces marked with the peace of a contented spirit". And without contentment, Bern Williams warned, "We may pass violets looking for roses."

However, it was an unknown contributor who supplied these insightful words: "Contentment is not the fulfilment of what you want, but the realisation of how much you already have".

Friday — **April 9**

GILBERT Duclos-Lassalle was a professional cyclist and regular competitor in the gruelling Tour de France. In preparation for the two thousand mile race over some of France's most mountainous terrain, he would cycle several thousand miles.

And what great prize was on offer for all that effort? A winner's jersey! So what made it worthwhile?

"Why, to sweep through the Arc de Triomphe on the last day," Gilbert said. "To be able to say you finished the Tour de France!"

Each of us has our own race to complete and, like Gilbert, we all want to sweep home to glory on the last day. Now, isn't that worth a little effort?

Saturday — **April 10**

I WILL love the light for it shows me the way, yet I will endure the darkness for it shows me the stars.   Og Mandino.

TULIP TIME

Sunday — *April 11*

WHAT is Spring? Well, think about pink cherry blossom seen against a blue sky, laughing children caught in an April shower, a carpet of bluebells, the gift of Easter, a countryside hazed with fresh greens, lambs in the fields, lengthening days — all these things surely uplift the heart and spirit in this season of promise and new life.

I am reminded of these centuries'-old words from Genesis 1:12:

"And the earth brought forth grass, and herb yielding seed after his kind, and the tree yielding fruit, whose seed was in itself, after his kind: and God saw that it was good."

Monday — *April 12*

I'VE been considering the Parable of the Talents, and three different quotations have come to mind. The first is to stir us into action:

"It is the greatest of all mistakes to do nothing because you can only do a little. Do what you can".
Sydney Smith.

The second is a reminder not to be stingy with our talents:

"When I stand before God at the end of my life, I would hope that I would not have a single bit of talent left, and could say, 'I used everything you gave to me'. "
Erma Bombeck.

And the third urges us not to underestimate our abilities:

"Every man has one thing he can do better than anyone else — even if it's only reading his own handwriting."
G. Norman Collie.

Tuesday — **April 13**

WE like to think of ourselves as independent, but each day we rely on lots of people. From the family who loves us, to the careful driver who stops in plenty of time; from the helpful shop assistant, to the stranger who catches your eye and smiles in passing, our days are often made special not by big events but by a hundred little things.

There's a Hawaiian saying that sums this up so well: "Cherish the small things. The prettiest kite only flies because of its tail!"

Wednesday — **April 14**

WHEN the storms of life are raging
With a tempest, fierce and wild,
Keep the joy of life within you
*   Keeping safe, the inner child.*
Storms will pass, the days grow calmer,
*   See the rainbow up ahead,*
Look for wonder all around you
*   Find the path the angels tread.*
Watch the waking of the Springtime
*   All that Mother Nature brings,*
Look for beauty, love and laughter,
*   Hear the song the skylark sings.*
See the colours of the Autumn
*   Golden leaves can stir our hearts,*
Looking forward, sharing friendship,
*   Every day adventure starts.*
So much beauty to discover,
*   Soon your soul will be beguiled,*
Keep the joy of life within you
*   Keeping safe that inner child.*
                     Iris Hesselden.

Thursday — **April 15**

A FAMILY heritage is all very well and good, but each generation must walk its own path and find something in themselves to be proud of.

I don't doubt that the family of young Martha thought likewise. Asked to introduce herself in primary school, she stood up and told her class:

"My name is Martha Bowers Taft. My great-grandfather was President of the United States. My grandfather was a senator. My daddy is ambassador to Ireland. And I am a Brownie."

Friday — **April 16**

DON'T ask God to guide your footsteps if you're not willing to move your feet.

Anon.

Saturday — **April 17**

THE shrubs looked bright and beautiful, their flowers a blaze of colour, the budding trees had turned a delicate shade of green and beds of tulips brought their own brand of beauty.

Everyone Ann met that day looked so much more cheerful. It was as if they had left behind a dark tunnel and stepped out into daylight. Spring had not quite removed a hint of chill from the wind, but the freshness of the day only served to lift everyone's spirits, it seemed. Ann was reminded of these words by Alfred Wainright:

"We live in a magical fairyland and it is given to us to enjoy as an absolute gift . . . We have more blessings than we could ever count."

Sunday — *April 18*

BROTHERS John and Charles Wesley, the founders of Methodism in the mid-eighteenth century, were men of letters in every sense of the word. Charles is remembered for some of his six and a half thousand hymns which his brother took pleasure in amending.

These include "Love Divine, All Loves Excelling"; "Gentle Jesus Meek and Mild" and "Hark The Herald Angels Sing". His brother, John, wrote forty thousand sermons in his eighty-eight years, covering a quarter of a million miles on horseback, addressing as many as thirty thousand people at a time.

He also managed to keep a daily journal, which records that on 26th May, 1776 he paid one of his many visits to the city of Dundee in Scotland, worshipping in St Andrew's Church and describing it as "cheerful, lightsome and admirably well-furnished".

The church was only four years old at the time, but I like to think that apart from the addition of its many stained glass windows, Wesley would still recognise that old kirk in the Cowgate and describe it as he did so many years ago.

Monday — *April 19*

WHEREVER you turn, you can find someone who needs you. Even if it is a little thing, do something for which there is no pay but the privilege of doing it. Remember, you don't live in a world all of your own. Albert Schweitzer.

Tuesday — **April 20**

I CAME across this blessing and would like to share its thoughtful sentiments with you today:

Hold on to what is good,
*   even if it is a handful of earth.*
Hold on to what you believe in,
*   even if it is a tree which stands by itself.*
Hold on to what you must do,
*   even if it is a long way from here.*
Hold on to life, even when it is easier letting go.
Hold on to my hand, even when
*   I have gone away from you.*

Wednesday — **April 21**

I LIKE the story from Ireland of St Kevin. He went to pray and, kneeling, stretched out his clasped hands. As he prayed, a blackbird came and laid an egg in his hands.

When St Kevin saw this, rather than disturbing the bird, he stayed where he was until the baby bird hatched. A lesson in patience and love!

Thursday — **April 22**

JOAN carries a card in her purse with this saying as a reminder to consider her words carefully each and every day. I think we would all do well to keep such wisdom in mind, don't you agree?

If it is not truthful and not helpful, don't say it.
If it is truthful and not helpful, don't say it.
If it is not truthful and helpful, don't say it.
If it is truthful and helpful, wait for the right time.

                              Buddha.

Friday — **April 23**

BORN to poor, black sharecroppers in the Deep South, country singer Charley Pride experienced his fair share of difficulties in life. When, in 1967, he performed at the Grand Ole Opry he was the first African-American to have done so. But none of this changed his outlook.

"A fan will grab you and hug you and not let go," he said, describing his concerts. "And when that happens — you wish it could be that way all over the world!"

Saturday — **April 24**

I'M sure most of us hope to make some small difference for good in this world, but Dame Daphne Sheldrick doesn't think small — she thinks jumbo size!

When her husband died in 1977, she founded the David Sheldrick Wildlife Trust in his memory, aiming specifically to look after abandoned elephants. Now she runs an "orphanage" in Kenya, housing as many as fourteen young animals at a time, each looked after by their own keeper until they are ready to return to the bush.

It has not been easy. Dame Daphne herself was once badly injured by an elephant in the wild, yet she can still say, "Their tremendous capacity for caring is, I think, perhaps the most amazing thing about them, even at a very young age. Their sort of forgiveness, unselfishness — they have all the best attributes of us humans and not very many of the bad."

Perhaps we need to think big a little more often!

Sunday — *April 25*

AGED only six weeks, Fanny Crosby was left blind after careless medical treatment. In the mid-1800s opportunities in life would in theory have been severely restricted, but she grew up to become a teacher in a school for the visually impaired, married a musician and wrote thousands of songs of praise.

Fanny Crosby's hymns are still hugely popular and include "To God Be The Glory" and "Blessed Assurance".

Her headstone, in Connecticut, bears the simple Biblical quote: *She hath done what she could.*

Monday — *April 26*

HERE are a couple of thoughts to share today:
Grass never grows on a path between friends.
Chinese Proverb.
Faithless is he that says farewell when the road darkens. J. R. R. Tolkien.

Tuesday — *April 27*

HERE are some anonymous words well worth remembering:
Drop a little word of cheer and kindness: in a minute you'll forget;
But there's gladness still a-swelling, and there's joy a-circling yet.
And you've rolled a wave of comfort whose sweet music can be heard,
Over miles and miles of water just by dropping one kind word.

WELSH WATERS

Wednesday — *April 28*

PRAYERS can be wonderful, even when short. When they seem to go unanswered they still serve a purpose in keeping us connected with the ultimate answer.

Mahatma Gandhi stressed the importance of prayer in a simple way. "It is," he said, "the key that opens up the morning and the bolt that safely closes the evening."

Thursday — *April 29*

HERE are some wise words by Anthony J. D'Angelo: "Wherever you go, no matter what the weather, always bring your own sunshine."

Remember that advice the next time you reach for your umbrella.

Friday — *April 30*

PEGGY had to spend a few days in hospital, and though her treatment went well and the medical staff were kind, she was more than happy to return home. She showed me a small poem she'd written not long afterwards:

It's been a normal kind of day,
A little work, a little play,
Some errands run, a friend for tea,
And then some time to just be me.
So I offer up my praise
For all the joys of "normal" days.

Sometimes it's good to remind ourselves of all the simple pleasures that we usually take for granted!

May

UBUNTU is an ancient Swahili term with no direct translation into English. Bill Clinton used this word in a speech about the importance of society, while according to Nelson Mandela, Ubuntu was central in the reconstruction of South Africa.

So what is this concept? Well, Ubuntu means "I am because you are." It means the well-being of others is important to our own well-being. It means showing humanity to everyone you meet because we are all connected.

Think about this today and I'm sure you'll agree it makes a great deal of sense.

I COULDN'T help but smile at a climber's awe-struck description of a Scottish mountain ridge.

"The slope on one side," he wrote, "is an overhang and infinite. The slope on the other side is even steeper and even longer!" Of course he was exaggerating — even the mountains are bounded by physical laws and everything in this world ends somewhere.

That is why it is so reassuring having a promise from beyond this world to depend on — forever.

"Heaven and Earth will pass away, but my words will never pass away." (Matthew 24:35)

THE FRIENDSHIP BOOK

Monday — *May 3*

YOU would never think it to look at them, but the words "compassion" and "womb" have the same origin. They both come from a term implying "new life" or "rebirth".

I admit I was puzzled at first, then I realised that if we show compassion by refusing to hold a person's situation or past deeds against them, we are giving them the gift of a fresh start. In our compassion we give them new life.

It seems there's much more to the word — and the deed — than I first thought.

Tuesday — *May 4*

BLOSSOM TIME

I STAND beneath the blossomed boughs
All touched with fairy lace,
And feel the wisp of fragile petals
On my upturned face.
A pretty froth of pink and white
In beautiful array,
Adorned like bridal finery
In delicate display.

As rays of light touch tiny buds
They open one by one,
And turn their dainty, petalled cups
Towards the morning sun,
And high upon the apple spray
A blackbird starts to sing,
Pouring out its praises 'midst
The blossoms of the Spring.
                                Kathleen Gillum.

PRIMULA
PERFECTION

Wednesday — **May 5**

RICHELIEU, the great French statesman, was renowned for his courtesy. The warmth of his speech delighted those he came into contact with and some even suggested it was worth having a request denied, just to hear how pleasantly he spoke, even when he was saying no.

Now, let's try to remember the words of this anonymous poet:

Speak gently! 'tis a little thing
Dropped in the heart's deep well;
The good, the joy, that it may bring,
Eternity shall tell.

Thursday — **May 6**

AN admirer once asked an award-winning journalist the secret of his success.

"I get up when I fall down," he replied.

It really is that simple.

Friday — **May 7**

"DID you know," asked the Lady of the House looking up from reading a favourite magazine, "that there's an event called a Festival of Faiths? It takes place every year, you know."

I hadn't heard about this, but was intrigued to learn that this annual gathering is held in order to focus on all the different faiths in the world, both celebrating their diversity and promoting their unity. It's a coming-together of various religions with the aim of overcoming fear and distrust and building bridges of understanding.

Now, that objective is surely to be applauded.

Saturday — *May 8*

GRETA loves baking and is often busy in her kitchen when visitors call. One day a friend watched her measuring out rice. Two or three grains fell on to the floor, so she picked them up, washed them under the tap and put them with the others.

She explained, "You'll remember I was in India last year. Well, in one very poor village I saw hungry children searching the ground for any spilt grains to eat. I vowed there and then I would never waste a single grain."

It was a lesson Greta has never forgotten.

Sunday — *May 9*

YOUNG Nicola came home from Sunday school with a list of prayers composed by children which her teacher had copied for the class. I hope these heartfelt sentiments turn your thoughts towards heavenly things today and raise a smile.

Dear God,
I didn't think orange went with purple until I saw the sunset you made on Tuesday.

Elaine.

Dear God,
If you watch me in church on Sunday, I'll show you my new shoes.

Robert.

Dear God,
Instead of letting people die and having to make new ones, why don't you just keep the ones you have now?

Jane.

Monday — **May 10**

PEOPLE with the resources to fulfil every little want ought to feel contentment, but rarely do. Usually it comes when we learn to lay aside our own worldly desires in favour of what's really important.

John Balguy put it this way in the 18th century: "Contentment is a pearl of great price, and whoever procures it, even at the expense of ten thousand desires, makes a wise and happy purchase."

Words which surely speak to us as clearly today!

Tuesday — **May 11**

I HAD to smile at this story I read — five times! A hotel chain interviewed five thousand people for five hundred jobs. The interviewers quickly cut that number down to size. They'd been told to reject people who didn't smile at least four times during the interview.

Hospitality may be a business, but it should also be a way of life. Now, that's surely one interview we'd all like to pass with flying colours!

Wednesday — **May 12**

ONLY forty-two years old when he died, Maltbie Babcock did not have a long life, but he did have one of the best definitions of life I have ever heard.

"Life is what we are alive to," he wrote. "It is not length but breadth. Be alive to goodness, kindness, purity, love, history, poetry, music, flowers, stars, God and eternal hope."

STEP THIS WAY

Thursday — *May 13*

JAN has always lived alone and when she retired from her job she thought she might be rather lonely.

Then a wonderful thing happened. A distant cousin she didn't know about turned up on her doorstep. She had been researching her family tree and had traced Jan!

She told Jan about other relatives she had found. Not only that but she encouraged her to join her local genealogical group and do some research herself.

"It has changed my life," Jan told me. "I'm in touch with so many relations and we all get on so well."

With all these visits, letters and phone calls, there is no fear of loneliness now!

Friday — *May 14*

ARTIST William Morris is possibly best known for his beautiful floral designs, but you may not know that the interior designer's maxim "Have nothing in your houses that you do not know to be useful, or believe to be beautiful" originated with him.

Yet while in theory this advice sounds wonderful, in practice I can't help but think that William Morris ignores the one thing that causes us to hoard in our homes – sentiment.

Those precious photographs, letters and gifts from family and friends aren't so easy to let go of, so I, for one, will never manage to live in a clutter-free home, surrounded merely by objects of beauty and usefulness!

Saturday — *May 15*

I LIKE acting legend Burt Lancaster's comment on upmarket places to eat. "I judge a restaurant," he said, "on its coffee and the bread."

In many American restaurants coffee refills and bread are free so he was judging them on their non-profit-making items.

In the same way a man or woman's character can't be summed up by their extravagant efforts on special occasions. It's the small courtesies and things done for no return that are the measure of a person — and a restaurant.

Sunday — *May 16*

PAT hadn't taken to her new neighbour. "The only time Eileen ever speaks to me is to complain," Pat told me with a sigh. "And yet I'd hoped that she'd become a good friend, just like my previous neighbour."

It was with some surprise therefore, that only a few days later I saw Pat helping Eileen to carry home her shopping, the two of them chatting away cheerfully. Afterwards, she explained:

"If the only way to have a friend is to be a friend, then that's what I'll do. After all, the more you get to know someone, then the fonder you usually become of them."

As Pat has discovered, not everyone is easy to like on first acquaintance, but we can always do our best to try. "A new commandment I give to you, that you love one another, even as I have loved you, that you also love one another. By this all men will know that you are My disciples."

(John 13:34-35)

Monday — *May 17*

EVER been tempted to give up on a goal, or an ambition because it just seemed unattainable? Well, imagine you were a clock!

If my arithmetic adds up, I reckon a clock will have to tick over thirty million times each year, a huge amount. But of course the clock doesn't have to worry about the enormity of its task, because it gets there — one tick at a time.

Now take another look at that impossible goal and ask yourself how far you might get, if you just go one tick at a time.

Tuesday — *May 18*

ONE night a man had a dream. In it he told God with great feeling that the cross he had been given to bear was too large and heavy. God showed him a room in which stood many crosses, some big, others small.

"Put down your cross then and choose one you have the strength to bear," God told the man.

"I'd like that small one," the man answered at once, pointing to a tiny cross close to the door.

"But," came the reply, "that is the cross you came with."

Wednesday — *May 19*

OUR friend Jeanette has green fingers, a sunny nature and a delightful sense of humour. In her garden she's put up a sign that says: *Step right into my garden. My roses want to meet you!*

What a welcoming way to invite someone into your world!

Thursday — *May 20*

IT'S a strange thing to be remembered for but St Alcuin, whose feast day is today, has been credited with inventing — of all things — joined-up writing!

It might sound like a rather unusual thing to be remembered for, but in an age of warfare Alcuin's new script meant that many important books were copied faster than they could be destroyed and for that we all owe him a debt of thanks. I'm also grateful to him for this tender prayer:

Lord, when we stumble, hold us,
When we fall, lift us up,
When we turn from goodness, turn us back,
And bring us at last to your glory.

Friday — *May 21*

AYRSHIRE-BORN Robert Service, who went on to become "the Bard of the Yukon", experienced the Gold Rush and learned a thing or two about hardship. He knew what made the difference between failure and success and his sound advice applies to us as much as it did to the challenges of gold prospecting.

"Be master of your petty annoyances," he wrote, "and conserve your energies for the big, worthwhile things. It isn't the mountain ahead that wears you out, it's the grain of sand in your shoe."

Saturday — *May 22*

THOSE who bring sunshine to the lives of others cannot keep it from themselves.

J. M. Barrie.

Sunday — *May 23*

ONE Sunday morning our dear old friend Mary noticed this invitation outside a local church:
Life is a puzzle — look here for the missing peace!

Monday — *May 24*

TWO teachers worked in classrooms side by side for many years. They were also longstanding friends, but it was widely known that their teaching styles were very different. One was renowned for the loudness of her voice, and indeed she could often be heard in the neighbouring classroom and the corridor.

In the infant class next door, however, Catherine's voice was never heard outside the room, and her pupils were always as quiet as proverbial mice. Someone asked her what her secret was.

"It happened by accident," she explained. "Once when I had just started teaching, I almost lost my voice. I could only whisper, yet I discovered that the softer I spoke, the quieter the children became, and the more closely they listened! I adopted that approach and it has held me in good stead for almost forty years."

Never underestimate the power of a whisper. In this noisy world, how good it is to know that you don't have to be loud to gain attention!

Tuesday — *May 25*

THIS Celtic proverb says a great deal in a few short words: *Say only a little but say it well.*

*Wednesday — **May 26***

I CAME across this intriguing list of things we can learn from a dog:

When loved ones come home, always run to greet them.
Take naps and stretch before rising.
Be loyal.
If what you want is buried, dig until you find it.
No matter how often you're scolded, don't scowl; run right back and make friends.
Delight in the simple joys of a long walk.
A few things to think about today!

*Thursday — **May 27***

WE are not permitted to choose the frame of our destiny. But what we put into it is ours.
Dag Hammarskjold.

*Friday — **May 28***

WHEN you're in the middle of sorrow, grief or loss it can be hard to imagine you will ever find anything worthwhile in life again. And nothing anyone says can convince you otherwise, it seems, unless perhaps they have been through what you have.

Well, I don't know who wrote these reassuring words but whoever they were, they've "been there" — and come out on the other side:

These things are beautiful beyond belief;
The pleasant weakness that comes after pain,
The radiant greenness that comes after rain
The deepening faith that follows after grief
And the awakening to love again.

MOTHER'S DAY

Saturday — **May 29**

WRITER and thinker Rubem Alves once said he believed that while the education of children to teach them to be adults was important, it was even more important to teach adults to be like children.

Just take time to think about it. Would we not all be better off seeing the world through the clear, unclouded eyes of childhood?

Sunday — **May 30**

SAINT THERESA is known as the Saint of the Little Ways, meaning she believed in doing the little things in life well. She is also the patron Saint of flower growers and florists. A correspondent sent me Saint Theresa's prayer and I'd like to share it with you today.

May today there be peace within. May you trust God that you are exactly where you are meant to be. May you not forget the infinite possibilities that are born of faith. May you use those gifts that you have received, and pass on the love that has been given to you.

May you be content knowing you are a child of God. Let this presence settle into your bones, and allow your soul the freedom to sing, dance, praise and love. It is there for each and every one of us.
Amen.

Monday — **May 31**

LIFE is like a journey and, like all travellers, we have to carry some luggage. Laughter is the name of the porter who is always there to help us carry it.

June

IT'S not often I'm greeted with the words "Happy New Year!" on a bright Summer morning, so I just had to stop and ask Hazel if her calendar had a misprint!

"No," she explained, smiling. "It's just that I came across a quotation yesterday that really made me think. It said: 'Life is a celebration of awakenings, of new beginnings, and wonderful surprises that awaken the soul'. I've decided to make these memorable words my new beginning this very morning."

It's a timely reminder that none of us has to wait until 1st January to start seeing and enjoying the world afresh — so let's make that our Right-Now Resolution!

YOU live in your own little corner of a small planet in an insignificant corner of space. How important can you make yourself out to be? Well, try looking at it all from a different point of view.

Recalling the view from the moon Colonel James Irwin said, "I thought, if Earth is that small, how small am I? Just a speck in the universe. But yet significant enough that God would create me and love me and touch my life."

That's how important you are!

Thursday — **June 3**

*D*O not believe in anything simply because you have heard it.

Do not believe in anything simply because it is spoken and rumoured by many.

Do not believe in anything merely on the authority of your teachers and elders.

Do not believe in traditions simply because they have been handed down for many generations.

But after observation and analysis, when you find that anything agrees with reason and is conducive to the good and benefit of one and all, then accept it and live up to it.

Buddha.

Friday — **June 4**

THE composer Frederick Delius believed that happiness came from creating and his greatest happiness came from creating music.

"Music," he said, "is an outburst of the soul."

Saturday — **June 5**

DANIEL, a lively twelve-year-old, was grinning when he announced: "Here's a puzzle for you! Can you guess the answer?

"It's something that makes you happy in the house, spells goodwill in business, takes up just a moment of time and stops anybody being sad.

"It's like sunshine when you're down, it costs nothing to buy, no electricity to operate, never loses power if topped up and makes you happy when repeated.

"Yes, that's right — a smile!"

Sunday — *June 6*

A GROUP of modern writers was asked to name their favourite books. Each was also asked to give a compelling reason why they read the ones they chose.

Author Malcolm Muggeridge's response sounded a little different. He said his favourite book was the Bible, because it was "the book that reads me".

Monday — *June 7*

HAVE you heard of the Nicholas Effect? It's a story that began in the worst possible way, when seven-year-old Nicholas Green was killed while visiting Italy on holiday, the random victim of robbery.

Although devastated by their loss, his parents agreed that his organs could be used to help others. What no-one foresaw, however, was the far-reaching effect their actions would have. The news that seven Italian recipients had been given back their lives touched and inspired all who heard the story.

Since then, not only has the rate of organ donation soared in Italy, but people around the world have become more aware of the benefits that can come from carrying a donor card. In the years since Nicholas' death, his parents have met those who were given new life — perhaps the most moving is the story of the young woman who received his liver.

Not only did she make a full recovery, she has since married and given birth to a son. She named the child Nicholas — a tribute to a boy and his parents and their generosity of spirit.

Tuesday — **June 8**

THE seventeenth-century author Thomas Fuller made this wise observation:

"Be a friend to thyself and others will be, too."

Wednesday — **June 9**

MY DAY OUT

I LEFT the house this morning,
My spirits soaring high,
My steps were light, my boots shone bright,
A gleam was in my eye.
The hills and dales were calling,
I yearned to walk each track,
Cast off all care, inhale fresh air,
Feel sunshine on my back.
By tea-time I was tattered,
By thorn and bramble mauled,
My feet were damp, my legs had cramp,
As back to home I crawled.
"Good time?" my neighbour asked me,
I paused to think it through.
I stood up straight, and answered, "Great!";
And what's more — it was true!

Margaret Ingall.

Thursday — **June 10**

THE lawyer, statesman, writer and philosopher, Francis Bacon, who was well acquainted with the ups and downs of sixteenth-century politics wrote these wise words:

"God Almighty first planted a garden. And indeed, it is the purest of human pleasures. It is the greatest refreshment to the spirits of man."

Friday — *June 11*

PEOPLE whose business it is to count such things tell me there are two hundred and six bones in the adult human body. All very scientific and interesting, but I prefer the opinion of football coach Duff Daugherty.

"You only need three bones to journey successfully through life," he insisted. "A wishbone to dream with, a backbone for the courage to get through the hard times and a funny bone to laugh at life along the way!"

Saturday — *June 12*

A MEETING was called in a town in the north of England to discuss race relations and see how they could be improved in the community.

Many suggestions were put forward and at last there was time for just one more. An elderly lady rose and said in her broad local accent, "Over the years we have all learned to live beside one another. Now it is time to live together."

There was nothing left to be said.

Sunday — *June 13*

AS the day ends many of us like a quiet time to ourselves. I came across these words recently, and made a note of them:

"Lord, dismiss us with Thy blessing, hope and comfort from above. Let us each, Thy peace possessing, triumph in redeeming love."

Surely this blessing is a perfect reflective thought. It is from R. S. Hawker; he was for forty years the Rector of Morwenstow Church in Cornwall.

Monday — *June 14*

YOU know those people who are always happy and eternally optimistic? Well, aren't they just a little annoying sometimes, if we are honest?

If they are, it's perhaps because of the challenge they represent to the rest of us. But what drives them — and how do we become more positive about life? Well, Rabbi Harold Kushner had some words that might help:

"When your life is filled with the desire to see holiness in everyday life, something magical happens. Ordinary life becomes extraordinary, and the very process of life begins to nourish your soul!"

Tuesday — *June 15*

A MAGAZINE asked its readers, "What are the most inspiring words you have ever been told?"

Some answers were predictable, some were flippant, some were deep and profound, but the one the Lady of the House liked best simply said, "You may not know where life's road will lead you, but keep moving . . . God is walking with you."

Wednesday — *June 16*

HERE is a memorable quote by Martin Luther King, Jr.: "Everybody can be great . . . because anybody can serve. You don't have to have a college degree to serve. You don't have to make your subject and verb agree to serve. You only need a heart full of grace and a soul generated by love."

Wonderful words to live by, don't you agree?

Thursday — *June 17*

WHAT could Australia's Great Barrier Reef possibly have to do with the everyday life we all share?

Well, it seems that tourists often notice a difference between the two sides of the reef. The landward, sheltered side is murky and dull, while the seaward side is vibrant and full of life. It's the seaward side that is challenged every day by ocean currents, tides and storms. Struggling against this, that side of the reef becomes stronger, brighter, more alive.

So, next time you feel beset by troubles, just think of the Great Barrier Reef. It's a natural wonder of the world — and so are you!

Friday — *June 18*

A LONG spell of rain had transformed the seed Joe had sown into fresh, new grass, and the rhubarb was thriving, as were the colourful lupins and delphiniums.

The garden chores were done so, looking for an excuse to stay in the sunshine a while longer, he brought a book of poetry outdoors. The words which fitted the scene belong to Rudyard Kipling:

Oh, Adam was a gardener, and God who
*   made him sees*
That half a proper gardener's work is done
*   upon his knees*
So when your work is finished, you can wash
*   your hands and pray*
For the Glory of the Garden, that it may
*   not pass away!*

Saturday — **June 19**

MAGGIE was telling me about a holiday in Edinburgh. "One of the most interesting places I visited was the Museum of Childhood," she told me. "It was such fun to see playthings that I could remember from my own young days. But among the toys, games and crafts I noticed a child's needle-case with this verse:

In friendship let me give this gift,
To show my best endeavour
To prove that friendship can be true
Though distance may us sever.

Isn't it good to see that whatever our age and whatever our century this sentiment never goes out of fashion?

Sunday — **June 20**

JO ANN HEIDBREDER'S Father's Day Prayer will strike many a chord today:
Mender of toys, leader of boys,
Changer of fuses, kisser of bruises,
Bless him, dear Lord.
Wiper of noses, pruner of roses,
Singer of songs, righter of wrongs,
Guide him, O Lord.
Mover of couches, soother of ouches,
Pounder of nails, teller of tales,
Reward him, O Lord.
Hanger of screens, counsellor of teens,
Fixer of bikes, chastiser of tykes,
Help him, O Lord.
Raker of leaves, cleaner of eaves,
Dryer of dishes, fulfiller of wishes . . .
Bless him, O Lord.

Monday — *June 21*

TRIBULATION — now, there's an evocative word which, in fact, derives from an ancient Roman threshing machine. The tribulum was a cart with rollers instead of wheels and each harvest time, sheaves of corn would be gathered together. Then the tribulum, with stones and lumps of metal attached to its rollers, would crush them.

But, of course, this wasn't wanton destruction — the tribulum was separating the grain from the husk, separating the wheat from the chaff.

Like the crushing of the corn, our own troubles might seem pointless at the time, but just as those early threshers brought out what was precious in their crop, so our tribulations help bring out what's precious in each of us.

Tuesday — *June 22*

THERE'S a story told of Thomas Jefferson that goes straight to the heart of the man. He and some friends on horseback found their way blocked by a raging river. Crossing it was a life-and-death matter and another traveller stood nearby to watch the first men struggle across.

Deciding it was worth the risk, the man asked the President if he would take him across on his horse. He agreed and carried him over safely.

Surprised by the man's audacity the other riders asked why he had asked the President for help and not one of them. The man was shocked by their hostile reaction and explained that he looked at them all and found that many wore a "No" expression on their face, but the man he asked had "Yes" on his.

Wednesday — **June 23**

WHEN Pra Acharn Chan learned that he had leukaemia, he made the decision to devote his remaining time to becoming a Buddhist monk. However, he could hardly have dreamed that thirty years later not only would he still be alive, but deeply involved in a most unusual monastery.

Situated in a remote part of Thailand, the monks there dedicate their lives to saving animals, giving sanctuary to a whole variety of injured creatures. It's truly, say visitors, a place where loving care towards all God's creatures can be seen in action.

This story is a reminder to us all that however little time we may think we have, it's always enough to do a little good in the world.

Thursday — **June 24**

THE west wind moves the grasses
And stirs the reeds and rushes,
He whispers through the branches
And sings of Summer days.
Then Autumn, creeping softly,
Fills every tree with splendour,
And countless leaves go swirling
With colours to amaze.
Impatient Winter blusters
As distant hills grow misty,
Low-lying fields are frosty
Where sheep now safely graze.
But Springtime soon awakens
Displaying golden beauty,
And we go forth rejoicing
With silent songs of praise.

Iris Hesselden.

TREESCAPE

Friday — **June 25**

"IT'S the worst district in London." That was the warning from the Bishop of London to Samuel Barnett when he took up a post in a Whitechapel church in 1873. But that was exactly the reason he had chosen to go there — he had new ideas for the East End neighbourhood.

He knew he could not cure the poverty but he aimed to open minds to knowledge and the arts. With the support of his wife he decided to run classes for young and old on a range of subjects.

Once these were up and running he opened Toynbee Hall, where volunteers could live and work to improve life throughout the community.

Sceptics said that such ideas would never work but Samuel Barnett and his wife, and the people of Whitechapel, proved them wrong.

Saturday — **June 26**

ALICE had been visiting Iceland, and she came to to show us her photos. When I complimented her she shook her head, smiling.

"It's not my expertise — it's the quality of light there which makes everything so clear. I'm sure it helped to make me see things with new eyes."

As Michael Strassfeld said: "Light gives of itself freely, filling all available space. It does not seek anything in return; it asks not whether you are friend or foe. It gives of itself and is not thereby diminished."

There are so many wonders of this world that we take for granted — let's make sure that light is one that we always see.

Sunday — *June 27*

THE Greek writer Lucian of Samosata was perhaps the most imaginative writer of his time. He had a vision of men sailing ships into space and fighting in a war between the moon and the sun! He saw even more amazing things on Earth.

Born less than a century after the death of Christ, Lucian could hardly believe the sense of fellowship amongst early Christians.

"It is incredible," he wrote, "to see the fervour with which people of that religion help each other in their wants. They spare nothing. Their first legislator (Jesus) has put it into their head that they are brethren."

"Therefore encourage one another and build each other up, just as, in fact, you are doing."

(Thessalonians 1 5:11)

Monday — *June 28*

IN Miguel de Cervantes' book "Don Quixote", the author's hero describes St John Chrysostom in a way that tells us nothing about him, yet tells us everything at the same time.

"He had a face like a blessing," the wandering knight says. Now you still don't know what he looked like, but don't you warm to what you've read?

Wouldn't it be wonderful if we could live each day with an attitude and expression that, like Chrysostom, made us a blessing to everyone we met? And his name, given to him because he was such an eloquent speaker, aptly means "golden mouthed".

THE FRIENDSHIP BOOK

OUR old friend Mary's mother used to quote this wise saying to her when she was a young woman: *The only place where success comes before work is in the dictionary.*

NEW BABY

WHAT will await you
When you open your eyes
To this strange and beautiful world?
Will you smile when you see your first bird;
When your fingers stretch forth
To pick your first daisy?
Will you be soothed by music,
Or have an ear for the beauty of words?

May your tiny feet
Lead you among bluebells.
The soft shells of your ears
Be shielded from harsh sounds.
May you be untouched by
Unlovely, unkindly things.

May your mornings be filled with birdsong,
Your evenings with starlight,
Your nights with untroubled sleep.
May your future paths
Hold the strength of courage,
The pleasure of humour —
And may an angel walk beside you
To point the way.

Joan Howes.

July

Thursday — *July 1*

EDWARD is head of a big business enterprise and a great believer in choosing his words with care. One day he was asked: "How do you deal with a crisis when it blows up?"

He grinned. "That's easy," he replied. "We never call it a crisis. To us it's a challenge and we don't stop until it has been fully overcome. We find that's an approach that works."

Friday — *July 2*

WE all have blessings in our lives,
We count them every day,
But now and then we have the urge
To softly steal away!
To find a new and open road
And follow where it leads,
To listen to the skylarks sing
As trouble all recedes.

To take a long and narrow boat
And glide the waterways,
To watch the countryside slip by
Where gentle cattle graze.
But if you just can't get away
To meadow, lake or stream,
Then close your eyes, shut out the world
And dream a little dream!

Iris Hesselden.

Saturday — **July 3**

THE simple, old-fashioned courtesy of sending a thank-you letter after receiving a gift, or some other treat or favour, sometimes seems to be a thing of the past. Yet when you consider how good a heartfelt "thank you" makes you feel, you realise why George W. Crane once said, "Appreciative words are the most powerful force for good on the earth."

A simple thank you can strengthen existing friendships and build new ones, but quite simply, it makes people feel appreciated and that's something we all need once in a while!

Sunday — **July 4**

ONE of our most enduring hymns, "Blest Be The Tie That Binds", was written by John Fawcett in 1782. He was born to poor parents in Yorkshire in 1740 and, at the age of sixteen, became a Christian. Aged twenty-six, the young man was ordained as a Baptist minister and accepted a call to serve a small, impoverished congregation at Wainsgate.

After spending several years there on a meagre salary, Fawcett was given the opportunity to take over a large church in London. However, on the day of their scheduled departure, he and his wife could not bear to leave their congregation; they unpacked and stayed.

Fawcett continued his ministry to the people of Wainsgate for more than fifty years and remained there until he died on 25th July, 1817. This man truly understood the meaning of brotherly love and the beautiful tie that binds us to one another.

Monday — *July 5*

TONY and Jenny had made an extended visit to India and, as well as an album full of photos, they showed friends the souvenirs they had brought home, attractive pieces of inlaid marble from Agra, home of the Taj Mahal.

"We chose them," Jenny explained, "not just for the craftsmanship that can be so clearly seen, but also because they reminded us of a Persian proverb that says, 'The best memory is one which writes kindness in marble, and injuries in dust'."

What an excellent sentiment!

Tuesday — *July 6*

MARCEL Proust wrote these words which our friend Dawn has framed in her hallway to welcome people into her home:

Let us be grateful to people who make us happy; they are the charming gardeners who make our souls blossom.

Words to remember, don't you agree?

Wednesday — *July 7*

"I LIVED on top of one hill and the school was at the top of another hill. Nobody ever went to school by car — we didn't have any cars."

You might be tempted to feel rather sorry for this schoolboy and his daily slog, but that little lad was Roger Bannister. "To and from school was training in itself," he admitted, after becoming the first man to run a four-minute mile.

Difficulties can often help us to achieve great things when seen from a later perspective.

Thursday — *July 8*

BARBARA was in a large second-hand bookshop, browsing through hundreds of titles.

"I don't know about you, Francis," she observed, "but there are one or two books that I read in childhood which have remained good companions right through my life. One of them was 'At The Back Of The North Wind', by George MacDonald and this quote has always stayed in mind:

"If instead of a gem, or even a flower, we should cast the gift of a loving thought into the heart of a friend, that would be giving as the angels give."

Friday — *July 9*

THE artist Jerry van Amerongen described his attitude to life as feeling "like a little bird with a great big song".

When we think of the Grand Scheme and realise that, tiny as we are, all the wonders of creation were made for us, I think we should join him in singing a huge song of gratitude.

Saturday — *July 10*

WHEN I met Megan on her way to work, I was surprised to see she was carrying a large tin. "Today's my birthday," she smiled, "so I've been busy baking cakes for my colleagues."

Her comment made me realise that most of us enjoy giving presents just as much as we enjoy receiving them. As Leo Buscaglia said: "Our talents are the gift that God gives to us. What we make of our talents is our gift back to God."

Happy giving!

*Sunday — **July 11***

WILLIAM BARCLAY, the Scottish theologian, said a better translation for the Hebrew word, often read as "tempted", would be "tested".

What's the difference? Well, there might, sometimes, be pleasure in giving in to temptation, but it leads us nowhere. There is so much more to be gained by passing a test. It's an achievement, especially when it brings you closer to God.

"But he knows the way I take; when he has tested me, I will come forth as gold."

(Job 23:10)

*Monday — **July 12***

SUPERHERO?

WHO wouldn't want to be the one
 To set the world to right?
To make the vital difference,
 And to turn the dark to light?
But life is not that simple and
 One single act won't do —
It's lots of small endeavours that
 Will change things through and through.

It's lots of little kindnesses,
 And little acts of care
That make the world a better place
 For everyone to share.
So don't despise the little things —
 Those little deeds of worth,
You won't be hailed a hero but
 You'll help save planet earth!

Margaret Ingall.

Tuesday — **July 13**

OUR friend John has a soft spot for Walt Disney's world of cartoons. "Pete's Dragon" is perhaps one of the lesser-known characters, but there's a song in it that always tugs at the heart. It goes:

I'll be your candle on the water
My love for you will always burn,
I know you're lost and drifting
But the clouds are lifting —
Don't give up; you have somewhere to turn.

"Somewhere to turn" must be the greatest gift one friend can give another, whether they're a man, a woman — or a big pink and green dragon!

Wednesday — **July 14**

FOLK who think that the grass is always greener on the other side spend so much time looking at the other side that they often neglect what they have.

Our friend Bill had an interesting take on the old saying. Resting on his hoe after busying himself in his garden, he observed, "You know, the grass isn't greener on the other side — it's greener where it's watered."

Whether it's gardens, relationships, or life itself, if you put the effort in, you'll surely get the pleasure out!

Thursday — **July 15**

DON'T wait for people to be friendly, go and show them how.

Anon.

*Friday — **July 16***

ELIZABETH Barrett Browning once said, "Earth's crammed with heaven and every common bush afire with God but only he who sees takes off his shoes."

The most ordinary things of life are really extraordinary. Nature is a wonderful teacher for those who will take time to seek her out.

Did you know that a tiny ant can carry twenty times its own weight? Surely the lesson here is that we can bear much more than we think. Ants live organised and efficient lives. They store their food for the Winter and are examples of industry and forethought. The Bible even refers to them as "exceedingly wise".

The spider, when spinning its gossamer web, demonstrates great patience and even the lowly caterpillar lying in its deathly shroud emerges as a beautiful butterfly, speaking of transformation and newness of life.

Let us see what we can learn from the most simple things, for Nature will reveal her secrets to those with a discerning eye, those who will take time to "stand and stare".

*Saturday — **July 17***

OUR friend Calum has a fund of wise and pithy sayings. Here are two I'd like to share with you today:

Always tell the truth: that way there's a lot less to remember!

A friend hears the song in my heart and sings it to me when my memory fails.

SAILORS' REST

THE FRIENDSHIP BOOK

Sunday — *July 18*

*E*ARLY morning; waking, yawning,
Sunday dawning, gold on grass.
Roused from dreaming, sun-rays gleaming,
Daylight streaming through the glass.
Birds are singing, church bells ringing,
Message winging on its way,
No more lazing, time for praising,
Thanking God for this new day.

M. J. Brison.

Monday — *July 19*

GEOFF was reading a newspaper supplement. "Did you know," he asked his wife Helen, "that the first aerial archaeology was carried out in 1906? Apparently a Lieutenant Philip Sharpe of the Royal Engineers Balloon Section went up in a tethered balloon and took three photographs of Stonehenge.

"The results were so informative that since then hundreds more sites have been examined from the air — all because it's often much easier to make sense of things from a distance." Geoff grinned. "A bit like life, don't you think?"

Sometimes we are so close to the things that puzzle or upset us, it's only when we're able to get a little perspective that we can begin to fully understand them. Perhaps next time we find ourselves caught up in confusion, we should try to remember that balloon.

It's reassuring to think that even though we can't always see an immediate answer, a bit of distance can work wonders.

Tuesday — *July 20*

ONE of the traditions of the Native Americans that still survives is the Yurok Brush Dance. It is held to create "good medicine" for children who are ill and anyone who wants to may join in. The only requirement is that each dancer must enter the dance circle with a good heart, intending only the best, leaving behind all ill-will, selfishness and bad feeling towards others.

These conditions are a truly worthwhile way of taking part in a bigger dance — the dance of life.

Wednesday — *July 21*

DO you ever feel there just aren't enough hours in the day to do all you have to do? If so, consider this: if you decide to get up just thirty minutes earlier each day for a year, you'll find you have approximately seven and a half more days to enjoy than if you'd spent the time sleeping.

And if you do find these extra hours, remember, what counts is not the number of hours you put in, but how much you put into the hours!

Thursday — *July 22*

A NEW school was being planned and a meeting was called to discuss what it should contain.

"A gymnasium," said someone at once.

"A science lab," suggested another.

"A music room," another person said.

Then a retired teacher stood up and spoke quietly. "It can have all of these and more," he said. "But all it really needs is four good, sound walls and tomorrow safely inside."

Friday — *July 23*

WHEN facing difficulty or adversity our old friend Mary said that her grandfather always gave this advice: "An oak is a nut that held its ground."

Wise words to keep in mind today.

Saturday — *July 24*

WITH the Scout movement having achieved over a century of good work, let's take a look at the principles laid down by founder Lord Baden-Powell. Amongst other things, he said, "A Scout smiles and whistles under all circumstances," and "The most worthwhile thing is to try to put happiness into the lives of others."

Principles well worth living by, I'm sure you'd agree, and not just for Scouts.

Sunday — *July 25*

"COULD do better." It's a comment which has appeared on many a school report at one time or another, and which sometimes, sadly, could be equally applied to aspects of our later lives.

Most of us are full of good intentions but find it just too hard to do as well as we know we could and ironically, awareness of our own shortcomings often makes us feel we're not confident enough to ask for help.

However, remember the words of Jesus as told in Mark 2:17: "They that are whole have no need of the physician, but they that are sick. I came not to call the righteous, but sinners to repentance."

So take heart. There is one great Teacher who never, ever gives up on us.

Monday — **July 26**

RED SKELTON left home to join a circus at the age of ten and was an entertainer for seven decades. He frequently ended his shows with these words:

"I personally believe we were put here to build and not to destroy. So, if by chance some day you're not feeling well and you should remember some silly little thing I've done or said and it brings back a smile to your face or a chuckle to your heart, then my purpose as your clown has been fulfilled. Goodnight and God bless."

Put that way, I can't think of a nobler calling than a clown!

Tuesday — **July 27**

KIND words can be short and easy to speak, but their echoes are truly endless.

Mother Teresa.

Wednesday — **July 28**

AT first glance the oyster wouldn't seem to have much going for it. It's an unattractive creature living in the silt at the bottom of the sea, yet it is capable of providing great beauty.

Harry Emerson Fosdick once told how even having a thick shell didn't stop irritations getting into the oyster's protected world. "And when it cannot get rid of them it uses the irritations to do the loveliest thing. If there are irritations in our life today there is only one prescription – make a pearl!"

Well, if an oyster can do it . . .

THE FRIENDSHIP BOOK

I'M sure that, like me, you've stood lost in admiration at some of the devotional scenes painstakingly portrayed in stained glass. But, have you looked at them from the outside at night?

Elisabeth Kubler-Ross wasn't referring to churches but those coping with death and loss, when she wrote:

"People are like stained glass windows; they sparkle and shine when the sun is out but it's when the darkness sets in that their true beauty is revealed — by the light within."

WHERE we love is home,
Home that our feet may leave,
But not our hearts.
Oliver Wendell Holmes.

"NANOOK Of The North" was a film made in 1920 about Eskimo life. Its director, Robert Flaherty, started off as a prospector. He failed to find gold but amassed seventy thousand feet of film showing his travels in the Far North. Friends encouraged him to make a documentary but a fire started, consuming the film and injuring him.

Most would have been tempted to give up but he dealt with his disappointment by heading north again, determined to make a film of Eskimo life "that people would never forget". He did just that!

Failure for this man wasn't a reason to stop — it was an incentive for future success.

August

Sunday — *August 1*

CLARA, the wife of composer Robert Schumann, often performed her husband's works after his death. But to do his music full justice she would first re-read old love letters which he had sent her. In this way she felt his spirit fill her; she had even greater understanding of his works and was better able to perform them.

In the Bible we have the greatest love letter of all. Through reading it we come closer to understanding the will of God and, like Clara with her husband's masterpieces, we are better able to carry out the work.

"But if anyone obeys his word, God's love is truly made complete in him. This is how we know we are in him."   (John 1 2:5)

Monday — *August 2*

A POPULAR family doctor told how anxious patients came asking him for a bottle of medicine or tablets.

"Of course," he said, "I often grant their wish because it is the right thing to do. To some, though, I say, 'I'll give you the best prescription for your trouble. Take it home with you and it will work wonders. It is called Hope!'"

"And you know," he said with a smile. "It rarely fails."

Tuesday — *August 3*

HAVE you ever doubted the power of friendship? Abraham Lincoln failed many times in his life, both in business and politics, but he rose to become a President the world will never forget. I had to smile at his explanation of how it all came about.

"If I am a success today," he explained, "it is because I had a friend who believed in me and I didn't have the heart to let him down."

Wednesday — *August 4*

BUS RIDE

SITTING on the top-deck
I am lord of all I see,
An ever-changing vista
  That's unrolling just for me.
The daisy-studded meadows,
  Where the quiet cattle graze,
The willows and the sturdy oaks
  That shade the Summer days,
The village green, the cottages,
  Small gardens growing high
With stocks and sweet delphiniums
  As blue as Summer sky.
And now the lanes give way to streets,
  The houses crowd in fast,
We're almost in the city now,
  My journey done at last,
But even though my day is mapped
  With errands by the score,
I'll still be looking forward to
  The journey home once more.

Margaret Ingall.

Thursday — **August 5**

I SAW this statement posted on an sign at a college and thought it was a bit of wisdom worth sharing: *Use the word impossible with caution.*

Good advice, don't you agree?

Friday — **August 6**

WHEN heavy showers put paid to gardening plans for the third time one week, it was difficult not to feel a bit disgruntled.

"Cheer up," the Lady of the House said. "Just think, if it never rained then none of us would exist. And water is not just life-giving, it's beautiful as well. Don't forget what John Ballantine Gough said: 'Everywhere water is a thing of beauty gleaming in the dewdrop, singing in the Summer rain'."

She smiled as she began to fill the teapot. "And remember, without rain, this 'cup that cheers' is another thing you wouldn't be able to enjoy!"

Saturday — **August 7**

HERE'S a way you can double the pleasure of a Summer's day!

When you're enjoying the feel of the lawn on your toes and a cooling breeze, try looking at it from another point of view. The poet Kahlil Gibran wrote this:

"And forget not that the earth delights to feel your bare feet and the wind longs to play with your hair."

THE FRIENDSHIP BOOK

Sunday — *August 8*

TRAVELLERS on London's underground trains are repeatedly warned to "Mind The Gap". These signs help because sometimes the gap between carriage and platform can be dangerously wide. We also might like today to think about narrowing that gap between us and God.

"Draw near to him and he will draw near to you." (James 4:8)

Monday — *August 9*

RACHEL'S Aunt Annie emigrated from Holland aged twenty. She had endured great hardship during the Second World War and arrived in Canada with very little. Her mother had died and she, her seven brothers and sisters and their father began the long and difficult process of making a fresh start.

Aunt Annie learned English, married, had two children and ran a successful business. She is surely a shining example of how to approach the unknown with courage. As it has been said — success is failure turned inside out.

"Come to the edge."
"We can't. We're afraid."
"Come to the edge."
"We can't. We will fall!"
"Come to the edge."
And they came.
And He pushed them.
And they flew.

Guillaume Apollinaire.

OVER HILL, OVER DALE

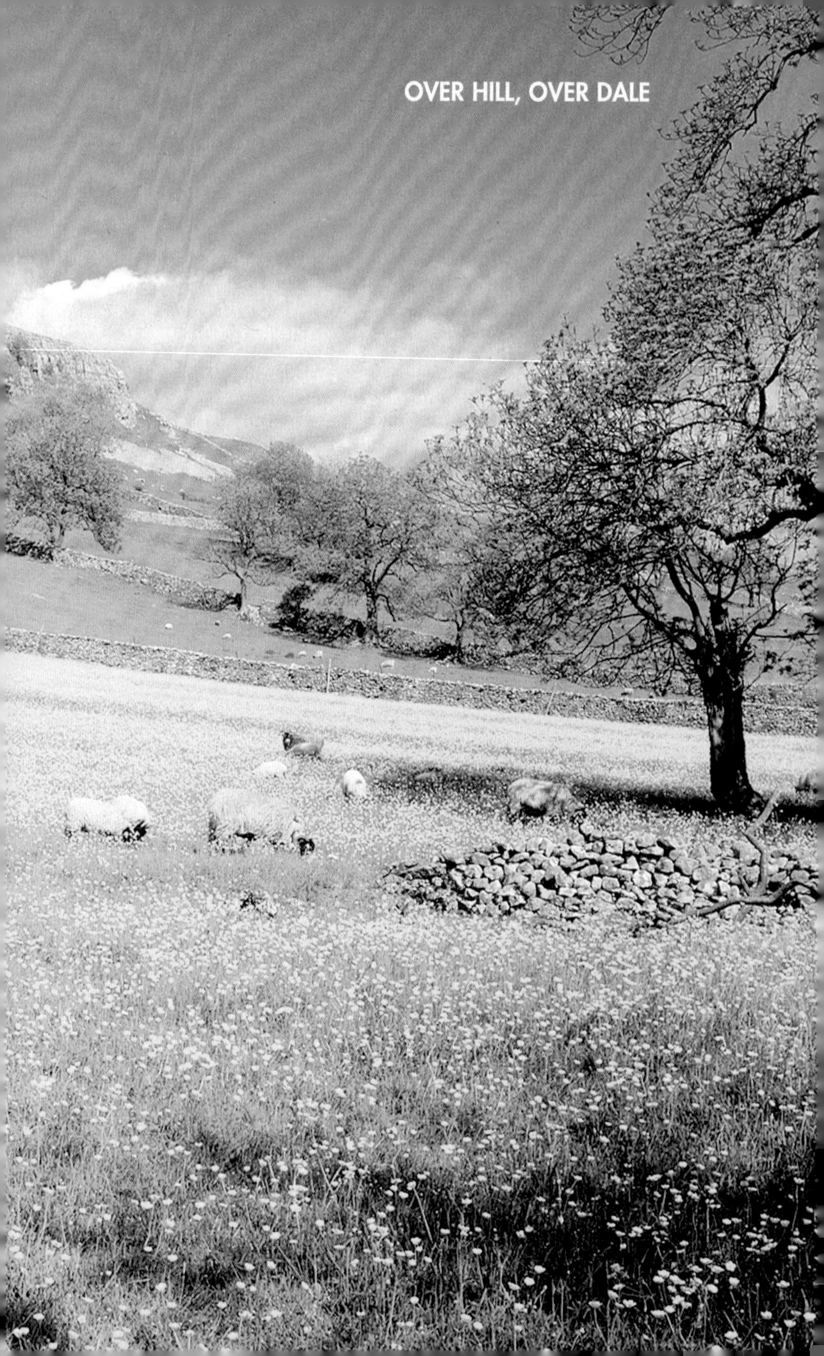

Tuesday — *August 10*

THERE is a school of thought that believes you're only as old as you feel, and that age has nothing to do with the number of candles on your birthday cake.

Actor John Barrymore had his own thoughts on the subject of growing older. "A man is not old until regrets take the place of dreams," he said.

To stay young keep your dreams alive leaving no room for regrets.

Wednesday — *August 11*

THERE used to be a sign frequently on display in hospitals at visiting times. A card pinned up in reception would advise:

Never utter a discouraging word in this hospital. You should come here only for the purpose of helping. Leave your hindering, sad looks at the door and if you can't smile don't go in!

If only we could put a sign like that at the beginning of each day! Well, we can but try . . .

Thursday — *August 12*

ONE of the delights of sending good deeds out into the world is that no-one can even begin to anticipate where they will end up or the wonders they will achieve on their way.

It's a thought summed up perfectly by an anonymous philosopher: "The blossom cannot tell what becomes of its fragrance as it drifts away, just as no person can tell what becomes of their influence as they continue through life."

Friday — **August 13**

MANY of us from time to time endure what is referred to as "one of those days" when everything seems to go wrong.

Then, just at the right moment we receive a telephone call with an encouraging message that puts things into the right perspective again, or perhaps we might have an unexpected visit from a friend.

Our friend Linda switched on her computer one evening and there, waiting for her after a tiresome day, was an e-mail from her son Lee. He had forwarded an uplifting quotation with a request: "Pass this on and brighten someone's day."

Then he'd added: "Remember — God answers *knee*-mail."

What a wonderful way to express the concept of prayer in this age of the Internet!

Saturday — **August 14**

BERRIES black or red on straw,
Purple elder, hip and haw,
Morrello cherries by the wall,
Netted lest the blackbirds call,
Grapes that turn to sparkling wine,
Their supporting arches twine,
Apple orchards, pear and peach,
Ripe and now within our reach,
So the gentle winds that sigh,
With flitting bee and butterfly,
Interplay, blend and combine,
To bring us fruits of Summertime.

Brian H. Gent.

Sunday — *August 15*

A WOMAN struggled into her post office one day carrying what was obviously a heavy parcel. She said that it contained a large family Bible which she was sending to a relative researching the family tree.

With great difficulty she placed it carefully on the scales.

"Is there anything breakable in this package?" she was asked.

"Yes," she replied, "the Ten Commandments."

Monday — *August 16*

A NNA had been enjoying a trip to a London art gallery, "Looking at those pictures made me wish I had artistic talent," she said later.

I smiled at her remark, for even if Anna can't paint, she's probably the best marmalade-maker I know. And although it's not the sort of talent that makes headlines, it's still a skill to be proud of, for Anna is generous with her produce and many a local bazaar has benefited from her numerous donations, and likewise, many a breakfast table has been brightened by a dish of her marmalade.

These words by Brenda Francis come to mind: "If you have talent, use it in every way possible. Don't hoard it. Don't dole it out like a miser. Spend it lavishly, like a millionaire intent on going broke."

Anna laughed when I told her. "So you think making pots of gold for the larder is better than making pots of gold and hoarding it all in the bank?"

Yes, I do!

THE FRIENDSHIP BOOK

Tuesday — **August 17**

OUR friend Alexandra had to go into hospital. Before she came home, the Lady of the House and I spent a rewarding few hours cleaning her cottage, doing shopping and weeding the garden so that everything was spick and span for her return.

Soon afterwards, a notelet arrived in the post. Inside Claire had written: "Good friends are like stars — even when you can't see them, they are still there."

Friendship could have no greater sentiment.

Wednesday — **August 18**

THREE candles disperse the darkness — truth, knowledge and the ways of nature.

Celtic Proverb.

Thursday — **August 19**

MOST of us know the old joke about the clergyman who remarked to a busy gardener, "You know, of course, that this is God's garden." And his reply, "Oh, is it, sir? You should have seen the state of it before I started work on it!"

The Lady of the House and I were admiring a neighbour's beautifully-designed garden — every shrub, tree, flower and, it seemed, almost every blade of grass meticulously sown or planted to create an amazing feast of nature's colours and fragrances.

We were overawed by his many hours of dedication and were also amused to see this small sign near his path:

A garden is a thing of beauty and a job for ever.

*Friday — **August 20***

THE great Blues guitar player Bo Diddley used to tell his audience, "I thank you in advance for the great round of applause you're about to give me!" His light-hearted words may hide a greater truth.

Don't you find that if you make your way through life expecting the worst of people, you usually get just that, but if you expect the best then more often than not people will exceed your expectations? Something to think about today.

*Saturday — **August 21***

WHEREVER there is a human being, there is an opportunity for a kindness.   Seneca.

*Sunday — **August 22***

ONE of the great pilgrimage routes of medieval times was the nine hundred-mile walk from Paris to Santiago de Compostela in Spain. Pilgrims completing the journey received blessings. After months of travelling they would come to the last stretch, rising up into the Cantabrian Mountains, but for many this was physically too much.

That's why, at the beginning of the slope, there's an ordinary-looking little building which houses the Door Of Pardon. Those who could go no further entered and were given the same blessings as if they had completed the journey.

We might fall short on our pilgrimage of life but Jesus makes sure we always have a Door Of Pardon whenever we stop. All we need to do is be on the right road. "For the Son of Man came to seek and to save what was lost." (Luke 19:10)

Monday — **August 23**

IS this just another ordinary day for you? Well, when you think of all that goes into making the sun rise, the flowers open, the dew evaporate and the birds sing, shouldn't each day be a chance to do — or appreciate — something wonderful?

Irma Bombeck showed her own appreciation of a new day with these memorable words: "Don't forget to stop and smell the roses today. Take time to tell a loved one how much you love them, do something nice for yourself, and stop to give God thanks for all of it."

Tuesday — **August 24**

I PARTICULARLY like this tender and thought-provoking proverb: "It is in the shelter of each other that the people live."

Some folk might seem more of a ramshackle lean-to, but a smile, an encouraging word or a helping hand can change all that, sheltering a troubled heart from the worst of the weather.

Wednesday — **August 25**

AFTER the Second World War, a famous French writer penned an inspiring story called "The Man Who Planted Trees". In it, a shepherd living in a remote area, yet one devastated by conflict, gathers acorns to plant in the bare earth.

Many thousands have been inspired by this tale and have carried out tree planting, sure that the shepherd must have been a living person.

In fact, he sprang entirely from imagination — but the tree-planting became real just the same!

Thursday — *August 26*

OUR friend John said to us, "For weeks I thought our new neighbour across the road wasn't the most friendly of people. He ignored several smiles with a blank look whenever I encountered him.

"But I later learned that the man's eyesight was very poor, and he found the world a shadowy and blurred place, so he seldom ventured far. Not surprisingly, he was waiting for an eye operation.

"Now I greet him warmly when I see him, and we have reached the stage of exchanging a few friendly words. It's seldom wise to jump to hasty conclusions about people or situations, for things often aren't what they seem."

Friday — *August 27*

TREAT people as if they were what they ought to be and you help them to become what they are capable of being.

Johann Wolfgang von Goethe.

Saturday — *August 28*

HOW I love morning —
Newborn skies of tender pink.
Rosy, shy, shining,
Wrapped in quilted gold and blue,
And ribboned with bird song.
How I love mornings —
When my soul stirs quietly
To the Father's whisper
And His loving touch,
Painted on a waking day for me.

Rachel Wallace-Oberle.

Sunday — *August 29*

IF your soul has no Sunday, it becomes an orphan.
Albert Schweitzer.

Monday — *August 30*

HE left school aged sixteen, joined a law firm, invested money unwisely and fell heavily into debt. Not a very promising start, you might say, yet young Benjamin Disraeli was not one to give up. Even after the collapse of a newspaper, his brainchild, his spirit saw him through.

He became a successful novelist, entered Parliament and rose to be Prime Minister, the only one in Victorian times who had not been to University and did not belong to the landed gentry.

When he died in 1881 Queen Victoria erected a memorial in his honour, describing herself as "his grateful Sovereign and Friend". A royal tribute indeed.

Tuesday — *August 31*

ALL faiths tell us to love one another. But it's not that simple, is it? People can be difficult. So just how do we go about achieving this fine aim?

Many minds have long pondered the same question and St Francis of Sales explains it in timeless terms:

"You learn to speak by speaking, to study by studying, to run by running . . . and just so you learn to love God and man by loving. Begin as a mere apprentice and the very power of love will lead you on to become a master of the art."

September

A MEMBER of the Mission to Seafarers, famous for their Flying Angel symbol, told me that he believed people fell into three categories.

"Some are like ancient canal barges because they only move forward when towed. Others are like sailing boats who only operate and function properly when there are favourable winds."

"And what's the third kind?" I asked.

"They are like lifeboats," he said. "They travel through all waters and all weathers, often against the tide, because they have not only the power within but a distant goal, too, that includes helping others out of trouble."

Let us try to be as single-minded as these lifeboats and their courageous crews.

COOKERY programmes and recipe books are all the rage these days, with celebrities also queuing up to pass on their recipes.

Jean Baptiste Moliere was a seventeenth-century playwright. He might or might not have known his way around a kitchen, but he did suggest an ingredient we might all stir into our life.

"It is a fine seasoning of joy," he said, "to think of those we love."

THE FRIENDSHIP BOOK

Friday — **September 3**

"**Y**OU know, Francis," observed the Lady of the House, "I think it is true that Autumn has something to please each of our five senses."

"For example?" I prompted.

"Well, there are the reds and golds of the trees to delight our eyes, the smell of the woodlands and the crunch of fallen leaves to satisfy our nose and ears, and the warmth of late sunshine to please our sense of touch."

"But what about our sense of taste?" I asked.

"How would you like some of my newly-made blackberry and apple jam for tea?" came the prompt reply.

And there was nothing more to be said.

Saturday — **September 4**

A GARDEN is a growing thing
  An ever-changing space,
A work in progress, not yet right
  Yet still a hopeful place.
And just as we would not condemn
  A garden's random flaws,
So let us just as soon forgive
  Our fellows, when we've cause.
For some of us are quick to bloom
  While others are more slow,
And all of us need love and care
  To help us as we grow.
With time and trust we all will reach
  Our own potential worth
And then, like every growing thing,
  We'll beautify the earth.

Margaret Ingall.

CRAFTED
WITH PRIDE

Sunday — **September 5**

"THANK God for stubble fields!" The clergyman was smiling as he said these words and of course he meant exactly what he said. A field of stubble may not be as beautiful as a field of waving golden grain but it tells us the harvest has been safely brought in and we can all share the farmer's relief and pride in a job well done.

Let's think of these words as we catch sight of the bare fields this Autumn.

Monday — **September 6**

GREG had just come back from a short trip to Scotland. "Did you know," he said, "that if it wasn't for an Edinburgh man, we might not have the Fire Brigade that we rely on today?

"It was started in the early 1800s by James Braidwood who, as a builder, was only too aware that the slums were fire traps, so he decided to form the world's first municipal Fire Brigade.

"He trained his recruits in safety procedures, encouraged them to enter buildings to tackle the seat of the blaze, and gave them climbing practice sessions on Edinburgh's North Bridge.

"The success of his methods became so widely known that more and more units were set up, and Braidwood himself was appointed Superintendent of the new London Fire Brigade. Sadly, he died in the line of duty. Thousands lined the route of his funeral procession, and later a London fire-boat was named in his honour."

This legacy lives on, embodied in every member of today's Fire Brigade who continues to risk their own life in the effort to save others.

Tuesday — **September 7**

HAVE you ever wondered where the expression, "A man's best friend is his dog," came from? Well, in Warrensburg, Missouri, in 1870, there was a court case about a dog that had been shot.

The lawyer for the animal's owner gave a long discourse on the qualities of a dog, including, "A man's dog will stand by him in prosperity and poverty, in health and sickness, will sleep on the cold, snowy ground if only he can be near his master, will kiss the hand that has no food to offer, will guard the sleep of his pauper master as if he were a prince . . . the one absolutely unselfish friend a man has in this selfish world is his dog."

The dog's owner won the case and Warrensburg adopted the motto: *Home Of Man's Best Friend.*

Wednesday — **September 8**

AUTUMN is a second Spring when every leaf is a flower.   Albert Camus.

Thursday — **September 9**

FEW of us will live a life such as Bob Hope enjoyed. He entertained millions of people worldwide and met royalty and heads of states. He won Oscars, a Congressional Medal and was made a Knight of the British Empire.

But was his life any better than yours or mine? He didn't think so.

"When we recall the past," he said, "we usually find that it is the simplest things – not the great occasions – that give off the greatest glow of happiness."

Friday — **September 10**

THERE was once a spoiled little boy whose father was rich. The young lad wanted for nothing, but despite this he stole from his elder brothers and from one of the gardeners.

He committed other misdeeds but had a change of heart when his father fell ill. Weeping, he wrote down all he had done and handed the list to his father.

His father tore it up and said, "I forgive you."

The boy grew up to be Mahatma Gandhi, the spiritual leader loved and respected throughout the world for his honesty and simplicity.

Saturday — **September 11**

THE Lady of the House and I were intrigued when we received an invitation to the home of our old friend Mary.

"Now, what should we bring?" asked the Lady of the House.

"Nothing," came the reply. "Just yourselves."

We were warmly welcomed on arrival and then taken into the dining-room where an elaborately-decorated celebration cake was placed in pride of place.

"What are we celebrating?" I enquired. "We know it's not your birthday."

"We are celebrating our long-term friendship," Mary replied. "Something that's given me so much pleasure over many, many years, a joy beyond words."

Beside the cake was a little note:
Make new friends but keep the old.
One is silver and the other is gold.

Sunday — *September 12*

*K*EEP me from shadows,
  Dear Father I pray,
From fears that dishearten,
And drive trust away.
Let foolish misgivings
Of challenges new
Not ever deter me
From seeing things through.
For though life brings trials
From which we can't hide,
I know I'll walk safely
With You by my side.

M. J. Brison.

Monday — *September 13*

I WAS visiting Ted when his nephew Kevin called round. "Now," he said as he caught sight of me, "my uncle has told me that you like to collect quotations. Well, I have a good one for you:

Time is a companion that goes with us on a journey. It reminds us to cherish each moment because it will never come again. What we leave behind is not as important as how we have lived.

I asked him where these memorable words had come from.

His smile grew wider. "It's wisdom from the stars — or to put it another way, it's from Captain Jean Luc Picard, in the television series 'Star Trek'. It's good, isn't it?"

It is indeed, which just goes to show that wisdom is still wisdom, even when it's beamed down from the Starship Enterprise!

Tuesday — *September 14*

MARIA was a Polish woman who spent two terrible years in a concentration camp when young. After gaining her freedom she moved to Scotland where one of the first things she did was to join the local church.

She was asked, "How can you still believe in a loving God after all you went through?"

"God did not do that to me," she replied. "Man did. God saved me."

Such is true faith.

Wednesday — *September 15*

RED and orange, yellow too,
  Followed by bright green and blue,
Vivid violet ends the flow,
  Just ahead of indigo;
What wondrous colours, hue and tint,
  Made manifest by sunlight's glint,
When sudden Autumn showers pass,
  And raindrops drip from leaves and grass,
God's miracle that mystifies,
  When a rainbow arcs the skies.

                              Brian H. Gent.

Thursday — *September 16*

THESE days we are not short of suggestions on how to keep fit. Usually these ideas tend to come and go, but the eighteenth-century writer Nicolas Chamfort had a health tip as valid now as it was then.

"If taking fruit does not keep you healthy enough, try more laughter! The most wasted of all days is that on which one has not laughed."

Friday — **September 17**

A NICE cup of tea for our friend Mavis is a delight to be savoured every afternoon at half-past three. The writer Jean Webster could have had her in mind when she wrote:

"It isn't the great big pleasures that count the most; it's making a great deal out of the little ones."

Saturday — **September 18**

YOU give but little when you give of your possessions. It is when you give of yourself that you truly give.

Kahlil Gibran.

Sunday — **September 19**

WE'VE all heard of the Dead Sea, but who killed it? Well, in a way it killed itself. There's a steady flow of water going into it from the River Jordan, but it gives nothing back. The water just stays there until it evaporates.

So there has been a slow but steady build-up of salts and minerals until the sea could no longer support life. You could almost say it died of stinginess. If it had given as much as it received the Dead Sea could be alive and well today.

The same thing happens to us if all we care about is what we receive. It's only by passing on our gifts that we keep our hearts and souls places worth living in.

"Give, and it will be given to you. A good measure, pressed down, shaken together and running over, will be poured into your lap."

(Luke 6:38)

Monday — *September 20*

ELLA spent her early years in an unhappy home, was orphaned as a teenager and followed a lifestyle that saw her placed in a remand home. But she also went on to become the First Lady of Song, win thirteen Grammy Awards and was presented with the National Medal of Art.

What carried her through? Well, perhaps these words, which might apply to each of us, can give us some insight:

"Just don't give up on trying to do what you really want to do," Ella Fitzgerald said. "Where there is love and inspiration, I don't think you can go wrong."

Tuesday — *September 21*

THIS witty item was seen in a church magazine: "Come work for the Lord. The labour is intensive, the hours are long, and the pay is low, but the retirement benefits are out of this world!"

Wednesday — *September 22*

IT'S all too easy to be dissatisfied with things. But there's a reason why we are where we are, reflected in these words by John Oxenham:

Is your place a small place?
Tend it with care! He set you there.
Is your place a large place?
Guard it with care! He set you there.
Whate'er your place, it is
Not yours alone but his
Who set you there.

GARDEN HARVEST

Thursday — *September 23*

DESPITE early insecurities about her appearance and speaking abilities, women's rights activist Susan B. Anthony grew into her role, giving thousands of speeches over a period of forty years. She learned that age was no barrier whatsoever to being effective.

"The older I get," she once wrote, "the greater power I seem to have to help the world. I am like a snowball, the further I am rolled, the more I seem to gain.

Friday — *September 24*

A POEM FOR WHISPERING

THE night is approaching
Long shadows now creep;
Through meadow and woodland
The dark stretches deep.

Up in the sky
The stars burn all pearl-white
And out from the hill edge
The moon climbs quite milk-bright.

Villages shine
Like clusters of fish
In a vast, shadowed ocean
With only one wish:

To float to the morning
So far out of view
Safe, sound and sleeping
Till the sun is made new.

Kenneth Steven.

Saturday — *September 25*

TO know someone here or there with whom you can feel there is understanding in spite of distances or thoughts expressed — that can make life a garden.

Johann Wolfgang von Goethe.

Sunday — *September 26*

MANY well-known hymns have been written by interesting people. An example was Julia Ward Howe, born in 1819, the daughter of a stockbroker father and a poet mother.

She married a much older man, Dr Samuel Howe, but their marriage was somewhat unhappy, because Samuel did not wish his wife to spread her wings. But Julia was determined, and attended lectures, studied foreign languages, and wrote.

The turning point in her life came when she wrote the much-loved hymn which became known as "The Battle Hymn Of The Republic". This rousing composition whose famous first line is: "Mine eyes have seen the glory of the coming of the Lord", was written to encourage the soldiers of the North who were fighting for the freedom of slaves during the American Civil War.

After the publication of this hymn in 1862, Julia became well known both as a writer and a speaker, and she devoted herself to various good causes including the improvement of educational and political opportunities for women.

She was ninety-one years old when she died and it was said of her, "she could always discover sunlight behind the shadows and the clouds".

Monday — **September 27**

ROSALINDE is a well-liked art tutor and a great encourager and motivator. Part of her home has been converted into a small studio and she never turns anyone away, regardless of their level of artistic ability. Rosalinde's philosophy has always been simple and is on the wall of her studio for everyone to see:

If you hear a voice within you say 'you cannot paint', then by all means paint, and that voice will be silenced.

Vincent Van Gogh.

Her students say these words have remained with them and inspire them in all sorts of situations and challenges.

Tuesday — **September 28**

TRAVELLING through the countryside there's a chance you might notice, somewhere in the distance, giant, white windmills, capturing the wind as a renewable source of energy. Of course, no matter how many wind farms we might have, only a tiny portion of wind can ever be caught this way.

We are searching for new sources of energy, and who knows where this might lead us. But I hope it takes us down the path predicted by Teilhard de Chardin, when he said:

"Someday after mastering the winds, the waves, the tides and gravity, we shall harness for God the energies of love, and then, for the second time in the history of the world, man will have discovered fire."

Thoughful words for us all to consider.

Wednesday — **September 29**

DO you have a favourite day of the week? It seems that nearly everybody does! Perhaps unsurprisingly, it appears that Monday is least liked, while Saturdays and Sundays predictably come top of the poll.

But one correspondent, Linda who lives in Georgia, left me bemused when she made a passing comment about Hump Day. "That's Wednesday," she explained, "the day when we get over the hump of the working week and can start sliding down towards the weekend."

It's a great thought, and one that left me smiling. Whether or not you have a favourite day of the week, let's remember to try to make the best of them one by one. A new day is a precious gift, so let's show we appreciate each and every one!

Thursday — **September 30**

IN "Roots", Alex Hailey's book about slavery, there is a chapter where Kunta Kinte is almost lost. He has been stolen from his home, transported across the world in terrible conditions and treated dreadfully by his new masters. Lying in his hut he has almost forgotten where he came from.

Then he hears a woman singing in the night. It's a song from Africa and that moment of grace reminds him he has a home and he was a free man. In his soul he's never a slave again.

As John Newton put it so well:

Through many dangers, toils and snares
I have already come;
'Tis grace hath brought me safe this far,
and grace will lead me home.

October

HECTOR was on his way home when I bumped into him. "I've been playing truant," he announced cheerfully. "This morning I'd intended doing paperwork indoors, but it was such a glorious day I couldn't resist going out for a walk."

There's something about a fine day in October that has its own magic. The sunshine is all the sweeter for knowing that Winter is on its way, and although we may be sad at the passing of Summer, it is the time to enjoy the fruits of the harvest.

So I could quite understand why Hector had seized his chance, for as he pointed out, "When God gives us a day like today — well, it's only good manners to accept it!"

CURIOUS people might spend a lifetime studying subjects such as philosophy looking for insights into life. George MacDonald, the Scottish writer who inspired both Mark Twain and C. S. Lewis, wrote these words on the theme:

"The good for which we are born into this world," he wrote, "is that we may learn to love."

It's a subject anyone can start learning at any age. We will be tested frequently, but never fail while we keep on trying.

Sunday — **October 3**

DOES it ever seem like your burdens are just too much to bear? Well, God has many names across the world and to the Ugandan tribe the Kiga, the Creator is Biheko, which translates as "God, who carries everyone on his back".

Burdens are heavy when you think you are the only one doing the carrying. When you realise a loving God is supporting you and your worries, things suddenly seem quite different.

"Even to your old age and grey hairs, I am he, I am he who will sustain you. I have made you and I will carry you."   (Isaiah 46:4)

Monday — **October 4**

TEN-year-old Daisy came home with this verse which her teacher had handed out to her class. These words provide much food for thought, whatever our age, don't you agree?

Be careful of your thoughts,
for your thoughts
become your words.
Be careful of your words,
for your words
become your actions.
Be careful of your actions,
for your actions
become your habits.
Be careful of your habits,
for your habits
become your character.
Be careful of your character,
for your character
becomes your destiny.

THE FRIENDSHIP BOOK

Tuesday — **October 5**

WE are all travellers in the wilderness of this world, and the best that we find in our travels is an honest friend.

Robert Louis Stevenson.

Wednesday — **October 6**

SOME people come into our lives
And fill an empty space,
And others smile and seem to make
This world a better place.

Some people let the sun shine in
Dispelling doom and gloom,
And some can make the stars come out
To light a darkened room.

Some people give us strength and hope
To make a bright, new start,
And walking through our lives they leave
Their footprints in our heart.

Iris Hesselden.

Thursday — **October 7**

AGED eighteen, Kim Linehan was the world's top amateur female distance swimmer. Attaining such success required a rigorous training schedule and when asked which part she found the most difficult, she replied, "Getting in the water!"

Many ambitions tend to fall by the wayside and we never find out what might have been achieved. There could be new skills to learn, help to give others, while adventures and travels may beckon.

But how will we know? Well, first we have to "get in the water".

THREADS OF GOLD

Friday — **October 8**

THERE'S never been a life without problems and when we're in the midst of trying to solve one it is sometimes hard to understand why it has to be that way.

The journalist and television presenter Malcolm Muggeridge had an opinion on that very matter.

"I can say with complete truthfulness," he wrote, "that everything I have learned in my seventy-five years in this world, everything that has truly enhanced and enlightened my experience, has come about through affliction, not happiness."

Let's not forget that life's challenges have their purpose, too.

Saturday — **October 9**

IT seems that not so many of us find time to write letters these days, and when we do the pace of modern life makes it likely that they will begin with something like: "Sorry for not having written for so long."

Author Garrison Keillor suggests that the first step in letter-writing is to get over the guilt of not writing. "Letters are a gift," he says, "a piece of handmade writing, not a bill, sitting in a friend's path as they trudge home from a long day."

Letters can convey both the good and not so good events in our lives — and they can even share things that don't get said in casual conversation, such as heartfelt thanks for a kind gesture or for precious, ongoing friendship.

So let's revive the art of writing letters, no matter how short — and brighten someone's day.

Sunday — **October 10**

WHEN the office where Jennifer had worked for many years closed, she lost her job. As the weeks went by and no new work could be found, she became increasingly concerned.

Throughout this uncertain time Jennifer kept firmly in mind one of her favourite Scripture verses: "Do not remember the former things, nor consider the things of old. Behold I will do a new thing, now it shall spring forth; shall you not know it? I will even make a road in the wilderness and rivers in the desert." (Isaiah 43:18-19)

She included this powerful promise in her daily prayers and believed that a new door would open. When she did find a job that turned out to be more rewarding than the one she had lost, she realised that her own road in the wilderness had opened up.

Faith is the vehicle that guides us through the barren, rocky places. But it is up to us to take the driver's seat, grasp the wheel and turn the key.

Monday — **October 11**

SHYNESS can often stop us putting ourselves forward when it comes to getting involved or helping out. After all, we tell ourselves, there's probably someone better placed to help.

But it's the so-called average, everyday abilities of ordinary folk which make the world go round. Henry van Dyke described that truth when he wrote these words:

"Use what talent you possess. The woods would be very quiet if no birds sang except those that sang best."

*Tuesday — **October 12***

MARIE CURIE, the Polish scientist, had an all too short life. However, in that brief space of time she made important scientific discoveries, found love and left these words of encouragement:

"Life is not easy for any of us, but what of it? We must have perseverance and confidence in ourselves. We must believe we are each gifted for something and that this thing must be attained."

You might not realise it, but you are gifted for something. Find your gift and you'll find fulfilment.

*Wednesday — **October 13***

INDIAN summer, most welcome of gifts,
The days when you wake, and your very
heart lifts
With pleasure at finding so perfect a morn,
As fresh as an apple, as crisp as the corn,
With sky that's as blue as a kingfisher's wing,
Sunlight so bright that it makes the world sing,
And trees with their branches scarce able to hold
The weight of the leaves that are dipped
all in gold.
Sweet Indian summer, you'll soon slip away
But long we'll remember your brief, lovely stay.

Margaret Ingall.

*Thursday — **October 14***

NO love, no friendship, can cross the path of our destiny without leaving some mark on it forever.

François Mauriac.

Friday — **October 15**

DONNA works for a well-known charitable organisation which employs disabled adults. She has this quote by Desmond Tutu on her desk:

A person is a person because he recognises others as persons.

It means no person is an island. Everything we do and every decision we make relies on the actions of others, and these should enrich our community.

An admirable philosophy of life, surely.

Saturday — **October 16**

A KIND word is like a Spring day.
Russian Proverb.

Sunday — **October 17**

IN the 1860s The Great Blondin amazed everyone by walking a tightrope across Niagara Falls. Sometimes he would make the perilous walk pushing a wheelbarrow, or even carrying his manager on his back.

What the public rarely noticed was the star at each end of the rope. While they were gasping at the depth of the drop, the narrowness of the rope and the rushing water, Blondin kept his focus on one thing, the star at the finish of his walk — he made it safely across each time.

When distractions tend to pull you down, find your own star and follow it: "To this you were called, because Christ has suffered for you, leaving you an example, that you should follow in his steps." (Peter 1 2:21)

Monday — **October 18**

THE novelist Charles Dickens is said to have based the ever-optimistic Mr Micawber in "Great Expectations" on his own father. John Dickens was a wages clerk with the navy and, after being made redundant, he fell into debt and was eventually locked up in jail.

John's ever cheerful response to hard times made sure his character lived on in the fictitious Mr Micawber and this attitude undoubtedly had a great effect on John's son, Charles.

A positive attitude is a real help in times of need.

Tuesday — **October 19**

HERE are some cheerful words for you today: "A good laugh is sunshine in a house."

William Makepeace Thackeray.

Wednesday — **October 20**

I CAME across a few encouraging lines, well worth passing on:
Just for today,
Let go of anger.
Just for today,
Let go of worry.
Just for today,
Count your blessings and honour your parents,
Teachers and neighbours.
Just for today,
Live honestly.
Just for today,
Be kind to all living things.
Why not send these thoughts to a friend today?

Thursday — *October 21*

THE Lady of the House was smiling when she arrived home one afternoon. "I've a riddle for you," she said. "What's the best thing to resolve a quarrel?"

But before I could even begin to consider a possible answer, she announced triumphantly, "A rain-storm! You see, I happened to catch sight of Cathy and Frances while I was out shopping. I knew that they'd had a disagreement, but they were both coming out of the newsagent's at the same time when the clouds burst.

"The next moment I saw Cathy helping to carry Frances' shopping, while Frances held her umbrella over both of them! It looks as if the rain-storm washed all that bad feeling completely away."

Well, it was an unusual sort of riddle, but I certainly liked the answer!

Friday — *October 22*

ASTRONAUT Donald Williams spent almost three hundred hours in space before retiring. With the possible advent of "space tourism" that impressive feat might soon come to seem quite commonplace, who can tell? But if tourists in the future get as much from their experience as Donald Williams did, then their trips will have been more than worth the fare.

"For those who have seen the Earth from space," he said, "and for the hundreds or perhaps even thousands more who will, the experience certainly changes your perspective. That's when you realise that the things we share in our world are far more valuable than those which divide us."

Saturday — *October 23*

IN the well-known film "Paint Your Wagon", Lee Marvin plays philosophical drunk Ben Rumstead. Near the end the rumour of gold to be found elsewhere has No Name City packing its bags to head off in search of riches.

A shopkeeper offers this opinion: "There are two kinds of people in this world, those who move on and those who stay. Ain't that the truth?"

Rumstead replies, "No, that ain't the truth. There are two kinds of people in this world. Them that's going no place and them that's going someplace."

Sunday — *October 24*

THE seeds that fall from some desert plants have shells so tough they keep everything out. They can lie dormant in the baking sun for years. Then a flash flood comes, the seeds are swept along, buffeted by the water and scratched by rocks.

When they settle in moist soil, they start to grow — but only because they can now take in water through the scratches and cracks in their shell.

A protective shell might seem a good thing, for a while. However, we're all subject to life's "flash floods" and, surprisingly, that's when many of us grow best. We choose not to be dormant any more and we take on board the water of eternal life through the cracks.

He said to me: "It is done. I am the Alpha and the Omega, the Beginning and the End. To him who is thirsty I will give to drink without cost from the spring of the water of life."   (Revelation 21:6)

HOME COMFORTS

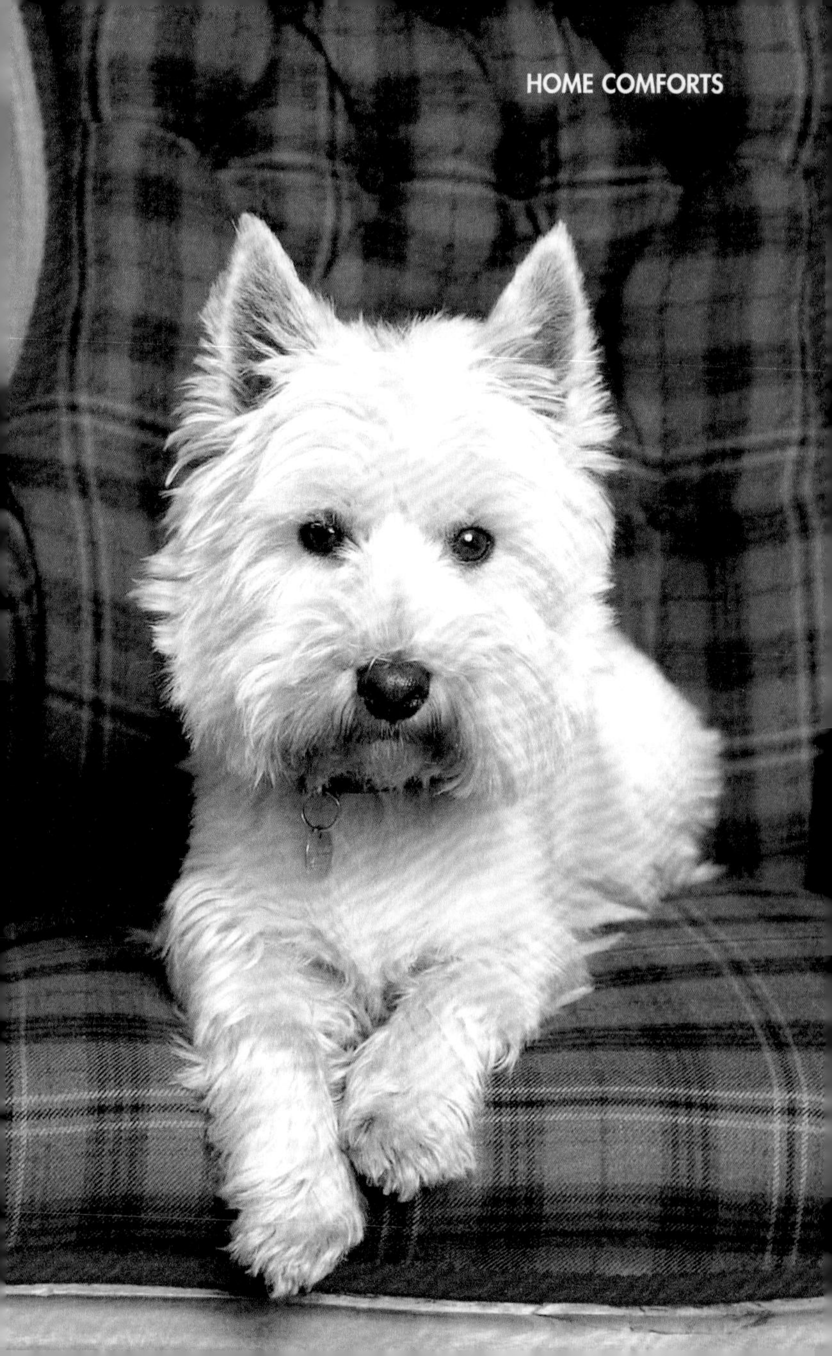

Monday — **October 25**

HOLD on to what is good,
even if it's a handful of earth.

Hold on to what you believe,
even if it's a tree that stands by itself.

Hold on to what you must do,
even if it's a long way from here.

Hold on to your life,
even if it's easier to let go.

Hold on to my hand,
even if I've gone away from you.

Pueblo Prayer.

Tuesday — **October 26**

I SUPPOSE we've all become accustomed to the sight of more and more road signs, but have you heard about the ones in Port Phillip, Australia?

They were put up by Mayor Janet Bolitho to count smiles per hour. Yes, that's right, smiles! The unusual scheme was monitored by volunteers, and a regular count was displayed to encourage even more people to smile or greet fellow pedestrians.

A silly idea? Not at all, for behind the experiment was the serious goal of trying to encourage people to become more connected, more trusting and to increase their quality of life.

And if all these benefits can be achieved by raising a smile or two, well, I'm willing to try. Are you?

Wednesday — **October 27**

HAVE you heard of Alice Herz Sommer? Not only was she one of Europe's most celebrated pianists but, born in Prague to a Jewish family, she was also a survivor of Nazi concentration camps.

Alice's long and varied life taught her a wisdom that she was happy to share with others. Possessions, she felt, were of little importance, something that "it's good to be able to detach yourself from". Friendship, however, was quite another matter:

"I have many old friends, but I have never stopped making new ones. Look for the best in them — everyone has something beautiful inside."

Thursday — **October 28**

THE Lord will drench you with showers, but He will dry you with His sun. Czech Proverb.

Friday — **October 29**

OUR friend Charles always has tales to tell about his youth when the world was younger and Summers were always sunny and warm — or so he would have you believe.

However, the last time we were chatting he made a comment when I remarked that he always seemed to be talking about the "Good Old Days".

"To tell you the truth, I'm beginning to realise that it is better to look ahead instead of looking back at the past," he admitted. "The future is there to explore, there's always a possibility of great things ahead, and if we have faith, 'the best is yet to be.'"

Nothing is better than faith and hope.

Saturday — **October 30**

IMAGINE standing beside Leonardo da Vinci watching him paint. I'd be lost in admiration, like a young student who once stood by this master, day after day, watching him bring one of his most famous works to completion.

When the painting was almost done da Vinci said, "Now you finish it."

The young man protested that he could not paint as skilfully. Da Vinci replied, "Will not what I have done inspire you to do your best though?"

Few of us are blessed with the talent of Leonardo da Vinci but, like him, each of us can live our lives in a way that will inspire others to do their best.

Sunday — **October 31**

JOSEPH SCRIVEN who penned the popular hymn "What A Friend We Have In Jesus", suffered personal tragedy and lived for a while as an itinerant worker carrying his saw and sawhorse wherever he went.

Legend has it a wealthy businessman saw him and suggested hiring him to cut some wood. A friend of the businessman's recognised Scriven and said, "He won't cut wood for you. He only cuts wood for those who don't have enough to pay."

How wonderful to think we might follow Scriven's example and even at our lowest ebb still find something in us for those worse off.

"The King will reply, 'I tell you the truth, whatever you did for one of the least of these brothers of mine, you did for me'".

(Matthew 25:40)

November

Monday — **November 1**

IN the short days and long nights of Winter I take some comfort from the wise words of Anne Bradstreet, a Puritan settler in the New World. Life would often have been difficult but she preferred to look at things a little differently.

"If we did not sometimes taste adversity," she wrote, "prosperity would not be so welcome. If we had no Winter, the Spring would not be so pleasant."

So when we do savour the brighter, longer days, remember that dull, grey days have served their purpose and added to the pleasures we enjoy.

Tuesday — **November 2**

THREADS and strands of many colours
Woven by an unseen hand,
Tapestry of life and living
Sometimes not the way we planned.
Threads of joy and expectation,
Strands of every rainbow hue,
Making pictures, forming patterns
With a promise running through.
Angel hands forever weaving
Through the laughter and the tears,
Adding threads of hope and comfort
Adding love throughout the years.
                    Iris Hesselden.

Wednesday — **November 3**

IN his novel "Les Miserables" Victor Hugo wrote these words: "I met in the street a very poor young man who was in love. His hat was old, his coat worn, his cloak was out at the elbows, the water passed through his shoes — and the stars shone through his soul."

Love will do that to you, and nothing else even comes close!

Thursday — **November 4**

OUR friend John is one of the most generous people I know. He always gives, whether it's of his time or money. One day I asked him how he's able to keep giving so cheerfully when it seems as though the needs around us will never run out.

He quoted a statement Martin Luther King Jr. made and said it has inspired him for many years: "Even if I knew that tomorrow the world would go to pieces, I would still plant my apple tree."

Making a difference may not be so much about the change we hope to see around us, as it is about the change we'll see in ourselves.

Friday — **November 5**

TODAY, consider these words by Anton Chekhov: "We shall find peace. We shall hear angels. We shall see the sky sparkling with diamonds."

There is beauty around us, in things large and small, in friends, family, the countryside, a singing bird. Stop to reflect, to give thanks, to contemplate the gift of another day. Touch the wonders of life and rejoice!

Saturday — *November 6*

ONE of the most dreadful sights anyone could ever witness must surely be a shipwreck, and certainly Henry Trengrouse never forgot watching the foundering of the *HMS Anson* in 1807.

Although able to assist in the rescue efforts, he still had to look on helplessly as more than a hundred people were drowned, unable to reach the safety of the nearby shore.

No doubt that's why, when attending a firework display some time later, he had the sudden inspiration that one method of getting a rope out to a ship in trouble might be to fix it to a light-weight line attached to a rocket.

Despite the fact it was to require a great deal of time and effort before his ideas on marine safety were taken seriously, eventually his device of a Bosun's Chair, a seat to pull people to safety on ropes tied between ship and shore, was put into use by around three hundred coastguard stations.

The folk museum in Helston celebrates Henry's achievement, but his real success must lie in the untold number of lives that have been saved — all thanks to, literally, a flash of inspiration.

Sunday — *November 7*

"LOOK everyone straight in the eye" was one suggestion offered for life's journey to the audience of school-leavers at their end of term prize-giving. Most, I'm sure, took the advice to heart, though not all would realise it goes back thousands of years.

"Let thine eyes look right on, and let thine eyelids look straight before thee." (Proverbs 4:25)

SAFE PASSAGE

THE FRIENDSHIP BOOK

Monday — **November 8**

*D*O not dwell in the past, do not dream of the future, concentrate the mind on the present moment. Buddha.

Tuesday — **November 9**

*T*HE wind was gusting hard outside
 This dark November night,
It whirls the clouds across the sky
 And hides the moon from sight,
It flings the rain against the doors,
 And rattles at the panes,
It strips the leaves from boughs and trees
 And blocks the flooded drains.
How blessed am I that I may lie
 In a bed so safe and warm,
May God embrace all those who face
 This wild November storm.

Margaret Ingall.

Wednesday — **November 10**

*L*ORD Shaftesbury was known as "the friend of the poor". He campaigned to free children from labouring in mines, set up ragged schools for the poverty stricken and provided better sanitation to prevent disease.

When he died, thousands of ordinary folk stood hatless in the rain at his funeral. His philosophy of life was summed up in these few words:

"Not one kind word is ever spoken, nor kind deed ever done, but sooner or later returns to bless the giver and becomes a chain binding men with golden bands to the throne of God."

Thursday — **November 11**

IN the United Kingdom today is Armistice Day or Remembrance Day, but in the United States since the year 1954, 11th November has been called Veterans' Day. Dedicating that special day in Congress President Eisenhower urged the world to "Remember the sacrifices of those who fought so gallantly and re-dedicate ourselves to promoting enduring peace."

We can all make sure those sacrifices weren't in vain. Why not, for example, reach out to someone you might not have talked to before? Let's make our own little corner of the world a place where enduring peace would feel right at home.

Friday — **November 12**

THIS Japanese proverb is a wise thought for today: *One kind word can warm three Winter months.*

Saturday — **November 13**

THE Shona people of Zimbabwe have this traditional greeting. "Maswera sei?" translates as "How has your day been?" and their response means, "My day has been good if your day has been good."

These words recognise a close kinship between people and a responsibility for each other's happiness and well being.

Cain was dismissive when God asked where Abel was. "Am I my brother's keeper?" he retorted. There are still places in the world where the answer to that question would be, "Of course!"

Sunday — *November 14*

*MY thanks, dear Lord, for everything
You've given me today.
For all those busy hours spent
At labour or at play,
For sticking with me when I moaned
That work was far from fun,
For giving me a sense of pride
When all my tasks were done.
I thank you for my leisure time,
For friends who made me smile,
For wisdom too, that came my way,
And made me pause awhile.
Dear Lord, the hours so quickly pass,
Both working and at play,
Please guide me through tomorrow
As you've helped me through today.*

M. J. Brison.

Monday — *November 15*

ART Fry had an idea that led to the invention of a best-selling product. When he sang in his choir the little bits of paper he used to mark the pages would end up fluttering to the floor.

Then Art remembered an adhesive developed by a colleague that was considered a failure because it didn't stick very well. He coated a piece of paper with the adhesive and discovered it was not only a good bookmark, but was ideal for writing notes. It stayed in place as long as was necessary and could be removed without causing damage.

This invention, the Post-it note, has become hugely popular, used by millions every day.

Tuesday — **November 16**

WHEN Keith retired after forty years of teaching, it was plain from the number of well-wishers at his party how much he would be missed. A colleague asked for the secret of his success.

He thought for a moment, then said, "The best advice I could pass on would be something told to me by my head of department when I first started out.

"It's a quote from William Arthur Ward: *Learn and grow all you can; serve and befriend all you can; enrich and inspire all you can*. And like all the best lessons, it's surprisingly simple."

Ten out of ten for that!

Wednesday — **November 17**

LIFE is short but there is always time for courtesy.   Ralph Waldo Emerson.

Thursday — **November 18**

JOY'S neighbours call her a "prayer warrior". When there is a need, they always ask her to pray for their families and friends. On her kitchen walls is a collection of inspiring quotes:

"We have to pray with our eyes on God, not on the difficulties."

Oswald Chambers.

"Prayer does not change God, but it changes him who prays."

Søren Kierkegaard.

"When you pray, rather let your heart be without words than your words without heart."

John Bunyan.

Friday — **November 19**

A SMALL travelling fair had arrived in a nearby village, and our old friend Mary was enjoying accompanying young Eve who was having lots of fun. "You know, I'd love to join her on the merry-go-round," Mary said, "but some activities are definitely for the young."

Sometimes it does seem that many of the best things in life are aimed at the younger generation, but we should remember that this is only part of the picture. As Dale E. Turner once pointed out:

"Dreams are renewable. No matter what our age or condition, there are still untapped possibilities within us, and new beauty waiting to be born."

So let's not give up dreaming those dreams and doing our best to fulfil them.

Saturday — **November 20**

WHAT makes a person great? Well, Marian Anderson was born into a poor black family at a time when racism was at its height. Her father died when she was a child and her mother worked hard to support the family.

Despite all this, she went on to become a great mezzo-soprano, singing in front of King George VI, Queen Elizabeth, Toscanini and John F. Kennedy. She was awarded the Medal of Freedom and the National Medal of Arts.

But when asked by a reporter to pick the best day of her life she chose neither of these awards. It was, she said, the day she told her mother she didn't have to take in washing any more.

I'd say Marian Anderson found true greatness, wouldn't you?

Sunday — **November 21**

HERE'S a prayer that a friend in Canada passed on. I hope that these words will guide your steps today.

May today be all that you need it to be. May the peace of God and the freshness of the Holy Spirit rest in your thoughts, rule your hopes and conquer all your fears.

May God manifest himself today in ways that you have never before experienced. May your joys be fulfilled, your dreams brought closer and your prayers answered.

May faith enter a new height for you. May your territory be enlarged and may you step into your destiny.

May you be filled to overflowing with peace, health, happiness and true love for God. Amen.

Monday — **November 22**

OUR friend Norman was warmly wrapped up in a fleece jacket and scarf one Winter's day and lifted up his face to catch the golden rays of the misty, late-afternoon sun.

That day the fireside had held no charms for him and he had walked briskly for an hour under a cloudless, clear sky. As Henry Thoreau wrote: "What fire could ever equal the sunshine of a Winter's day?"

Later, Norman paused in his garden enjoying the last of the daylight hours, anticipating a brilliantly-coloured sunset foretold by a sky already colouring in the west.

Such days are diamonds in the crown of Winter.

Tuesday — *November 23*

"**Y**OU sound happy!" It's a comment often made to anyone overheard singing and I can understand why, for it's a cheerful sound, even coming from those who are not the most tuneful!

However, it would be a pity, surely, if we had to wait until we felt happy before we began to sing; I've been reading how the very act of singing is good for us.

It releases endorphins, chemicals which have a positive effect on our moods, and it also improves our breathing and posture. It can boost confidence and can bring us together, especially if we are a regular member of an amateur musical group.

Best of all, singing is free, so don't keep it under wraps. Sing and make a joyful noise!

Wednesday — *November 24*

*T*HE Lord is my shepherd. These are words we all know well, but why a shepherd? Why not a baker? Or a farmer?

One day, I was chatting to a shepherd, a man who had spent his whole working life on the hills. He recalled one Winter when the snow was so bad it had covered the whole flock — all except their ears, that is. Later, the rescue operation began.

"We nearly found them all," he said. "We brought three hundred and ninety-nine safely home." He slumped a little in his chair and bit his lower lip for a moment. "But we never found that other one."

This had happened over half a century before. Now aged over ninety, the shepherd still keenly felt the loss of that one stray creature.

That's why the Lord was a shepherd.

Thursday — **November 25**

THERE are various patterns and sequences occurring in the world of nature that often intrigue the best academic brains. This one was pointed out to me, not by a scientist, but by our friend Lisa.

"The phrase, From The Heart," she explained, "contains twelve letters which can be rearranged to form the words *Mother* and *Father*."

A coincidence? Who knows? But isn't it a lovely thought all the same?

Friday — **November 26**

BELIEVE: When someone says it can't be done,
Remember the sun, moon and earth
And all her stars
Were fashioned for you,
And are cheering for you.

Choose: When someone says it can't be done,
Swim bravely through the river of words;
Swim upstream,
Breathe deeply
And open your eyes.

Press On: When someone says it can't be done,
Learn to hear your heart,
To use your wings,
To own your truth.
Press on, friend;
Take Faith's warm hand in yours
And press on.

Rachel Wallace-Oberle.

Saturday — **November 27**

BRENDA had just returned home after enjoying a trip to some well-known gardens. "I'd been looking forward to visiting them for weeks," she said, "so I was really disappointed when the day turned out to be so wet.

"In fact," she continued, "like most of my fellow visitors, I was tempted just to spend most of my time in the café and shop. Then I decided that having come so far, it would be silly not to at least try a little walk outside — and I'm glad I did.

"Everything smelled so fresh, the colours were vibrant, and the raindrops just seemed to make everything look even more beautiful. When I eventually arrived back at the coach, the other passengers were sympathising with me for getting drenched, but I couldn't help feeling that I'd had a far more satisfying day."

Sometimes it takes a little effort to make the best of a bad situation, but as Brenda discovered it can set the whole world blooming!

Sunday — **November 28**

IT'S strange that whatever our age there are times when we feel rather lost, unsure of ourselves and our ability to cope. At these times we long for the reassurance that we are not alone. Let's keep in mind these words from Isaiah 41:13:

"I am holding you by your right hand — I, the Lord your God. And I say to you, Do not be afraid. I am here to help you."

Words to bring comfort to us always.

THE FRIENDSHIP BOOK

Monday — **November 29**

WHEN Fred Lebow went to consult his doctor, complaining of tiredness, a course of exercise was prescribed. Fred took up running and gradually started to feel much more energetic. It was then that he decided to share his "discovery".

He set about organising a race that has since seen thousands of people sharing Fred's elation at successfully crossing the finishing line — the New York Marathon.

We each have our own race to run. It might be short or long but, like Fred Lebow, let's make up our mind to run it in style!

Tuesday — **November 30**

SOMETIMES the demands of everyday life seem so overwhelming that we never have time just to be ourselves.

So I was intrigued to read about an idea called Mindfulness — in other words, the art of reclaiming the pleasure of simply being alive by concentrating all our attention on the moment.

The writer of this article suggested that we should try to put aside our worries about what tomorrow might bring, and enjoy the stillness and beauty of what we have here and now.

I think that's wisdom well worth sharing with you today. In the memorable words of the artist Georgia O'Keefe:

"When you take a flower in your hand and really look at it, it's your world for the moment. I want to give that world to someone else."

Now, that's a priceless gift to receive! And, in turn, you can pass it on.

December

IT'S such a crime that Summertime
Goes fleetly skipping past,
While Winter weeks, like dull antiques,
Just last and last and last.
But wait a tick, let's not be quick,
For Winter's not so bad,
There's hot mince pies and starlit skies
To make our hearts feel glad.
There's frosty walks and firelight talks,
There's crumpets for our tea,
There's dancing snow and candle glow,
Yes, that's the stuff for me!
So am I down, or wear a frown?
Oh no, I'll not complain.
I'll just give praise for all the days
Till Summer's here again.

Margaret Ingall.

A GAME of American football consists of four quarters, complex strategies, time-outs and overtime. But when Chicago Bears player Mike Singletary was asked what his favourite part of the game was, he replied, "The opportunity to play!"

We might not all be athletes or star players, but in this life we all have the opportunity to play. Let's make it a good game!

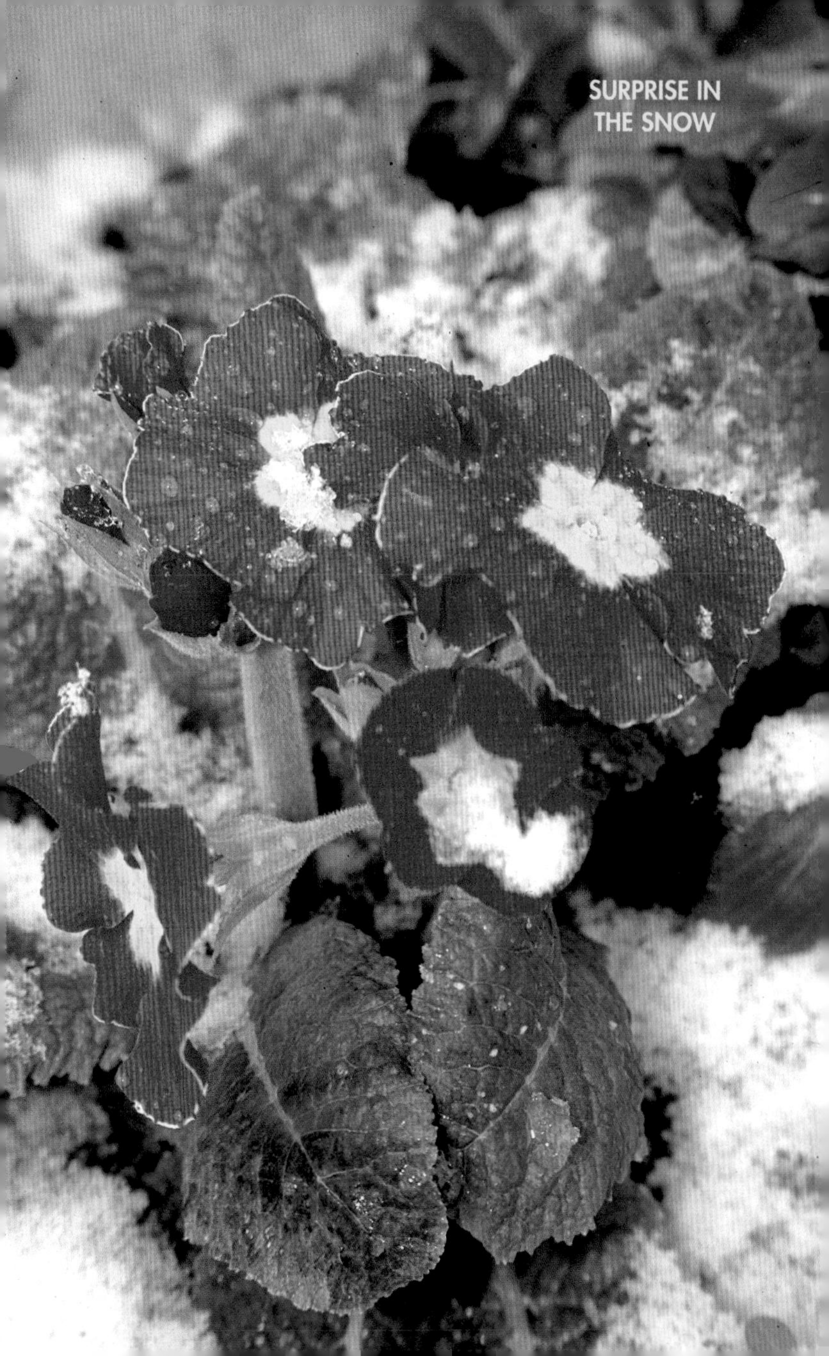
SURPRISE IN
THE SNOW

Friday — **December 3**

IN 1956 Erich Stegmann, established MFPA (the Mouth And Foot Painting Artists) by bringing together a small group of disabled artists from eight European countries. Their dream was to make a living through their creative talents.

MFPA has grown to become an international organisation which helps artists to meet their financial needs by reproducing their work in the form of cards, calendars and books. Today the group represents some seven hundred members from more than seventy countries worldwide.

As the poet and novelist Kahlil Gibran wisely observed, "All you have shall someday be given; therefore give now, that the season of giving may be yours and not your inheritors'."

Saturday — **December 4**

A TELEVISION series which showed the efforts of neighbours who banded together to restore their local churches was a "must-see" for many viewers, including the Lady of the House and myself.

It was our friend Peter who summed up the aspirations behind the various restoration efforts in a quote from Vista M. Kelly: "Snowflakes are one of nature's most fragile things, but just look what they can do when they stick together."

I doubt if any of these cheerful volunteers would have thought of themselves as snowflakes, but everyone who willingly lends a hand, whatever the project, makes the world a better place.

THE FRIENDSHIP BOOK

Sunday — December 5

HOW can weakness make you strong? Think of a steam train's whistle — that long blast of noise is powered by steam. You might say that's a waste of power best kept in the engine.

But an engineer once explained that boiling water leaves behind many impurities which cling to pipes, making the engine less efficient. The steam whistle blows impurities out of the pipes making the engine more efficient, more powerful.

Belief in our own abilities can often lead to the impurity of pride. Prayer can be the equivalent of a good blast on the steam whistle, seeming to give away power, but making us immeasurably stronger in the process.

"But he said to me, 'My grace is sufficient for you, for my power is made perfect in weakness.'"
(Corinthians II 12:9)

Monday — December 6

TIME is the greatest thief we know
He steals our lives away,
Don't let him rule you, let him go
And cherish every day.

"Time is a healer" people say
And "Only time will tell",
But love can take the hurt away,
And whisper, "All is well".

Keep all your dreams within your heart
And never let them die,
Make every day a brave new start —
And let the time go by!

Iris Hesselden.

HIDDEN DEPTHS

Tuesday — *December 7*

THERE is a story told of Niccolo Paganini, the great virtuoso violinist, who was born in 1782 in Genoa. While performing to a packed house with a full orchestra, a string on his violin suddenly snapped. But Paganini continued to play, improvising beautifully.

To everyone's surprise a second string broke. And then, a third . . . Paganini stood there with three strings dangling from his Stradivarius, but instead of leaving the stage, he calmly completed the music on the one remaining string. It became one of the most memorable concerts of his career.

Another great man, Louis Pasteur said, "Let me tell you the secret that has led me to my goal. My strength lies solely in my tenacity."

Often genius is perseverance in disguise.

Wednesday — *December 8*

WHAT is the shortest prayer you have ever heard? For me it is the one said by a mystic called Meister Eckhart in the fourteenth century. His simple words were: "Thank you."

After all, what else need we say?

Thursday — *December 9*

A STORY is told of the cathedral in Strasbourg. After a wartime bombing raid a statue of Christ remained almost intact — except for the hands.

Both had been blown off, and the sculptor offered to re-work the statue. But the congregation decided that they wanted the statue just as it was for, as they said, Christ had no hands but their hands in the world.

Friday — **December 10**

WHEN George Washington was a young army commander he made a derogatory comment to a Mr Payne. He promptly knocked Washington to the floor.

When they heard about this Washington's men were incensed and ready to set out for revenge, but their commander sent them back to barracks and instead met his opponent with a good bottle of wine and two glasses.

"Mr Payne," said Washington. "To err is human, but to correct our errors is always honourable."

When you think of the satisfaction that comes from doing the right thing and the pleasure that comes from mending a grievance, we should perhaps aim to do this more often.

Saturday — **December 11**

AT this time of year The Lady of the House fills a copper jug with an arrangement of seasonal evergreens, and places it on our hall table, a welcoming sight for visitors.

We call this "dressing up the hall" in celebration of the Twelve Days of Christmas. And not only does the copper jug contain red-berried holly and trails of ivy, there are also sprays of golden Winter jasmine to remind us of warm sunshine on chilly days, and sprigs of aromatic, evergreen rosemary for remembrance of the birth of Christ.

There is mistletoe, too, which the Romans believed brought peace to enemies, hence the well-known custom of kissing under it. Such traditions reflect the continuity of the great festival of Christmas.

Sunday — *December 12*

A UNIVERSITY did a study on "peace of mind". Amongst the attitudes they felt contributed to that happy state were these:

Staying engaged with the living world, even when you feel like shutting yourself far away; accepting that pain and disappointment are not failures, they are part of everyday life; cultivating virtues such as love, humour, compassion and loyalty.

Last, but certainly not least on the list was having something bigger than yourself to believe in: "I will grant peace in the land, and you will lie down and no one will make you afraid." (Leviticus 26:6)

Monday — *December 13*

WHEN you see a field of crisp, new snow, don't you just long to walk across it? In its clean freshness Russian author Anne Sophie Swetchine saw something we could all aspire to.

"Let our lives be pure as snowfields," she wrote, "where our footsteps leave a mark, but not a stain."

Tuesday — *December 14*

JANE'S mother has treasured this little poem on her writing desk for many years and its quiet wisdom has made a huge impression on her. I'd like to share it with you today:

Happy moments, praise God.
Difficult moments, seek God.
Quiet moments, worship God.
Painful moments, trust God.
Every moment, thank God.

THE FRIENDSHIP BOOK

Wednesday — **December 15**

I BUILT a birdfeeder on my lawn and waited.
Waited for the music of feathered wing
And glad song.
Waited for grace and glory to anoint the air,
Waited for colour to drench my yard.
And then, they came!
Countless precious creatures,
Black, brown, red, yellow, blue, speckled, grey,
Rejoicing, sharing, celebrating.
I watched and my heart overflowed
With the lesson winging joyfully across my lawn –
Our differences are beautiful,
But even more breathtaking and miraculous
When we come together.

Rachel Wallace-Oberle.

Thursday — **December 16**

JULIA has written a self-help book and at her signing event she inscribed this quote on the inside cover for readers to share:

"The world is a looking glass and gives back to every man the reflection of his own face. Frown at it, and it will in turn look sourly upon you; laugh at it and with it, and it is a jolly kind companion."

William Makepeace Thackeray.

Helpful advice, indeed!

Friday — **December 17**

EVERY tomorrow has two handles. We can take hold of it with the handle of anxiety or the handle of faith.

Henry Ward Beecher.

Saturday — *December 18*

CHRISTMAS Pudding — it has to be one of the best and most British of desserts, surely. Well, no, it's not, for, as a chef friend pointed out to our friend Eileen, in order to make a traditional Christmas pudding we actually need a great deal of help from other countries.

Sultanas, raisins and currants have to be brought from places such as Greece and Turkey, citrus fruits from India and China, say, while the various spices travel all the way from eastern Asia.

It's only then that we can combine all these ingredients, steam well and serve topped with a sprig of holly, perhaps from our own garden.

I like the thought of so many ingredients coming together from all over the world. It's just the kind of mix that adds flavour to all life's best things!

Sunday — *December 19*

DURING a Sunday service Helen's clergyman remarked that when we display our heavenly Father's character, we leave behind His influence wherever we go and in whatever we do.

To illustrate his point, he read aloud this verse:

My life shall touch a dozen lives
Before this day is done,
Leave countless marks for good or ill,
Ere sets the evening sun;
This is the wish I always wish,
The prayer I always pray:
Lord, may my life help other lives
It touches by the way.

Alice E. Clark.

THE FRIENDSHIP BOOK

Monday — **December 20**

I REMAIN a firm believer that most people are essentially . . . well . . . wonderful! Eddie Guest, who became known as The People's Poet in the first half of the twentieth century, summed this up beautifully:

A man is at his finest towards the finish
    of the year;
He is almost what he should be when the
    Christmas season's here.
Then he's thinking more of others than he's
    thought the months before,
And the laughter of his children is a joy
    worth toiling for.
He is less a selfish creature than at
    any other time;
When the Christmas spirit rules him,
    he comes close to the sublime.

Tuesday — **December 21**

HOW the sending and receiving of cards brightens up the festive season! A neighbour told me how in his student days he worked as a temporary postman to help deliver the large seasonal mailbag and there had even been a morning delivery on Christmas Day then.

With his payslip he had received a letter from the Postmaster General which he still treasures. It reads:

Your job in the Post Office is finished for this year. You will be going home to enjoy your Christmas in the knowledge that you have helped to bring cheer and happiness into many homes.

Wednesday — **December 22**

IT was the most beautiful view over the valley, and Rose wasn't the only one who had taken time to admire it. However, among the many comments of "glorious" and "superb" that she overheard, she was puzzled to hear one man stop and say to the woman beside him, "Well, I think this is another one to put on the list."

He explained that when he and his wife were first married they had so few material goods that they decided to make an inventory of all their blessings that money couldn't buy.

"We have never lost the habit of keeping the list," he continued.

Now, I've heard of people keeping lists of all sorts of things, but this one caught my fancy. In fact, I'll definitely put it on my list of "things to do"!

Thursday — **December 23**

IT was the early nineteenth century in an isolated village in the Swiss Alps and a teacher and a priest were bemoaning the lack of good songs for Christmas. The priest, Joseph Mohr, had other problems, because the church organ had collapsed and was beyond repair.

Rather than disappoint his parishioners he began to write a composition suitable for an unaccompanied choir. When he showed it to the teacher, he exclaimed, "Friend Mohr, you have found it, the right song — God be praised!"

What was it, that song which would capture the essence of Christmas on an evening devoid of organ music? Appropriately enough, it was "Stille Nacht" — or, as we know it, "Silent Night".

Friday — **December 24**

JUST now the earth is strangely still,
And moonlight silvers every hill;
The patient trees wait, stiff with rime,
To hear the joyful church bells chime.
Like beacons burn the hearts of men —
For midnight nears: a clock strikes ten;
The old, old carols thrill the skies —
Two thousand years! A baby cries . . .

Glynfab John.

Saturday — **December 25**

THERE is a small island off the west coast of Sweden with an old house near the shore. A fisherman and his family once lived there.

One Christmas Eve a storm erupted, driving the tide right up the shore so that the sea washed the walls of the house. The youngest child brought out the big Bible and gave it to her father, while the rest of the family gathered in the front room to hear him read the Christmas story.

Suddenly, the bowsprit of a ship crashed through the window. The candles blew out, sea-spray poured in and the room was a confusion of broken glass and frightened children.

The fisherman and his two eldest sons ran out to help rescue the sailors. The crew was English. They couldn't speak a word of Swedish, and the fisher family knew no English, but that didn't matter.

While the storm raged outside, Swedish and English carols were sung by candlelight and enough food was found for all. Although it was called a disaster, it turned out to be the most joyous Christmas anyone there could remember.

WHILE SHEPHERD
WATCHED

Sunday — **December 26**

OUR friends, David and Pat, had a canary which was almost ten years old. Because of her age she seldom sang and was content to sit quietly during the day.

But on Christmas morning she amazed them. When they opened their Bible to read the story of Christ's birth she plumped her feathers, filled her lungs with air and sang for almost five minutes.

David and Pat were filled with wonder. It seemed as though even a little creature like their canary felt the joy of the season.

"And suddenly there was with the angel a multitude of the heavenly host praising God and saying, 'Glory to God in the highest and on earth peace, goodwill toward men'!"   (Luke 2:13,14)

Monday — **December 27**

OUR old friend Anon. shares this thought today: *A faithful friend is the medicine of life.*

Tuesday — **December 28**

IF Paradise on earth you'd seek
  You'll find some places quite unique:
There are hills and lakes, and shining seas,
    And vistas that can't fail to please,
There are rivers wide and streams galore,
    Tall snow-capped peaks, and so much more . . .
And yet — somehow, I have no doubt,
    That in the end we all find out
That Heaven is no place apart
    But lives in every loving heart.
                    M. J. Brison.

Wednesday — **December 29**

JIM and Anne were invited to attend their son's school sports day and became absorbed watching the obstacle race.

Eventually there was a winner, but no one really lost because all the competitors managed to overcome the various impediments placed in his or her path. They accepted the challenges and succeeded, sometimes after several attempts, in eventually reaching their goal.

As Maurice Maeterlinck wrote: "An obstacle is not a discouragement. It may become one, but only with our consent. So long as we refuse to be discouraged, we cannot be discouraged."

Thursday — **December 30**

YOU will find, as you look back upon your life, that the moments you have really lived are the moments when you have done things in the spirit of love.

Henry Drummond.

Friday — **December 31**

SO, the year is almost over and who knows what the year to come will hold for us? One thing is certain, however — good as the next year may be, there will still be occasional dark days and trying times. Rev. Robertson of Ardrossan told me this:

"Do you know that the Bible tells us, 'Do not be afraid,' three hundred and sixty-five times? The same number of days there are in the year."

With that thought in mind we can welcome a New Year and face every day with faith.

Photograph Locations and Photographers

THE CALLING — *Santorini, Greece.*
HOLY ISLAND — *Lindisfarne Castle.*
TULIP TIME — *Victoria Park, Glasgow.*
WELSH WATERS — *Llyn Cregennan near Dolgellau, North Wales.*
STEP THIS WAY — *Galloway Forest Park.*
HOME FARM — *Sidlaw Hills, Angus, Scotland.*
TREESCAPE — *Masai Mara, Kenya.*
SUMMER SPECTACLE — *Easton, Somerset.*
SAILORS' REST — *Kennet and Avon Canal, Great Bedwyn, Wiltshire.*
SPREADING OUT — *Leliefontein, South Africa.*
OVER HILL, OVER DALE — *Littondale, Yorkshire.*
CRAFTED WITH PRIDE — *Drummond Castle Gardens, Perthshire.*
SAFE PASSAGE — *Kessock Bridge, Inverness.*
HIDDEN DEPTHS — *Loch Glow, Fife.*

ACKNOWLEDGEMENTS: **David Askham;** The Cat's Whiskers, Garden Harvest, While Shepherd Watched. **Chris Cole;** Sailors' Rest. **Colin Garthwaite;** The Calling, Treescape. **Dennis Hardley;** Summer Spectacle. **Douglas Kerr;** Crafted With Pride. **C. R. Kilvington;** Over Hill, Over Dale. **Colin Mathieson;** Safe Passage. **Duncan McEwan;** Spreading Out, Threads Of Gold. **Polly Pullar;** Holy Island, Primula Perfection, Mother's Day, Home Comforts. **Phil Seale;** Finding A Path. **Willie Shand;** The Way We Were. **SW Images;** Step This Way. **Sheila Taylor;** Spring Serenade, Tulip Time, Home Farm, Surprise In The Snow. **Robert Walker;** Frosty Fingers, Hidden Depths. **Jack Watson;** Sound Of Music. **Arch White;** The Visitor, Down To Earth, Building For The Future. **Andy Williams;** Welsh Waters.

Printed and Published by D. C. Thomson & Co., Ltd.,
185 Fleet Street, London EC4A 2HS.
© D. C. Thomson & Co., Ltd., 2009

THE KINGFISHER BOOK OF THE
HUMAN BODY

Dr Patricia Macnair

Consultant:
Richard Walker

KINGFISHER

KINGFISHER

Kingfisher Publications Plc,
New Penderel House,
283–288 High Holborn,
London WC1V 7HZ
www.kingfisherpub.com

First published by Kingfisher
Publications Plc 2005
10 9 8 7 6 5 4 3 2 1
1TR/0605/PROSP/PICA(PICA)/140MA/C

ISBN–13: 978 0 7534 1201 5
ISBN–10: 0 7534 1201 2

A CIP catalogue record for this book
is available from the British Library.

Printed in China

Author: Dr Patricia Macnair
Consultant: Richard Walker
Editor: Clive Wilson
Designer: Peter Clayman
Illustrators: Sebastian Quigley, Guy Smith
Picture researcher: Kate Miller
Senior production controller: Lindsey Scott
DTP coordinators: Carsten Lorenz,
  Sarah Pfitzner, Jonathan Pledge
Indexer: Sue Lightfoot

NOTE TO READERS
The website addresses listed in this book are
correct at the time of publishing. However, due
to the ever-changing nature of the internet, website
addresses and content can change. Websites can
contain links that are unsuitable for children.
The publisher cannot be held responsible for
changes in website addresses or content, or
for information obtained through third-party
websites. We strongly advise that internet
searches should be supervised by an adult.

Contents

CHAPTER 1
Building Blocks

Cells, organs and body systems

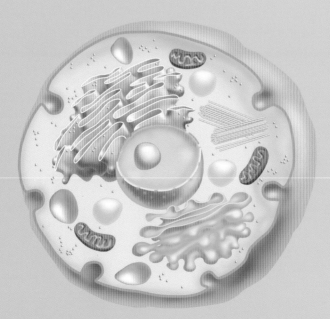

Our bodies

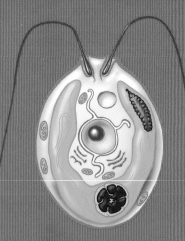

▲ Humans are made of millions of cells but some microscopic living things, such as this one, only have a single cell.

Every person in the world is unique. Humans come in many shapes and sizes. We have different skin colour, different colour eyes and different hair. But under the skin our working parts are much the same as everyone else's.

The smallest unit

▼ Only humans have the skills and intelligence needed to create buildings like this art gallery in Bilbao, Spain.

All living things are made up of cells. These are so tiny that they can only be seen with a microscope. Some organisms, such as bacteria, are made of just one cell. It takes millions and millions of cells to build an organism like the human body.

Busy body

The human body is as complex as a large town. Food and oxygen supplies must be taken in and carried to every part, and waste has to be taken away. Messages are sent around the body and to the outside world, and defence against invaders is vital.

Let's create

Although we are made of cells like every other living thing, we have features that set us apart. Our brains are highly developed and, because we stand on two legs, our hands are free to carry out complicated tasks. This has allowed us to shape our surroundings, to build civilizations and to explore space.

Groups

In the body, cells of the same type group together to form tissue, such as fat or muscle. Organs, such as the heart, are formed when tissues join together. A group of organs working together on one task, such as breathing or digestion, is called a system.

infolab

- The first living organism appeared on the earth about 3.8 billion years ago.

- The human body contains about 100 trillion cells.

- There are over six billion people on our planet.

Cells

The cell is the smallest unit of life. Tiny parts inside each cell work together like machinery to make it come alive. A control centre, or nucleus, tells this machinery what to do. Tiny power stations, called mitochondria, release energy to keep the cell running.

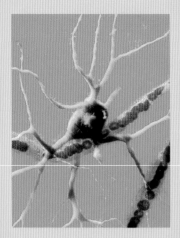

▲ A nerve cell has many branches that make contact with other nerve cells.

Cell shapes

Cells come in many shapes and sizes, depending on the job they are designed to do. Nerve cells, which stretch through the body and carry important signals, are usually long and thin. Fat cells are often round and packed full of stored energy from food.

cytoplasm, a watery jelly that supports organelles

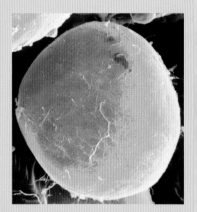

▲ This is a fat cell, magnified 700 times. A layer of fat cells under the skin helps to insulate the body, keeping you warm.

Recipe for life

Every cell nucleus contains tiny packets of information, called chromosomes. These are made of a substance called DNA. DNA is like a recipe book that has all the instructions needed to make a whole human body.

◄ If you could unravel a chromosome, it would look like a spiralling ladder.

mitochondria
supply energy

cell membrane

▲ Underneath the membrane, or surface, of a cell, tiny structures, called organelles, are hard at work.

nucleus controls the cell

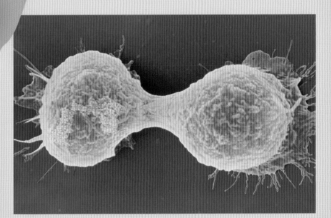

▲ This picture, magnified hundreds of times, shows a cell dividing into two. In this way, the body can replace cells that become damaged or die.

Red and white

Most cells stay firmly in one place. But some cells can roam around the body. Red blood cells in the blood carry oxygen to cells around the body and remove waste from them. White blood cells can move through the tissues to attack invaders, such as bacteria.

Cycle of cells

Every second, millions of cells in your body are dying or becoming damaged. Some cells, such as those in your skin or lining your intestines, are lost very quickly. Fortunately, almost all the cells in the body are able to reproduce, or divide to form new cells.

From cell to system

Cells are the body's building blocks. The billions and billions of cells that make up your body are carefully organized. Cells of a similar type group together to form tissues. And different types of tissues work together to form organs.

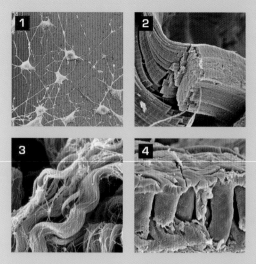

▲ The body has four main types of tissue – nervous tissue (1), muscle tissue (2), connective tissue (3) and epithelial tissue (4).

◄ Cells are the smallest units that make up the human body.

◄ Tissues are made from a group of cells of the same type, packed together.

◄ An organ, for example the liver, is formed from two or more types of tissue.

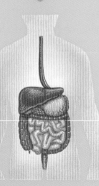

◄ The body has several systems. Each system contains two or more organs that work as a unit.

Different jobs

Each kind of tissue performs its own task. Connective tissue supports and joins together parts of the body. Another kind, called epithelium, lines the inside and outside of the body. This stops invaders getting in and liquids flowing out.

Listen up!

Most organs are tucked inside your body where you cannot see them. But you may be able to feel or even hear them at work. Listen to your stomach rumble when you are hungry, or feel your heart thump after you have been running.

Teamwork

When two or more organs work together to get a particular job done, they are called a system. For example, the respiratory system is made up of all the organs that help to bring oxygen into the body. This includes the nose, breathing tubes and the lungs.

infolab

- Cells are held together in the tissues by a glue-like substance.

- Without stretchy fibres in the connective tissues, our bodies would tear every time we moved.

- The brain is the softest tissue in the body. Bone is the strongest.

lung

heart

◄ Exercise hard and you will feel your lungs heaving air in and out of the body, and your heart thumping as it pumps blood.

Creatures at home on your body

Get ready to squirm! You share your body with millions of other living things. Your insides are teeming with bacteria, and your hair and skin are home to tiny mites and other organisms. Most, you'll be pleased to know, are harmless.

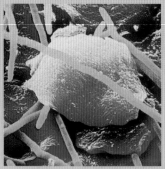

▲ These orange threads are a fungus that causes 'athlete's foot'. This makes the skin between the toes very itchy.

▼ Billions of bacteria, of all shapes and sizes, cover the skin. They help to keep out more harmful micro-organisms.

Invasion of the fungi

Most people have tiny fungi growing on their skin, feeding on the oils that skin makes. But if the surface of the skin is broken by a cut or scrape, then these organisms can turn nasty and cause problems such as 'athlete's foot'.

▲ You share your body with a host of creatures including bacteria in your intestines (1), skin fungi (2), eyelash mites (3) and sometimes head lice (4).

Wash your hands

Some bacteria that live in the intestines are good for you, releasing vitamins. But if you don't wash your hands after going to the toilet, bacteria can end up on the food you touch and make you sick.

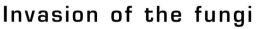

▶ Rod-shaped bacteria (yellow) help to digest food (blue-grey) inside the large intestine.

◀ An eyelash mite, here magnified nearly 1,000 times, feeds off oil made by the skin.

▲ This terrifying monster is actually a head louse, clinging to a human hair. Head lice are common and rarely cause harm.

Power stations

In every cell of your body mitochondria can be found, working hard like tiny power stations to release energy for the cell. But millions of years ago, these were quite separate creatures – an ancient type of bacteria.

Minute mites

Tiny mites live in the pores of the skin and in the roots of hairs, especially on the face and in the eyelashes. The mites feed off dead skin cells and oil made by glands. Most people have these mites, but they rarely cause problems.

Blood

Blood is the liquid of life. It flows around the body in tubes called blood vessels, taking food and oxygen to every cell, and collecting waste. Blood also helps to keep the body at a steady temperature. Blood contains millions of tiny cells that float in a liquid called plasma.

▲ This bag of blood could save someone's life! But it can only be given to a person who has the same blood type.

▼ A white blood cell surrounds and destroys harmful bacteria (red).

Red is the colour

Almost all the cells in your blood are red blood cells, which give blood its colour. These cells carry oxygen around the body. A red blood cell is shaped like a doughnut without a hole. This shape helps them to collect oxygen in the lungs and give it to cells in the tissues.

Search and destroy

White blood cells keep you safe from infection. They prowl around the body, hunting down germs such as bacteria. Some white blood cells make chemicals that can kill the germs. Others surround the germs and swallow them.

▲ Blood, made up of red and white blood cells, rushes through a blood vessel. The blood cells are carried in plasma.

16

Blood givers

Without enough blood, the tissues in the body are starved of oxygen and die. If you are hurt in an accident and lose blood, you could be saved by a blood transfusion. This is blood given by other people which is then stored, ready for emergencies.

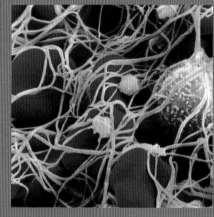

► To make a clot, tiny blood cells, called platelets (pale green), trigger the formation of a net of threads that trap both red and white blood cells.

► If you cut your skin, blood cells escape from damaged blood vessels.

► A blood clot quickly forms, making a plug that stops the bleeding.

► As the skin repairs itself, the clot shrinks to a scab on the surface.

Heal yourself

If you fall over and graze your knee, the wound will stop bleeding after a little while. This is because blood can form a sticky lump, or clot, that plugs the holes in the broken blood vessels.

Sending blood around the body

▲ A doctor checks this boy's pulse. Every time the heart beats, it makes a blood vessel pulse on the inside of the wrist.

Every minute of every day, blood travels once around your body, through a network of blood vessels. Blood is pumped through the blood vessels by the heart, which is found in the middle of your chest.

Two sides

The heart is a strong muscular bag, about as big as your clenched fist. It is divided into two halves, left and right. Each half is made up of two chambers. The upper chamber is called the atrium and the lower chamber is the ventricle.

Pumping machine

Each time the heart beats, it squeezes blood out through blood vessels known as arteries. This pushing force, called blood pressure, is very strong, so the arteries have thick walls. Blood returns to the heart in the veins. It is no longer under much pressure, so veins do not need to be as strong as arteries.

right atrium

valve

right ventricle

◄ Blood from the veins flows into the heart's upper chambers, or atria.

◄ Blood moves through valves in the atria into the lower chambers, or ventricles.

▲ The heart has thick walls that are made of muscle, and valves which open and shut to control the flow of blood.

◄ The ventricles pump blood back out to the lungs and body.

heart

major artery carrying
blood to legs

aorta

major vein
carrying
blood
from legs

left atrium

left ventricle

capillaries

▲ Arteries (red) carry blood from the heart to the rest of the body. Veins (blue) carry blood back to the heart.

Branching out

The main arteries divide like the branches of a tree into smaller arteries and then into the capillaries. As blood passes through the capillaries, it gives up food and oxygen to the cells, and collects waste.

▲ When you exercise, more blood is pumped by the heart to the skin. This helps to prevent the body from overheating – and it also turns your cheeks pink.

Get active

Give your heart a workout! When you exercise, your muscles use up more oxygen and food, and your heart has to work much harder to keep them supplied with blood. It may pump up to five times more blood around the body.

◄ Blood flows between the arteries (red) and the veins (blue) through a network of tiny tubes, called capillaries.

19

Fighting infection

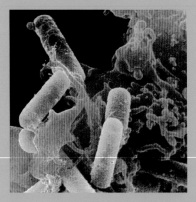

▲ These rod-shaped bacteria are being swallowed up by a white blood cell (orange).

There is a war going on in your body. It is constantly under attack from germs that can cause infections and make you ill. But your body has lots of ways to protect itself, including barriers, killer cells and chemicals that are poisonous to germs.

On the defence

To get into the body, germs such as bacteria and viruses have to get through a number of defences. The skin forms the first line of defence. Here, the cells are packed closely together to stop micro-organisms getting through. In the nose, thick mucus traps germs. Body fluids, including tears, saliva and sweat, contain chemicals that kill bacteria.

The hunters

White blood cells are natural killers! Some cells move between the bloodstream and the tissues, looking for germs. When they find one, they may release chemicals that kill the germ, or they wrap themselves around their prey and digest it.

▼ These bacteria, called streptococci, can cause serious infections. They build an outer shell to protect themselves against the body's white blood cells.

◀ Your body has a number of defences against invaders. These include the skin (1), as well as mucus found in the nose (2), windpipe (3) and intestines (4). Acid in the stomach (5) kills most harmful bacteria.

▲ This girl is being given a vaccine by a doctor. The vaccine will protect her from germs that can cause life-threatening infections.

Vaccines

For centuries, people greatly feared infectious diseases that spread very quickly, such as smallpox or plague. Since the development of vaccines, in the late 1700s, and antibiotic medicines, in the 1920s, millions of lives have been saved.

► The first microscope was invented over 300 years ago. It allowed scientists to see bacteria.

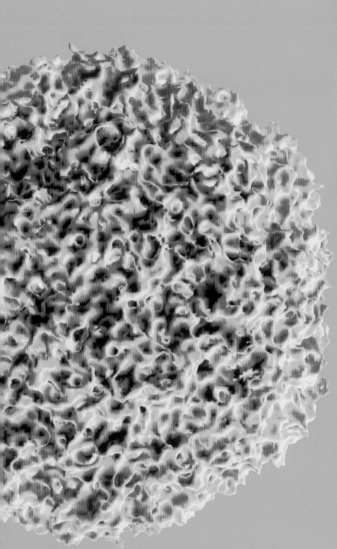

▲ Enemy alert! Viruses such as this one, here magnified thousands of times, can invade your body through the nose and cause a cold.

Antibodies

When germs enter the body and cause an infection, special white blood cells, called lymphocytes, learn to recognize the intruders. The next time the same type of germ invades, the lymphocytes spot them and release chemicals called antibodies to put the germ out of action.

infolab

■ Breast milk contains antibodies that protect a baby from infection.

■ Your temperature increases during an infection to try to stop the germs from reproducing.

21

Digesting food

Your body needs food for energy, growth and repair. But first the food needs to be digested, or broken down. This is the job of your digestive system. The mouth, stomach and intestines work together to break down food into tiny particles, called nutrients.

◀ Digestion begins in the mouth. Teeth cut up and crush food. The lips and tongue help to hold food or move it around.

◀ After you swallow food, strong muscles in the wall of the oesophagus squeeze it down towards the stomach.

oesophagus _____

liver _____

Food crushers

Your teeth are powerful crushers that can chew and cut through tough lumps of food. Saliva, or spit, contains chemicals that also help to digest the food.

Stretchy stomach

The stomach is a stretchy but strong muscular bag. It churns and squeezes the food that you have swallowed. Fluids, called digestive juices, help break up the food, which can stay in the stomach for several hours before passing into the intestines.

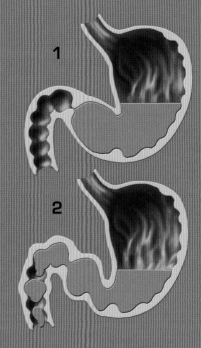

1

2

infolab

- Food takes between 20 and 45 hours to get from one end of the digestive system to the other.

- If you look after them, your adult teeth should last all your life.

- There are three pairs of glands that pour saliva into your mouth.

stomach

A balanced diet

Every day, we need lots of carbohydrates for energy, some protein for growth and repair, a small amount of fat and sugar-rich food, and lots of water. We also need special chemicals, called vitamins and minerals, to make the body work properly.

▲ The muscular walls of the stomach contract to churn the food (1) and then squeeze it through into the intestines (2). The stomach can hold up to four litres of food.

◀ The oesophagus takes food down into the stomach, which digests and stores the food.

▼ These unhealthy foods contain lots of sugar, fat and salt. Fresh fruit and vegetables are better for your body as they contain fibre, as well as vitamins and minerals.

The intestines

When food leaves the stomach, it enters the small intestine where it is broken down into smaller and smaller particles. The food, now in the form of tiny nutrients, moves through the small intestine and into the bloodstream. The waste matter that is left is pushed out through the anus.

Down the tube

The small intestine is a six-metre-long tube where food is taken into the body, or absorbed. It is lined with millions of tiny hair-like projections, called villi. These make a large surface through which nutrients can pass into the blood vessels beneath.

liver

pancreas

small intestine

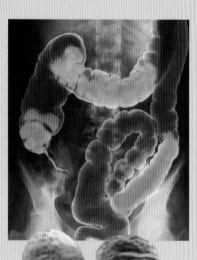

◄ The large intestine is about 1.5 metres long. Its main job is to get rid of waste.

▼ Tiny villi cover the inside of the small intestine. Nutrients pass through them into the blood.

- Together, the small and large intestines are almost eight metres long – nearly the length of a bus.

- Food stays in the large intestine for up to 12 hours before it is pushed out of the body.

Hard worker

The liver is the biggest and busiest organ inside the body. Its main task is to collect and process the nutrients as they come in through the blood from the intestines.

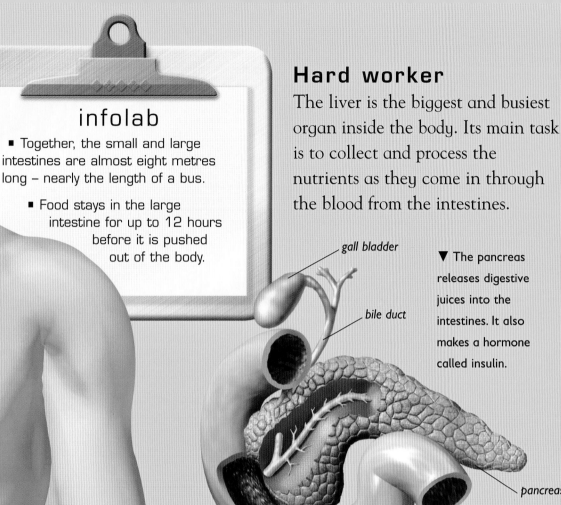

gall bladder

▼ The pancreas releases digestive juices into the intestines. It also makes a hormone called insulin.

bile duct

pancreas

duodenum

large intestine

Bile

Underneath the liver, a small bag called the gall bladder makes bile. This green, gooey fluid is squirted into the intestines, where it makes fat from the food easier to digest.

In the end

The large intestine is a long, wide tube at the end of the digestive system. The lining of the large intestine is very smooth, and produces slimy mucus. This helps the food waste, called faeces, to slide along easily and pass out of the body through the anus.

Breath of life

Your breathing system, which includes the nose, throat and lungs, takes oxygen from the air and into your blood. The oxygen is then delivered to your body's cells. Without this gas, your cells would die – they need oxygen to release energy from food.

nose

mouth

throat

larynx (voicebox)

windpipe (trachea)

Breathe in

Put your hands on your chest as you breathe in, or inhale, and feel your lungs fill with air. Two sets of muscles draw air into your lungs – the muscles of the ribcage and a large flat muscle under the lungs, called the diaphragm.

▲ When you breathe in, the space inside your chest becomes larger and pulls air into the lungs.

▲ When you breathe out, the space in your chest becomes smaller and air is pushed out of your lungs.

No entry

The larynx, or voicebox, sits at the entrance to the windpipe – the main tube into the lungs. A flap of tissue inside the larynx prevents food from getting into the lungs. This flap is called the epiglottis.

Making sound

The voicebox also contains two folds called the vocal cords. When you breathe, air is squeezed past the folds, making the vocal cords vibrate. This produces sound that can be shaped into words by moving your tongue and lips.

▼ When you sing or speak, the vocal cords inside your voicebox vibrate to make sound. The vocal cords are two folds in the shape of a V.

lungs

ribs

diaphragm

The lungs

Your lungs are a pair of large spongy organs inside the chest. They are protected by the bones and muscles that form the ribcage. Inside the lungs are millions of tiny air bags that pass oxygen into the blood. The lungs also breathe out a waste gas, called carbon dioxide.

Forest of tubes

Your lungs are connected to the outside world by your windpipe. The lower end of this long tube divides into two parts, each one entering a lung. Here, the tubes continue to divide like the branches of a tree into smaller and smaller tubes. The narrowest ones end in tiny air bags called alveoli.

windpipe (trachea)

right lung

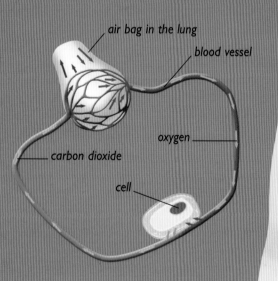

air bag in the lung

blood vessel

oxygen

carbon dioxide

cell

▲ Oxygen in the lungs is carried by the blood to the body's cells. Waste carbon dioxide is removed from the cells and breathed out.

▼ Once air has been cleaned and moistened in the nose and throat, it is carried down into every corner of the lungs through a series of branching tubes. At the end of the tubes are grape-like clusters of alveoli *(below)*.

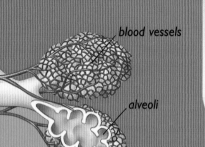

blood vessels

alveoli

left lung

tubes

Gas exchange

Your lungs contain over 300 million alveoli. Each one is covered in a network of blood vessels that carry oxygen into the bloodstream. The alveoli also take carbon dioxide from the blood into the lungs, where it can be exhaled, or breathed out.

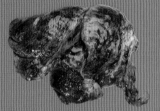

▲ This is a lung from a person who smoked. It is full of harmful chemicals, which have turned the lung black.

▲ Healthy lungs are clean and pink.

Dirty habit

Healthy lungs are smooth, pink and shiny. But the lungs of a smoker are dark and dirty. Smoking damages the lungs and prevents them from working properly. This makes breathing more difficult.

Cleaning up

While your body is busy making energy, building new cells and repairing old ones, it needs to get rid of waste products. If these are allowed to build up, they poison the body. However, you have some clever cleaning systems to get rid of this waste.

Cleaning blood

Waste chemicals are carried away from the cells by the blood. The blood is cleaned by your two kidneys. Each one contains more than half a million tiny filters that sift out harmful substances and remove excess water. The waste fluid, called urine, drains out of the kidney through the ureter into the bladder.

▶ Inside the kidney (shown here cut in half lengthways), the medulla and cortex contain tiny filters. These clean the blood and remove water that is not needed by the body.

medulla

cortex

artery

vein

ureter

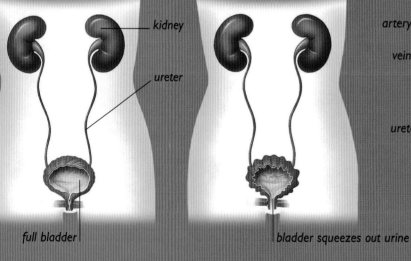

kidney

ureter

full bladder

bladder squeezes out urine

▲ Urine drains from the kidneys down long tubes, called ureters, into the bladder.

▲ As the bladder becomes full, it sends signals to the brain that it needs to be emptied.

The liver

Some waste chemicals or cells are broken down by the liver, which is the recycling factory of the body. The ingredients are then used again to make new cells. The liver also breaks down chemicals that may be dangerous, such as alcohol or drugs.

▶ In the liver, blood flows through channels between rows of liver cells. As well as breaking down poisonous chemicals, the liver stores vitamins.

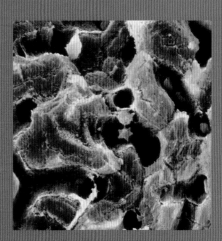

Hot and sweaty

When we are hot, more blood is sent to the surface of the body so that heat can be lost through the skin. We also sweat, which helps to cool the skin and remove extra water, salt and an important waste chemical called urea from the body.

▶ The body gets rid of excess heat through the skin. In this picture, called a thermogram, the hottest areas, such as the cheeks, show up as red, while cooler skin appears blue.

The skin

Imagine being a tiny creature on a person's skin. You would have to struggle through a jungle of hairs, avoiding dozens of potholes or pores oozing sweat! Skin is the body's largest and heaviest organ. It is tough and waterproof, and it helps to stop germs and dirt from entering the body.

▲ We each have a unique pattern of fingerprints, on the tips of our fingers. Try comparing yours with your friends' fingerprints.

Fingerprints

Everybody's fingerprints are unique. Even if you damage your fingers, the fingerprints will grow back into the same pattern. The ridges that form fingerprints have hundreds of sweat glands that help to keep your skin cool.

▶ This is a magnified picture of hairs emerging from skin on the face. Hair can grow up to 15cm a year.

◀ There are many different shades of skin colour. But beneath the top layer, or epidermis, we all look very much the same.

Tool kit

Fingernails provide a set of tough tools that are very useful for jobs that involve scraping and gripping. Nails are made from dead cells and a very tough substance called keratin.

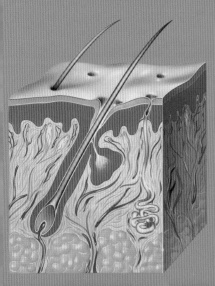

◀ The skin has a range of different sensors. Light touch and pressure are detected by sensors near the surface.

Body hair

The hair on the top of your head is thick, but much finer hairs cover most of your body. These let you sense very light touch. Your eyebrows help to keep sweat from dripping into your eyes, and eyelashes protect them from dust.

So sensitive

The skin is packed with millions of tiny nerves. The endings of these nerves work as sensors that can detect pressure, pain and other sensations. This information is sent to the brain.

▶ Fingerprints can help catch criminals! The police take fingerprints from suspects and see if these match prints found at the scene of the crime.

CHAPTER 2

Brain Box

The brain,
nervous system
and senses

Control centre

Every movement, every thought and every feeling you experience is controlled by your nervous system. This is made up of your brain, spinal cord and a network of nerves. The nervous system is always switched on – even when you are asleep, millions of signals are travelling along the nerves.

▲ You need precise and rapid finger movements to play the harp. The brain controls every one of these movements.

Central station

Together, the brain and the spinal cord form the central nervous system. This is the body's main control centre. Cable-like nerves carry messages between the central nervous system and the rest of the body.

The natural order

The brain works out what movements the body needs to make and what order they should follow. It then sends out commands to the muscles through the nerves.

◄ This boy's body is not moving, but his brain is hard at work. The brain uses up large amounts of energy.

▲ Signals travelling around the nervous system reach speeds of up to 350km/h. This makes them even faster than the super-quick Japanese Bullet train.

Outside information

In order to control your body's movements, your brain needs to know what is happening in the world around you. Information comes in from the sense organs. These include your eyes, ears and even your skin.

brain

spinal cord

◀ Instructions from this boy's brain pass down the spinal cord and along the nerves to different parts of his body. These signals control the muscles that allow him to keep his balance.

Communication

Most animals can communicate with each other but only humans, with our complex brains, have highly developed languages. With speech and writing we can share our thoughts and feelings, and work together. We also use other signals, from facial expressions to body posture, all controlled by the brain.

nerve

▶ These Egyptian picture-signs are an example of hieroglyphics – one of the world's oldest forms of writing.

Inside the brain

Your brain is packed with tiny nerve cells called neurons. A piece of brain the size of a grain of sand contains 100,000 neurons! These neurons connect up to make your brain the most powerful and intelligent machine in the universe.

▲ The outer layer of the brain has a huge number of folds. This allows a lot more of it to fit inside the skull.

skull protects the brain

Grey matter

The outer part of the brain, which does your thinking, is called the cerebral cortex, or grey matter. Its folds give the brain a wrinkled look. Below the grey matter, millions of neurons carry signals between different parts of the brain.

It's all relative

You do not need a big brain to be a genius! Albert Einstein's brain was smaller than an average person's. People who are very intelligent may simply be using their brain in a different way.

cerebellum controls muscle movement and balance

breathing is controlled by the brain stem

▶ The brain has three main areas — the cerebrum, the cerebellum and the brain stem.

◀ Albert Einstein made amazing scientific discoveries, but his brain was on the small side!

Special protection

Because the brain is soft and delicate, it needs to be protected. The brain floats in a layer of fluid, which cushions it inside the skull. The bones of the skull provide the brain with a natural crash helmet.

cerebrum controls language, thought and movement

infolab

■ If the folds of the brain were ironed out flat, it would be the size of a pillowcase.

■ Nearly 80 per cent of the brain is water.

■ About half a cupful of clear, colourless fluid surrounds the brain and spinal cord.

Messenger system

Neurons carry electrical signals around the brain and also the body. They come in all shapes and sizes. Although most neurons are no longer than a full stop, some are the longest cells in the body, stretching from your toe to your spine.

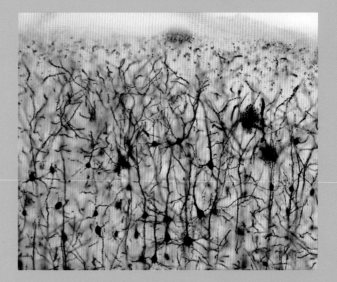

▲ These black dots are neurons. Each one is connected to hundreds and sometimes thousands of other neurons.

Active brain

Your brain is in charge of your body – it's the boss! Different parts perform different tasks. Some areas receive information, others send out messages to the muscles. The brain also has areas to process information so that you can think, remember and make plans for the future.

◄ Messages from the brain's movement area control this rock climber's muscles.

◄ These girls are using the right side of the brain to sing together.

speech area

vision area

sensory area

hearing area

cerebellum

Left and right

The largest part of the brain, called the cerebrum, is divided into two. The left half controls the right side of the body and helps you to solve problems, to speak and to write. The right half controls the body's left side and may help you to think about things that are hard to describe using words, such as music.

Heat control

Hidden deep inside the brain is an area called the hypothalamus. It is no bigger than the tip of your thumb. If the weather gets cold, the hypothalamus turns up your internal central heating. It also controls your appetite.

▼ The cerebrum is divided into areas that control different activities. This picture shows the right half of the cerebrum.

movement
area

Auto pilot

As you concentrate on reading this book, hundreds of other activities are going on in your body. Breathing, digesting food and the beating of your heart are just a few of the things that are automatically controlled by your brain.

Coordination

At the back of the brain is a very wrinkly area, called the cerebellum. This helps you to keep your balance. The cerebellum also makes sure that your movements are smooth and not jerky.

thinking
area

► This chess player is using an area right at the front of his brain to work out his next move. This area is involved in problem solving.

▼ The images that enter this boy's eyes through the telescope are turned into signals that are passed to an area at the back of the brain.

infolab

- Over 300 million nerve fibres connect the left and right sides of the brain together.

- 'Cerebellum' means 'little brain'.

Reflexes

The spinal cord is the main highway carrying information between the brain and the rest of the body. The spinal cord is packed with millions of nerve fibres and neurons, but it is more than just a pathway for messages. It also controls many automatic reactions in the body. These reactions are called reflexes.

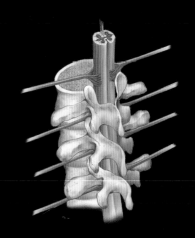

▲ The spinal cord (pink) is protected by the bones of the spine. Pairs of spinal nerves (green) connect the spinal cord to the rest of the body.

Action stations

Whenever the body needs to digest food, go to the toilet or speed up the heart, a special set of nerves from the spinal cord goes into action. These nerves automatically control many organs and glands.

◄ An automatic reaction, called the withdrawal reflex, allows this footballer to move his head out of the path of a fast-approaching ball.

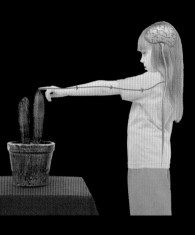

◀ As soon as this girl touches the cactus, pain sensors in her skin send a signal to the spinal cord.

◀ Before the signal reaches her brain, the spinal cord has sent another signal back out to the muscles, pulling back the girl's arm.

In the tunnel

The spinal cord travels from your brain to just below your waist. The vertebrae, or bones of the spine, keep it safely in place. Nerves going to and from the rest of the body leave and enter the spinal cord through spaces between the bones.

Ouch!

Touch something very hot or very sharp and you will pull your hand away almost instantly. Your brain does not even have time to think about it! This reflex action can be controlled by the spinal cord without any help from the brain.

infolab

■ Babies are born with some reflexes, such as grasping, which disappear after a few months.

■ The spinal cord does not reach all the way down the bony spinal column.

■ An adult's spinal cord is about 44cm long.

Knee jerk

Try testing one of your own reflexes. Sit on a desk with your legs dangling over the edge and ask a friend to gently tap just below your knee. Your leg should jerk upwards whether you want it to or not!

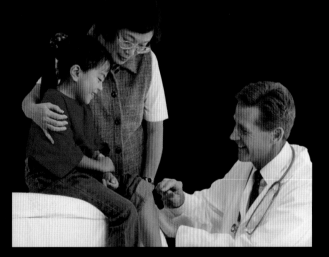

▲ A doctor tests the stretch reflex by tapping just below the kneecap. This reflex makes the muscle tighten and pull up the lower leg.

Vision

▲ In dim light, the pupil becomes as wide as possible (top) to let in light. In bright light, the pupil narrows to prevent too much light getting in.

A huge amount of information about the outside world comes to you through your eyes. The eye works like a camera, gathering in patterns of light from objects. These patterns are turned into signals. The brain uses the signals to create a picture of your surroundings.

pupil

In focus

As rays of light enter the eye, they are bent by the cornea. This starts to focus the light into a sharp image. The rays then pass through a clear lens that does the fine tuning, accurately focusing the picture onto the retina at the back of the eye.

iris controls how much light enters the eye

lens changes shape to focus light

cornea lets light into eye

▲ The parts at the front of the eye focus light and control how much light enters. At the back, light is turned into signals, which are sent to the brain.

Changing size

The pupil is a dark circular opening in the iris, or coloured part of the eye. It controls how much light reaches the back of the eye. The muscles of the iris make the pupil smaller so that you can see in bright light, or wider to help you see in poor light.

▲ When the light from an object is focused by the cornea and lens, the image appears upside down on the retina. The brain turns it the right way up.

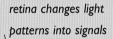

retina changes light
patterns into signals

optic nerve carries
signals to the brain

muscle controls
eyeball movement

infolab

- People who are colour-blind may not be able to tell the difference between red and green.

- Your eyes contain about 120 million rods and 7 million cones.

- Six bands of muscle around the eye control its movement.

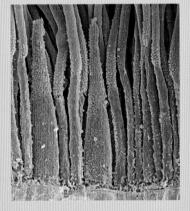

▲ Millions of light-sensing rods (purple) and cones (orange) are packed into the retina.

Bit of a blur

If the eyeball is too short or too long, the eye cannot focus properly to produce a sharp image. The result is blurred vision and the person is said to be long sighted or short sighted. Wearing glasses or contact lenses corrects this very common problem.

Rods and cones

The retina is a layer of special cells at the back of the eye. These cells detect light and then send signals to the brain. Some cells, called cones, sense colours. Other light-detecting cells, called rods, can only detect black and white. In dim light, the cones do not work very well and the rods take over.

▶ A nearby object, such as this face, looks fuzzy to people who are long sighted. They cannot focus light properly onto the retina.

45

Tricking the brain

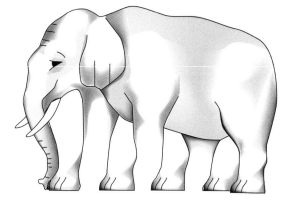

▲ How many legs does this elephant have? In trying to create a three-dimensional (3-D) image, your brain sees this image in more than one way.

Look closely at this page and prepare to have your brain boggled! When you look at an object, the brain must work out the patterns of light detected by your eyes. It is easy to trick the brain into seeing a picture in a certain way. These tricks are called optical illusions.

▼ Which is the bigger of the two central circles? If you think the circle on the right is bigger, you are wrong! They are actually the same size. Your brain is fooled by the size of the surrounding circles.

The third dimension

Our brains are used to seeing the world around us in three dimensions. But pictures printed or drawn on paper are only two-dimensional, as they have no depth. Even so, your brain can make it appear that you are looking at three dimensions.

▲ These rows appear to slope but, in fact, they are parallel. The brain is tricked by the uneven edges and the contrast between the black and white bricks.

▲ These identical twins are actually the same height, but the distorted shape of this Ames room tricks the brain. The girl on the left is much farther away than her sister.

Check again

The brain estimates the size of an object or shape by comparing it with other objects nearby. If a small object is surrounded by larger objects, the brain judges the smaller one to be less important. You will, in fact, see it as smaller than it really is.

Seeing isn't believing

Many optical illusions work by sending confusing information to the brain. Shapes can be made to move or shimmer and parallel lines can appear to bend. If a picture is not complete, the brain 'fills in' the missing information – but it does not always get it right!

Curiouser and curiouser

When you see a room, you expect it to be a regular shape. But in a special room called an Ames room, the floor and ceiling slope and the walls are sharply angled. A person moving from one corner to another will appear to shrink or to grow dramatically in size!

Hearing

Every noise, soft or loud, that reaches your ear is made up of sound waves. Inside the ear, the sound waves are turned into signals. These are sent to the brain, which lets you 'hear' the sound. Hearing helps us to communicate, to pick up warning signals and to enjoy good music!

▼ The ear has three main parts. The outer ear collects sounds. These pass through the middle ear and into the inner ear, which sends signals to the brain.

◄ Even a short burst of very loud noise can damage your hearing. In certain jobs it is very important to wear ear protectors.

bones of the middle ear carry sound to the inner ear

inner ear

cochlea turns sound into signals

eardrum lies between the outer and middle ears

Turn it down!

Your ears can detect the faintest of noises to the loudest of sounds. Sound is measured in decibels – a finger brushing over skin is around 10 decibels. The sound of a jet engine is a billion times louder and can measure over 130 decibels.

Good vibrations

Sound waves pass down the ear canal and make the eardrum vibrate. Behind the eardrum is the middle ear. Here, the vibrations of the eardrum are passed on through tiny bones that carry the sound across to the inner ear.

◄ Our hearing is so sensitive that we can pick up the quietest of whispers.

outer ear channels sound into the middle ear

ear canal carries sound waves to the eardrum

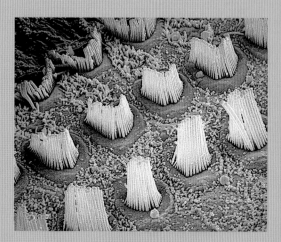

▲ Sound waves arriving in the fluid-filled cochlea form ripples. These bend the tiny 'hairs' (yellow) which send signals to the brain.

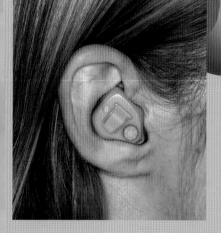

◀ If you have problems with your hearing you may need to wear a special device called a hearing aid.

Ripple effect

The main part of the inner ear, called the cochlea, forms a spiral chamber which is filled with fluid. Here, tiny ripples, caused by the vibrations in the middle ear, are turned into electrical signals. These are sent as messages down the hearing nerves to the brain.

Balance

If you want to dance, ride a bicycle or just stand upright, you need balance. In order to balance, the brain has to work out in which direction the body is moving. Much of this information is provided by your inner ear.

◄ Information from her eyes, ears and sense of touch helps this tightrope walker to stay balanced high above the ground.

Secret chambers

A system of chambers and canals, called the vestibular system, is found inside the inner ear. It detects the tiniest of changes in your body's position, and sends information to your brain. The brain can then adjust the muscles to control your balance.

semi-circular canal

saccule

utricle

◄ The vestibular system is made up of semi-circular canals and jelly-filled chambers. Together, they help your brain detect the movement and position of your head.

▼ Tilting your head downwards bends tiny hairs in the utricle and saccule. This movement triggers signals that provide the brain with information about the head's position.

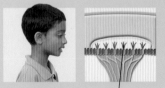

hairs stand upright

hairs bend downwards

▲ Construction workers need to have a good head for heights as well as perfect balance! In the USA, the Mohawk people were famed for this and many helped to build skyscrapers.

Travel sickness

Sometimes your eyes and ears tell the brain two different things. If you have ever been seasick, it is usually because the balance organs in your ears tell the brain that your body is moving from side to side. But your eyes, which are looking at the deck, tell the brain that the boat is steady. This causes you to feel dizzy and sick.

▲ Seasickness is caused when the brain is confused by different information coming from the sense organs.

Use your eyes

Close your eyes and try standing on one leg. Not so easy, is it? This is because your brain uses information from the eyes as well as the ears when you want to balance.

Smell

Our noses sniff out the world around us, from freshly baked bread to a pair of old trainers. Each smell is made from a unique recipe of millions of tiny particles, or molecules, which float in the air. With every breath you take, these smell chemicals are carried into your nose. Here, they trigger sensors that send signals about the smell to the brain.

▲ Perfume makers can choose from up to 3,000 different plant and animal smells when they create a new fragrance.

Memory lane

Sometimes a particular smell can unlock old memories. This is because the nerves from our smell sensors are directly linked to the parts of the brain involved in storing memory.

Mood change

Smells can affect how you are feeling, because of links between the nose and the area of the brain that controls your emotions. Lavender, for example, has been found to help people relax when they are feeling stressed.

◀ Dogs have many more smell detectors than humans and can pick up very faint smells.

Warning system

You can detect at least 10,000 different smells. Your sense of smell can help to protect you from danger, by warning about leaking gas or rotten food.

◀ Smells can have powerful effects on the brain and body. Aromatherapists use perfumed oils to relax people and to treat health problems.

Smell experts

To make a perfume, dozens of different smells are combined together. Each perfume has its own individual scent. The highly trained expert who creates this is known as a 'nose'.

▼ Smells are picked up by sensors high up in the nose.

nerve carries signals to brain

smell molecules are breathed in through the nose

smell sensors

Taste

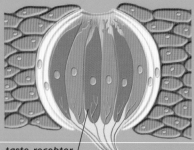

taste receptor

▲ Taste receptors are packed together inside a taste bud. They detect chemicals dissolved in saliva.

Imagine if everything you ate, from sweet, juicy oranges to chocolate ice cream, tasted of cardboard. Fortunately, your tongue has thousands of special taste sensors, or taste buds. Your tongue and lips can also detect heat, cold and the texture of food. These all add to the sensation and pleasure of eating.

Bumpy surface

Look closely in a mirror at the surface of your tongue. The tiny lumps and bumps that cover it are known as papillae. These protect the delicate taste buds, which can be easily damaged. On the papillae are thousands of taste buds.

▶ Four main tastes – bitter, salty, sour and sweet – can be sensed by taste buds buried in the surface of the tongue.

bitter

salty

sour

sweet

A matter of smell

You need your sense of smell as well as your sense of taste to pick up the flavours in food. Your smell sensors are much more sensitive than your taste sensors. When you eat, the brain receives information from both sets of sensors.

▶ Thousands of tiny spikes on the surface of the tongue help to grip food. The pink bump, or papilla, is packed with taste buds.

Some like it hot

Some people love spicy foods such as chilli peppers. A chemical in the chilli pepper triggers pain sensors in the mouth. This sends signals to the brain that boost sweet flavours in the food and make it taste hot.

▶ Chilli peppers are a popular ingredient in many dishes because they boost the sweet flavours in food.

◀ Temperature sensors in the tongue tell the brain if the food you are eating is hot or cold.

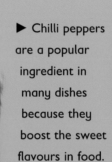

Colour and taste

The colour of food can affect taste. Most people avoid blue or grey foods – we usually think of these colours as a sign of rotten or poisonous food. Food manufacturers often add artificial colouring to their products to make them look tastier.

Touch

Close your eyes and touch the objects in front of you. Do they feel smooth or rough, cold or warm, soft or hard? Your sense of touch tells you a great deal about the world around you. Your skin is packed with millions of sensors that can detect tiny changes in movement, temperature and pressure. They can also sense pain.

▲ Babies often use their mouths to feel objects. The lips and tongue are packed with sensors and are extremely sensitive.

Touch sensors

Some parts of the body are more sensitive to touch than others. The skin on the fingers and lips contains many more sensors than the skin on the back. Much more of the brain is used to detect touch signals from these sensitive areas than from other areas of the body.

▲ This is what your body would look like if the different parts were in proportion to the number of sensors they contain.

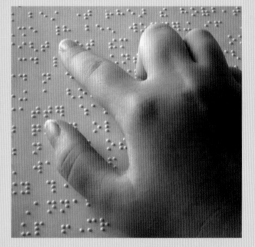

▲ This person is reading a Braille book. With practice, people can read Braille as fast as printed words.

The point of pain

Pain is not much fun, but it is a very good warning system that helps to prevent injury. For example, the eye's delicate covering, the cornea, is easily damaged, so even tiny flecks of dirt ring warning bells of pain.

Fingertip reading

Peope who are blind or partially sighted can use the Braille system to read. Special patterns formed by raised dots stand for each letter of the alphabet. People read the words by running their fingers over the dots.

The gentlest touch

Some of the skin's sensors are made of a bare nerve fibre wrapped around the base of a hair. These sensors can be triggered by the lightest touch, such as a feather brushing against hairs.

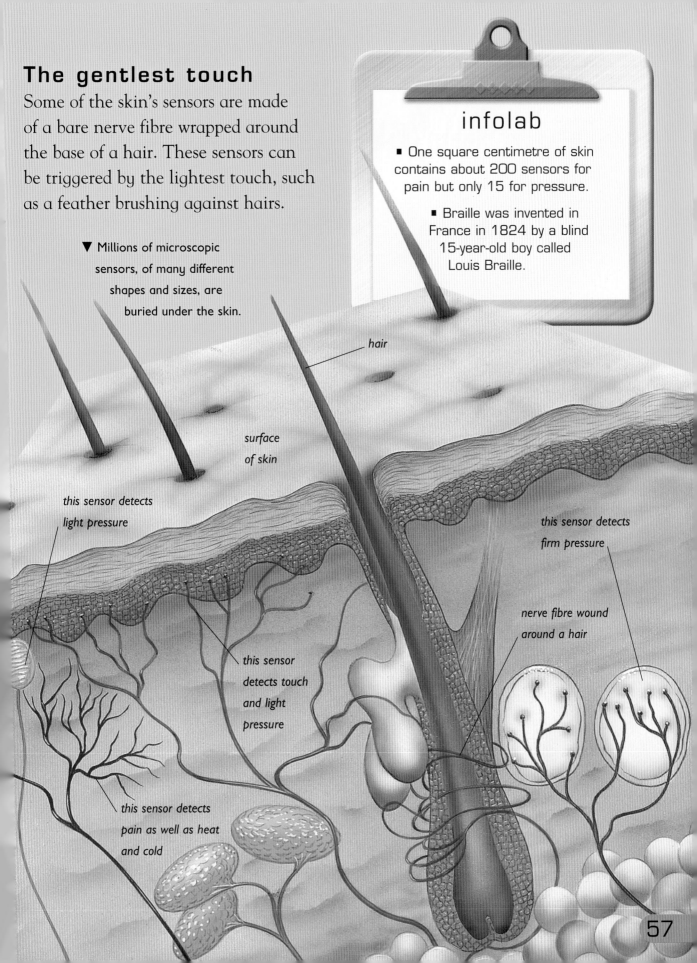

▼ Millions of microscopic sensors, of many different shapes and sizes, are buried under the skin.

hair

surface of skin

this sensor detects light pressure

this sensor detects touch and light pressure

this sensor detects pain as well as heat and cold

this sensor detects firm pressure

nerve fibre wound around a hair

Hormones

The nervous system is not the only route for messages to be sent around the body. A second system, called the endocrine system, uses chemical messages called hormones. These are in charge of growth, energy supply, reproduction and many other important activities.

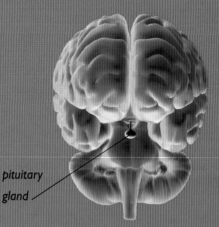

pituitary
gland

▲ The pituitary gland is found just under the brain. It makes six different hormones and controls the release of other hormones.

Supply and demand

Hormones are made in small factories called the endocrine glands, which are found all around the body. Tiny amounts of the hormone are released into the bloodstream, when needed, to do their work a long way from the gland itself.

► The excitement and fear experienced when you ride a rollercoaster release adrenaline. This hormone prepares the body to face danger.

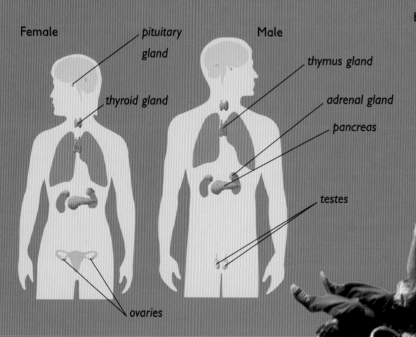

Female

pituitary gland

thyroid gland

Male

thymus gland

adrenal gland

pancreas

testes

ovaries

▲ The body makes more than 100 hormones. They are produced in the endocrine glands, which are found in different parts of the body.

The master gland

Just below the brain is a small but very important gland called the pituitary gland. The pituitary gland makes growth hormone – without this chemical, your body would not grow.

infolab

- Hormones travel much more slowly than messages carried by the nerves.

- Laughter can lower your levels of stress hormones.

- The pituitary gland is joined to the hypothalamus – the part of the brain that controls body temperature.

Under pressure

If the body is put under stress, it produces adrenaline. This hormone makes the heart beat faster, sending more blood to the muscles and brain. It also speeds up breathing and releases sugar into the blood for energy.

▲ Hormones control puberty – the period when children begin to develop into adults.

Mind over matter

Sometimes, in extreme situations, the brain can drive the body past its normal limits, overcoming hunger, pain, weakness or exhaustion. With practice we can also use our minds to relax our bodies, control our fears and even keep illness at bay.

◄ This boy uses his mind to remain calm and keep his body still as a large spider crawls up his arm.

Phobias

Many people suffer from phobias, or irrational fears. There are all kinds of phobias, from a fear of spiders to a fear of flying. Hypnotism, in which the person is put into a trance, is often used to help people with phobias.

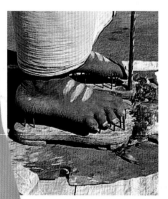

◄ Overcoming extreme pain is a sign of religious devotion in some cultures. Here, an Indian man is standing on nails.

The pain barrier

One of the greatest challenges for the brain is to ignore pain. Many cultures have rituals or festivals that involve acts in which people must test their limits – by lying on a bed of nails, for example.

Ancient practice

For over 5,000 years, people have practised yoga to stay well. Yoga uses meditation in order to focus the mind. Most people find it very relaxing, and it can even help to keep your heart in good shape.

◀ This Indian man is practising yoga to enter into a very calm state and clear his mind of distractions.

Remote control

A scientist called Andrew Junker has steered a boat by thought alone! A special headband picks up electrical signals from his brain and sends them to a computer that controls the steering.

▶ The performer David Blaine stood inside a block of ice for over 60 hours. He used meditation to withstand extreme cold, exhaustion and hunger.

CHAPTER 3

Movers & Shapers

Bones, muscles and joints

Movement and support

Imagine your body without bones. You would be floppy and unable to move. The bones form a framework, or skeleton, that supports the body and protects the internal organs. Muscles cover the bones. Together, they give the body shape and allow you to move.

► This diver is about to launch herself into the air. Her body is supported by the bones that make up her skeleton.

◄ You need to use over 60 muscles and bones in each hand and arm just to lift a glass.

▲ Hundreds of muscles, of different shapes and sizes, cover the bones.

Pulling power

In order to make a movement, the muscles and bones must work together as a team. When muscles contract, or get shorter, they pull on the bones. This makes different parts of the body change position. Most movements are controlled by the brain.

No rest

Your muscles and bones never stop working. Even when you are standing still, they are busy holding the body in the correct position. And day and night, the muscles and bones in your ribcage are moving to help you breathe.

▶ This picture, called a CT scan, shows the inside of a person's head. The bones of the skull protect the brain. The left-hand side of the brain is not shown in this scan.

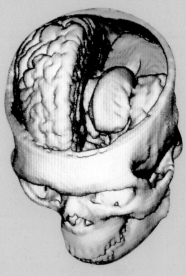

◀ ▼ During the dive, the muscles pull on the bones. This makes the body bend or straighten.

Guard duty

Bones and muscles also have the important job of protecting the organs inside your body. The skull forms a hard box around the brain. Your ribs shield the heart and lungs, and the bones and muscles of the pelvis protect the bladder and organs of reproduction.

infolab

■ Bone is stronger than a steel bar of the same weight.

■ Over half the bones in your body are found in your hands and feet.

■ Muscles are grouped in pairs.

■ Muscles make up about half of the weight of your body.

▶ To stand to attention, these soldiers are using muscles in their necks, backs and legs.

Bony framework

The skeleton is made up of bones of all shapes and sizes. Arm and leg bones are long and thin, while hand bones are small and rounded. Although bones are hard and rigid, they can grow and change their shape.

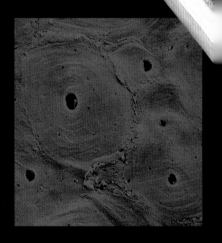

▼ Long bones such as the femur, or thigh bone, are filled with marrow. The blood vessels provide bone cells with food and oxygen.

blood vessel

compact bone

spongy bone

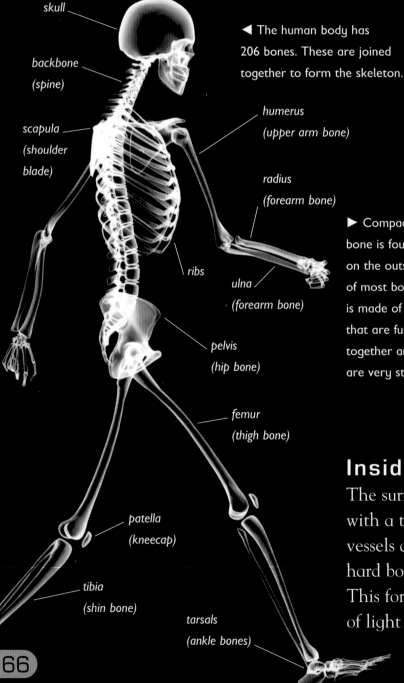

skull

backbone (spine)

scapula (shoulder blade)

◄ The human body has 206 bones. These are joined together to form the skeleton.

humerus (upper arm bone)

radius (forearm bone)

ribs

ulna (forearm bone)

► Compact bone is found on the outside of most bones. It is made of tubes that are fused together and are very strong.

pelvis (hip bone)

femur (thigh bone)

Inside a bone

The surface of each bone is covered with a thin layer containing blood vessels and nerves. Underneath is hard bone called compact bone. This forms a shell around a layer of light but very strong spongy bone.

patella (kneecap)

tibia (shin bone)

tarsals (ankle bones)

► The shape of the skeleton helps the body to balance upright, leaving the hands free. Bones in the feet make a wide base. The pelvis, formed from the hip bones, supports the upper body.

infolab

■ At birth, babies have more than 300 bones.

■ Adults have 206 bones – many of the bones you are born with fuse together as you grow older.

Bone marrow

Spongy bone is packed with jelly-like red bone marrow. This is where blood cells are made. As a child grows into an adult, the red bone marrow in long bones is replaced by yellow bone marrow, which stores fat.

bone marrow

spongy bone

Getting it right

Over time, bones can change their shape because they are made of millions of living cells. This is why it is very important to have your feet measured when you buy shoes. Shoes that are too tight can damage the bones of your feet.

► Special scans can detect if the bones of a living person are diseased. This picture shows a healthy skeleton.

▼ Spongy bone is not solid. It is made up of a network of bony struts. The spaces are filled with bone marrow.

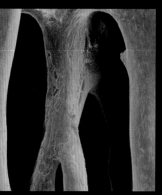

The joints

Wherever two or more bones meet up, you will find a joint. In some joints, the bones are fixed tightly together. In others, the bones can move freely, allowing different parts of the body to bend or twist. Without this flexibility, it would be almost impossible for you to move.

Smooth operators

Joints have to work smoothly to prevent wear and tear. In joints such as the knee, the bone ends have a slippery coating called cartilage. A fluid, in between the layers of cartilage, stops the bones rubbing together.

pelvis
(hip bone)

femur
(thigh bone)

fluid

cartilage

▲ This picture was taken with an endoscope. It shows the cartilage inside a knee joint.

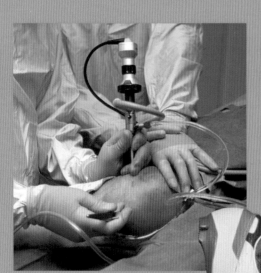

▲ Joints and other parts of the body can be examined by a special instrument called an endoscope.

▲ Two bones meet at the knee, forming a joint. Fluid in the space between the cartilage lets the joint work smoothly.

Chain of bones

Your spine is often called the backbone, but if it was just one rigid bone you would be unable to bend over. Instead, it is made up of many small bones, or vertebrae, with narrow joints in between each of them.

▼ The joints between each vertebra of the spine can move slightly apart.

infolab

- The body contains more than 400 joints. Most of them allow a wide range of movements.

- The ligaments holding the hip joint together are very strong, so it rarely dislocates.

- If you twist your ankle suddenly you may tear and stretch the ligaments in the ankle joints. This is known as a sprained ankle.

vertebra

joint

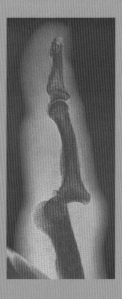

► This x-ray shows a dislocated finger joint, or knuckle. You can see how the two bones have been pushed apart.

Dislocation

Bones are held very tightly in place at the joint by tough bands called ligaments. If a bone is knocked hard enough, it may move out of place. This is called a dislocation, and the joint will not bend properly until the bone is put back into the right place.

How joints move

Joints move in many different ways. Some joints work like a hinge – bend your knee to see this in action. Others, such as the shoulder, let you make movements in most directions.

a ball and socket joint is in each shoulder

Ball and socket

Your hip and shoulder are examples of ball and socket joints. One bone rotates just like a ball inside a cup-like socket formed by another bone. Ball and socket joints are the most moveable of all joints.

Hinges and pivots

The knee, elbow, fingers and toes contain hinge joints. These move backwards and forwards in one direction only. The elbow also contains a pivot joint, which lets you turn your hand over and back again.

the saddle joint is only found in the hand

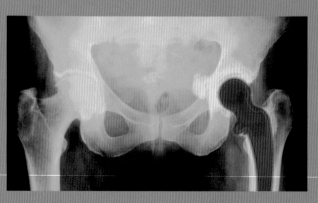

▲ If a hip joint becomes diseased, it can be replaced with an artificial joint made of metal (shown in red).

infolab

- People with 'double joints' do not have extra joints – they are just more flexible.

- Every step you take involves the 33 joints in each of your feet.

- In some of the ankle and wrist joints, the bones glide over each other.

the pivot joint at the top of the spine allows the head to turn

▲ This perfomer can twist and turn her body into this shape because she has very flexible joints.

Thumb power

The saddle joint is found at the base of the thumb. This joint lets you move your thumb in a wide circle. Along with your fingers, your thumb helps you to grip objects in your hand.

in the knee is a hinge joint

Flexibility

Imagine being able to tuck your feet behind your ears! Some people have extremely flexible joints, so they can bend their bodies into unusual and extreme positions.

◀ The body has several different kinds of joints. Each one allows a different movement, from bending the knee to moving the arm in a circle.

Bendy bits

Try folding your ears forwards. They should bend easily and spring back when you let go! This happens because they are made from a flexible tissue called cartilage. Your nose and voicebox, which is the bumpy part in your neck, also contain cartilage.

On the nose

Your nose is made of several pieces of cartilage. They form the sides of your nose and give your nostrils shape. A central piece of cartilage, called the septum, divides the inside of the nose into two chambers.

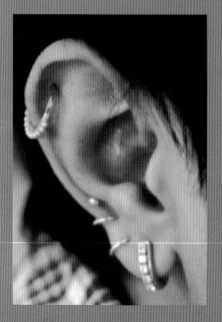

◀ Cartilage is soft enough for an ear to be pierced.

▲ The upper part of the nose is made of hard bone. Plates of cartilage (grey) form the rest of the nose.

cartilage

two-year-old child

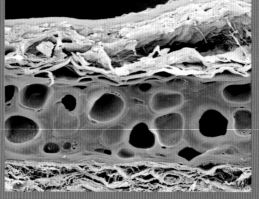

◀ In this picture, taken with a microscope, you can see a layer of cartilage (green) surrounded by skin. The holes contain cells that make cartilage.

◄ You can wobble your nose from side to side and squash it out of shape because the sides and lower part are made from cartilage.

infolab

- Breastbone cartilage does not turn to bone until at least the age of 40.

- The larynx, or voicebox, is also known as the 'Adam's Apple' in men.

- The folds of your ear, which are made of cartilage, help the ear to catch sounds.

bone

Soft skeleton

For the first six weeks, a baby developing in its mother's womb has a skeleton made of cartilage. Cartilage is softer and more flexible than bone and allows for rapid growth and change.

bone

seven-year-old child

adult

◄ These x-rays show a hand at different stages of development. By the time adulthood is reached, the cartilage (lighter areas) has been replaced by bone (blue).

Growth and repair

Cartilage is easily damaged, especially in the knee joint. Many athletes have to retire because of cartilage injuries. But scientists are now able to grow new cartilage in the laboratory, giving hope to injured athletes.

Cartilage into bone

In young children, the bones still contain large areas of cartilage in between more rigid bone. These pieces of cartilage are called growth plates, because they let bones grow. Over time, most cartilage is replaced by bone.

Muscles that get you moving

Without muscles you would not be able to scratch your head, open a door or turn a single page of this book! The muscles you use for these and most other movements are joined to the bones. Muscles work by pulling on the bones.

Under the skin

There are almost 650 muscles in your body that you can control and move. This type of muscle, called skeletal muscle, is connected firmly to the bones by tough, string-like cords. These are the tendons.

this muscle wrinkles your forehead

chest muscles pull the arm forwards

this muscle twists the body

the thigh muscle straightens the knee

▶ Underneath your skin are hundreds of overlapping muscles. Most are attached to your skeleton.

muscle fibres

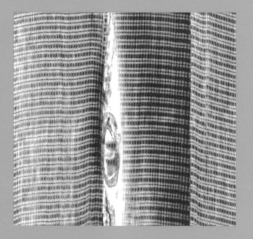

▲ ▶ Muscle is made from long muscle cells, called fibres, packed together in bundles (right). Under a microscope, these fibres look striped (above).

the trapezius muscle pulls the head and shoulders back

the deltoid muscle raises the arm

How muscles work

Muscles move the body because they are attached to the skeleton. When a muscle contracts, it gets shorter and pulls on a bone. Try bending your arm. If you put your hand on the upper part of the arm, you should feel the muscle become fatter as it gets shorter.

Muscle pairs

The muscles we use for movement are controlled and co-ordinated by the brain. Most muscles work in pairs. One pulls in one direction and the other pulls in the opposite direction.

the buttock muscle straightens the thigh

the calf muscle bends the foot downwards

biceps

◀ ▼ The biceps muscle at the front of the upper arm bends the arm up at the elbow. The triceps, at the back, straightens the arm out.

triceps

The skull

The skull is a hard box, made of bone. It contains and protects the brain and other soft parts, such as the eyes, ears and tongue, which can be damaged easily. Nerves and blood vessels go in and out from the brain through holes in the skull.

▲ This decorated skull mask is used during the Mexican Day of the Dead festival. Ancestors are remembered and celebrated on this day.

parietal bone forms the top and side of the skull

Bone head

The skull is formed from 22 bones. Eight of these are large, flat bones that make up a domed box called the cranium. This surrounds the brain. The remaining bones give shape to the face. Only one skull bone can move – the jaw bone, or mandible.

▲ An exploded view of the skull shows how the bones fit together like a jigsaw. The jagged edges lock the bones into place.

▲ This cyclist is taking no chances. A helmet protects his skull and brain from knocks and blows.

Balancing act

The bones of the cranium fit together very tightly and cannot move or slip unless the skull is hit with great force. The skull is balanced on top of the backbone. The spinal cord runs through the backbone and into the brain through a large opening at the base of the skull.

*frontal bone forms
the forehead*

*zygomatic bone
(cheek bone)*

infolab

- The bones around the nose are hollow, to keep the skull as light as possible.

- The fontanelles of a baby become bone between 12 and 18 months.

Safety first

Although the skull is strong, sometimes it needs extra help to protect its precious contents. In many sports, such as cycling, skateboarding or American football, it is important to wear protective headgear.

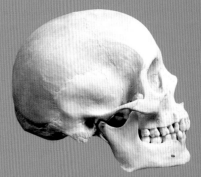

▲ At the front of the skull there are two large openings called orbits. These hold the eyes.

▲ The jaw bone is the strongest and largest bone in the skull. You use it to chew food and to help you speak.

*mandible
(lower jaw)*

*maxilla
(upper jaw)*

Fontanelles

In small babies, the bones of the skull have not yet knitted together. Instead, the bones are connected by a stretchy material. The gaps between the bones are called fontanelles. These allow the skull to get bigger as the baby's brain grows.

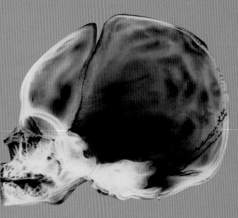

▲ This x-ray of the side of a baby's skull shows the gaps, or fontanelles, that close up as the skull grows.

77

The face

If you have ever had an injection at the dentist, you will know what happens when the muscles of the face are out of action. You cannot speak clearly and you begin to drool! The facial muscles help you to eat, to speak and to communicate without words.

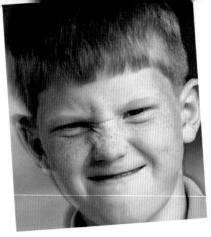

Pulling faces

If you want to know what kind of mood someone is in, just look at his or her face. Facial expressions show others whether we are happy or sad, excited or angry. Many of these expressions, such as a smile, are understood in the same way by people around the world.

▶ The muscles of the face pull on the skin to make all kinds of different expressions, from anger to a look of surprise.

Kissing muscle

A ring of muscle around the mouth pulls your lips into different shapes. This muscle is sometimes called the kissing muscle! We use this muscle to suck, to whistle and to form words when we speak.

◀ When you drink through a straw, a ring of muscles around the mouth goes into action.

frown with
this muscle

wrinkle your
forehead with
this muscle

In the blink of an eye

Your eyes have an automatic safety feature. Every time you blink, the eyelids wipe dust and dirt away from the eyes. If any other object gets too close, the same muscles instantly close the eyelid to protect the surface of the eye.

close your eyelids
with this muscle

smile with
these muscles

the masseter muscle
closes the mouth

the 'kissing' muscle lets
you shape your lips and pout

when you feel sad,
this muscle pulls
down the corners
of the mouth

infolab

■ There are more than 40 muscles in the face.

■ You need most of the muscles in the face to frown, but less than half of them to smile.

■ The masseter muscle is the strongest muscle in your body.

▲ Facial muscles are used to express feelings as well as to eat and to speak.

▼ A performer from the 1920s demonstrates the power of the masseter muscle, which opens and shuts the jaw.

Spine and ribs

Feel the bumps running down the middle of your back. Each one is a ring-like bone called a vertebra. These bones form the spine, or backbone, which is the central part of the skeleton. Twelve pairs of curved rib bones are also attached to the spine.

seven cervical vertebrae in the neck support the head

twelve thoracic vertebrae are connected to your ribs

five large lumbar vertebrae carry most of your body weight

these five fused vertebrae form the sacrum, which secures the spine to the pelvis

four fused vertebrae form the coccyx, or tailbone

◄ ▲ The spine has 33 bones – 24 separate vertebrae and nine that are fused together.

Support system

The spine is made up of curved sections. Each one has a different job to do, from supporting the head to carrying the weight of your body. The different sections of the spine together form a gentle 'S' shape. This helps to make the spine flexible and strong.

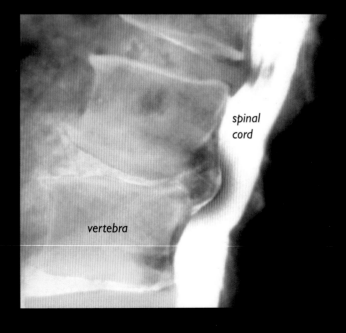

▼ Here, part of a vertebra has broken off in an accident and is pressing against the spinal cord.

spinal cord

vertebra

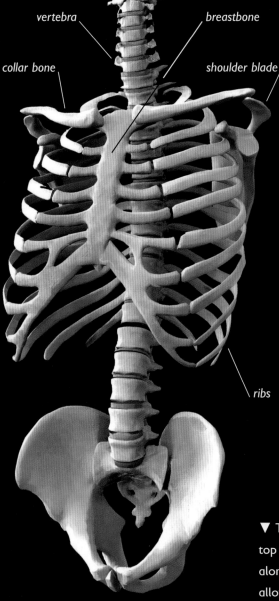

vertebra

breastbone

collar bone

shoulder blade

ribs

▲ The ribs curve around the chest from either side of the spine. Most are connected to the breastbone, or sternum, at the front.

Anti-shock

When you move, stand or jump, you put pressure on your spine. Between each vertebra there are padded discs of cartilage. These cushion and protect the bones of the spine from damage.

The ribs

The ribs form a protective cage around your lungs and heart. When you breathe, your ribcage moves up and down, helping your lungs to suck in air and squeeze it out again.

▼ The atlas is found at the very top of the spine. This vertebra, along with the one below it, allows you to shake and nod your head.

▶ The atlas, which supports your head, is named after a character from one of the myths of Ancient Greece. This sculpture shows Atlas carrying the Earth on his shoulders.

Legs and feet

When you are walking, running or just standing still, your legs and feet have to carry the weight of your whole body. The femur, or thigh bone, in the upper part of the leg, is connected to the body by the pelvis. The femur is the largest and strongest bone in the body.

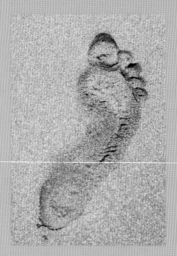

▲ Look at a footprint and you can see that the sole is not flat. Arches of bone raise the inner part of the foot off the ground.

tibia (shin bone)

femur (thigh bone)

Bone basin

The basin-shaped pelvis is where the upper and lower body meet. The pelvis is made from two curved hip bones, joined together at the front. At the back, the hip bones are connected to the backbone.

Under pressure

When you are on the move, your feet push your body forwards. They also stop you from falling over! The bones and ligaments of the foot form curves called arches. These can bend under the weight of the body and they turn the feet into excellent shock absorbers.

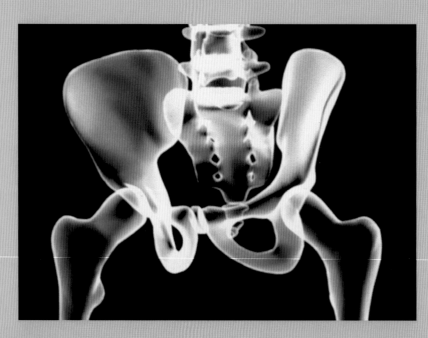

◀ The legs are joined to the spine by the pelvis. The pelvis also surrounds the reproductive and digestive organs.

infolab

- There are 26 bones, 33 joints and more than 100 muscles, tendons and ligaments in each foot.

- The muscles of your feet expand slightly during the day.

- The bones and muscles of the arms and legs are very similar.

◀ The bones and muscles in this gymnast's left leg support the body, while his right leg is stretched out.

All in a name

The sartorius muscle is the longest in the body. Found in the thigh, it is about 30cm long and pulls the knee up and rotates the thigh outwards. The sartorius also lets you sit cross-legged. Ancient Roman tailors, called *sartors*, sat like this when they sewed.

sartorius muscle

▲ A triple jumper winces in pain as the Achilles tendon, which connects the calf muscle to the heel, suddenly tears.

tarsals (ankle bones)   *metatarsals (sole bones)*   *phalanges (toe bones)*

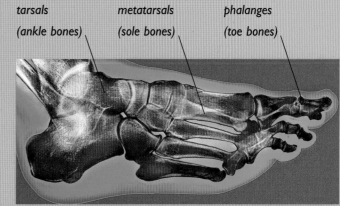

▶ Each foot contains seven tarsals, or ankle bones, five metatarsals, or sole bones, and 14 phalanges, or toe bones.

83

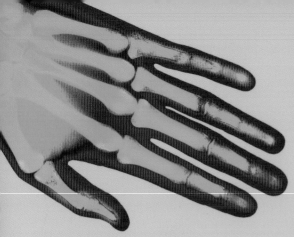

◄ This x-ray shows how the hand bones are arranged. Each finger is made up of three bones called phalanges. The thumb only has two.

▼ Most of the muscles that control the hand are in the forearm. They are connected to the fingers by tendons.

this muscle straightens the fingers

this muscle bends the wrist

Hands

Your hands are one of nature's most amazing tools. From operating complex machinery to catching a ball, our hands are designed to hold and control objects with great accuracy. Each hand has 27 bones and 29 major joints.

Success story

One of the reasons that the human species has been so successful is down to the thumb! The thumb can move across the palm to press against the fingertips. This means that we can perform a huge range of tasks using our hands.

Tendons

Every time you make a hand movement, dozens of tiny muscles are at work. Most of these movements are made by muscles in the arm, as there is not enough space in the hand. The muscles pull on long tendons. The ends of these are attached to your fingers.

On the left

Most people are right-handed. But one in nine of us is left-handed. If you are left-handed you may find it difficult to use scissors and other tools designed for right-handed people.

► Wrapping the fingers and thumbs around a rope in a game of tug-of-war gives a strong and powerful grip.

*fibres called
ligaments hold the
tendons in place*

*tendon from
the muscle that
straightens the fingers*

▲ To play an electronic game you need to make rapid and precise movements with your thumbs.

▼ Special hand shapes and movements are used in sign language. It allows people to communicate without spoken words.

Hand signals

Hands play an important part in human communication – we shake hands, wave goodbye or clap in appreciation. Many people who have problems with their hearing communicate by using special hand movements, called sign language.

infolab

■ In the USA, sign language is the fourth most widely used language.

■ In 1989, two million people joined hands to form a human chain across three countries in eastern Europe.

■ Each hand contains over 120 ligaments.

The story of a broken bone

Your bones are some of the toughest parts of
your body, but they can be broken if they are
bent, twisted or receive a very hard knock. Arms
are often broken when people fall and stretch
their hands out to break the fall. Once a bone
is broken it must be fixed back into position.

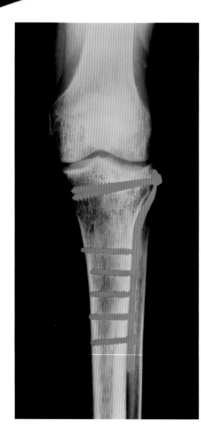

◄ If a bone is
broken in several
places, screws
might be needed
to hold the bone
together while
it heals.

Fractures

A broken bone is called a fracture.
Sometimes the broken bone breaks through
the flesh to open a wound in the skin. This
is known as a compound fracture and can
be very painful. If the skin is not torn, the
fracture is called a simple fracture.

X-ray vision

Doctors check to see if a bone has
been broken by taking a special
picture called an x-ray. This can
see through the skin to the bone
itself. Bones are hard and dense,
and show up very clearly in an x-ray.

► In this x-ray, the two bones below the elbow are broken. At the break, the jagged ends of the bones have moved out of line.

Joining the ends

For a bone to heal properly, the two broken ends must be brought back together. To keep the bones in exactly the right place, the arm or leg is put in a cast. This is a special bandage that turns hard and stops the bone ends from moving.

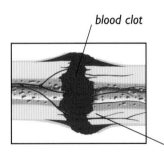

blood clot

◄ A broken bone heals in several stages. First, a blood clot forms around the two ends of the bone.

broken bone

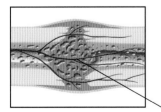

◄ Over the next few weeks, new bone is made and fills the space between the broken ends.

new blood vessels

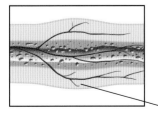

◄ After several months, the bone has healed. It is as strong as it was before the break.

new bone

► A plaster bandage, or cast, will set rock hard to hold the girl's broken bones in position.

On the mend

The two ends of the broken bone produce millions of new cells. These cells build up layers of new bone. Eventually, the two ends meet and join up. It can take up to 12 weeks for bones to repair themselves. Once the x-ray has been checked to see that the bone has healed, the cast can be removed.

Get active!

If you want to stay in shape, then you need to make exercise a regular part of your life. From playing football to dancing, exercise strengthens growing muscles and bones. It can also stop you from becoming overweight. And best of all, exercise can be great fun!

▲ These Chinese children keep fit by exercising every day. Fitness gives you energy, flexibility and strength.

Use it or lose it

The more you use a muscle, the stronger it gets. The best kinds of exercise involve moving lots of different muscles. Swimming, cycling and running are ideal for this.

Body fuel

For your body to work properly, it needs healthy foods. You should eat a variety of different foods, including lots of fresh fruit and vegetables. These provide many of the vitamins and minerals that your body needs.

◀ Swimming gives your heart, lungs and muscles a good workout.

◀ ▶ Exercise is great fun, but some people take sport very seriously. To be one of the best in the world, you need to train for many years and be in peak physical condition.

Keeping safe

Get the right kit, or accidents and injuries will spoil your fun. It is important to wear the right sort of protective gear. Helmets are needed for many sports and should fit snugly to protect your head.

infolab

- A balanced diet and regular exercise will help you to live longer.

- Exercise makes the body release chemicals in your brain that make you feel happy.

- To stay fit, you should exercise for at least half an hour, five days a week.

▲ For some sports, you need proper protection, such as padding and a helmet.

► Many sports injuries can be prevented by doing gentle stretches.

Stretch those legs

Always warm up properly before any sporting activity. This will help prevent damage to your muscles and tendons. Warming up means stretching your body and doing gentle exercise to get the muscles moving.

CHAPTER 4

Life Story

Birth, growth and development

All in a lifetime

Just like every other person on the planet, you will go through many changes during your lifetime. These changes are part of the human life cycle, which begins with birth and ends with old age. A new baby marks the beginning of a new life cycle.

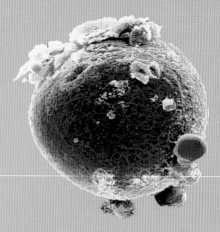

▲ Every person develops from a tiny human egg like this one, seen under a microscope. Each egg is smaller than a full stop.

▼ This baby girl is welcomed by her family. When she has grown up, she may have children of her own.

The circle of life

In order to create a new generation of children, men and women reproduce. Around the world, more than 14,000 babies are born every hour, or four every second! Most will survive into adulthood and become parents themselves.

▲ This baby zebra is up and about soon after being born. It can look after itself without its mother's help.

Bringing up baby

Unlike many baby animals, human babies are completely helpless when they are born. It takes many years, first as a child and then as teenager, to learn the skills that you need as an adult. During this time, your parents take care of you, providing support and love.

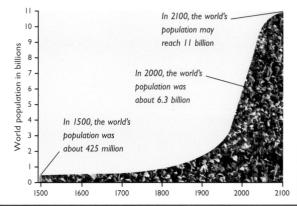

World population in billions

In 2100, the world's population may reach 11 billion

In 2000, the world's population was about 6.3 billion

In 1500, the world's population was about 425 million

▲ More than six billion people live on our planet. By 2100, there may be 11 billion.

Child of our time

One hundred years ago, many children did not live past their fifth birthday. Today, with cleaner water and better health, most children reach adulthood. In a developed country, such as the USA, a baby girl born today can expect to live for 80 years.

◄ Strapped to his father's back, this baby is safe from danger. It will be many years before he is able to look after himself.

93

The male reproductive system

In order to reproduce, a man must make special cells, called sperm, and pass these on to a woman, to join with one of her eggs. To do this, a man has several reproductive organs. They include the testes, where sperm are made, the penis and the prostate gland.

Sperm factories

Every single day, about 300 million new sperm are produced inside a man's testes, a pair of oval-shaped organs. Before the sperm leave the body, they are mixed with fluids from the prostate gland. This provides them with fuel for the journey to the woman's egg.

Keeping cool

Sperm need to be kept cool – at about 34°C. This is 3°C below the temperature inside the body. So the testes hang outside the body, where it is cooler, inside a pouch of skin called the scrotum.

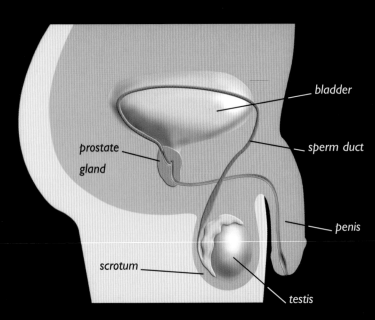

prostate gland

scrotum

bladder

sperm duct

penis

testis

◄ Sperm travel from the testes, along the sperm duct and out through the penis. The reproductive system does not become fully developed until the teenage years.

▼ This microscopic picture of sperm shows their whip-like tails. The sperm use these to swim towards the woman's egg.

Being a man

The male reproductive system is controlled by hormones, or chemical messengers. One of these hormones, testosterone, makes men look different to women. It causes the voice to deepen, muscles to develop and thick hair to grow on the face and body.

▼ ▶ Inside the testis (right) sperm develop from cells inside special tubes (below).

sperm made in tightly coiled tubes

sperm stored here

▶ Testosterone, which is produced in the testes, makes hair grow on a man's face. It can also cause baldness.

Female reproduction

A woman's body has special organs that allow her to become pregnant and to have a baby. These organs form the reproductive system. They include the ovaries, the fallopian tubes, the uterus or womb, and the vagina.

The ovaries

A woman has two ovaries, each the size and shape of a large almond. They are packed with thousands of cells called eggs, or ova. Each month, several eggs ripen but only one is released. The egg travels down one of the woman's fallopian tubes towards the uterus.

egg begins to grow in follicle

egg ripens

egg is released from follicle

remains of follicle break down if fertilization does not happen

◀ Inside the ovary, each egg grows inside a bag called a follicle. When the egg is ripe, it will burst out of the follicle. This is called ovulation and it happens, on average, once every 28 days.

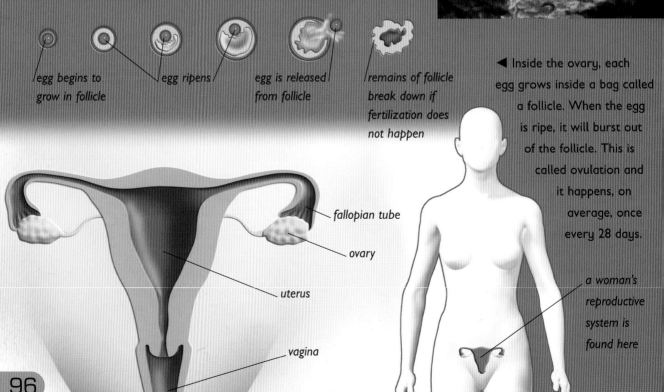

fallopian tube

ovary

uterus

vagina

a woman's reproductive system is found here

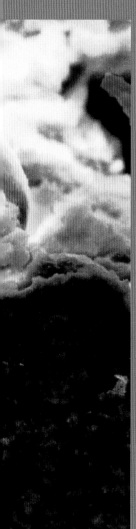

▶ Each month, eggs start to grow in the ovary. After two weeks, one ripe egg is released. If this egg is not fertilized, a new monthly cycle begins.

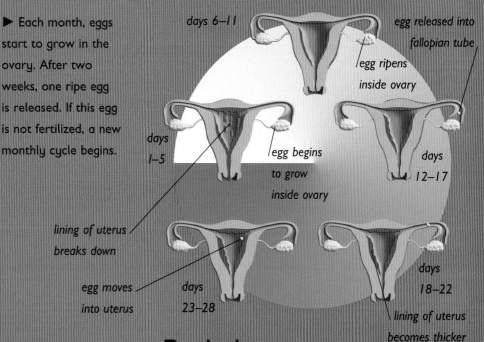

days 6–11

egg released into fallopian tube

egg ripens inside ovary

days 1–5

egg begins to grow inside ovary

days 12–17

lining of uterus breaks down

egg moves into uterus

days 23–28

days 18–22

lining of uterus becomes thicker

Periods

In most months, the woman does not become pregnant. Instead, the lining of the uterus falls apart and is shed with the unfertilized egg through the vagina. This causes bleeding, or a period. About five days later, the lining of the uterus begins to thicken again.

▲ An egg (pink) bursts out of an ovary. It will move down a fallopian tube and may be joined, or fertilized, by a sperm.

▲ Most girls begin to have periods, or to menstruate, between the ages of 11 and 14 years. These will continue until the age of about 50 years.

Getting ready

While the egg is maturing in the ovary, the lining of the uterus becomes thick with blood vessels. This prepares the uterus for pregnancy, which takes place if the egg is fertilized by a sperm.

infolab

■ When a baby girl is born, her ovaries contain between one million and two million eggs, or ova.

■ A woman will release more than 400 eggs during her lifetime.

■ By the age of 50, most women have stopped ovulating. This is called the menopause.

In the beginning

Every human life begins in the same way, when a sperm from a man joins with an egg from a woman. To do this, the man puts his penis inside the woman's vagina. Millions of sperm are released which swim towards the egg. If one gets through the egg's outer layer, fertilization takes place.

The long voyage

To reach an egg, sperm must swim up the uterus and into the fallopian tubes – a journey several thousand times their own length. Of the millions of sperm that set out, no more than a fraction will reach the egg, and only one will fertilize it.

Let's divide

Once the egg has been fertilized, it continues to travel along the fallopian tube. As it does so, the new cell divides into two, then four, and so on. About three days after fertilization, a ball of 16 cells arrives in the uterus.

▶ This sperm has broken through the surface of the egg. It will lose its tail and fuse with the nucleus at the egg's centre.

▶ This is a fertilized egg after six days.

infolab

- It takes several hours for sperm to journey to the egg.

- Sperm can survive for several days in the uterus or fallopian tubes.

*the egg divides
into two cells*

the egg divides again...

*fertilization
happens here*

...and again

▶ After the egg is fertilized,
it travels down the fallopian
tube and into the uterus.

*the egg settles into
the lining of the uterus*

Seeing double

Sometimes, more than one egg is
released and fertilized by the sperm.
This results in twins or even more
babies developing in the pregnancy.
If a single fertilized egg divides in two,
the twins will be identical because they
are from the same egg and sperm.

▲ Several hundred sperm
surround an egg. In order
to attract sperm towards
it, the egg releases a
special chemical signal.

▶ Identical twins
are born when a
single fertilized egg
divides to start
two new lives
rather than one.

The journey ends

Six or seven days after fertilization, the
egg has grown to about 100 cells. It is
now ready to bed down into the lining
of the uterus. This is the beginning of
pregnancy. The cells on the inside of
the egg will grow into the new baby.

Early pregnancy

During the first three months of pregnancy, the tiny baby and its mother both go through dramatic changes. In just a few weeks, the ball of cells grows hundreds of times in size. By the fifth week, the baby's heart has begun to beat. After twelve weeks, the baby has a face, can frown and move its limbs.

▶ Inside the womb, the 12-week-old fetus floats in a bag of fluid. This liquid, called amniotic fluid, cushions the baby.

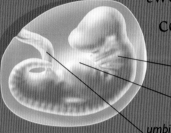

buds will become limbs

heart is beating

umbilical cord

▲ At four weeks, the embryo is the size of a pea.

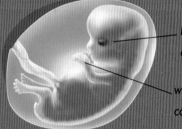

bones of the face are forming

wrists and elbow can bend

▲ By eight weeks, the fetus is about the size of a strawberry.

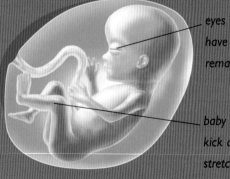

eyes and eyelids have formed but remain closed

baby can kick and stretch

▲ Twelve weeks after fertilization, the fetus is about the size of a lemon.

Four weeks

A month after fertilization, the ball of cells is called an embryo. It has a tail and looks more like a tadpole than a human! The heart and other organs are forming, but the arms and legs have not yet developed.

Eight weeks

The embryo is now called a fetus. It has a face, with eyes that are closed, along with a mouth and tongue. Fingers and toes have now formed. Inside its body, the organs are growing fast.

Twelve weeks

All the organs, limbs, muscles and bones are in place. The head is still large compared to the rest of the body, but the fetus now looks like a baby. It is also possible to tell if it is a boy or girl.

placenta

umbilical cord

Life support system

The developing baby needs to be supplied with food and oxygen. This is the job of the placenta, a large spongy disc that grows in the uterus during pregnancy. The placenta is connected to the baby by the umbilical cord. Your tummy button is what is left of this lifeline.

infolab

- Pregnancy is divided into three stages, called trimesters. Each lasts three months.

- From eight weeks until it is born, the baby is called a fetus.

- The umbilical cord grows to more than half a metre in length.

Later pregnancy

▲ Between 16 and 22 weeks of pregnancy, the mother may start to feel the baby moving inside her.

After three months of pregnancy, all the baby's organs, muscles and bones have formed. But it is still very small and would not be able to survive in the outside world. During the next six months, the baby must grow 100 times in weight before it is ready to be born.

Growing fetus

At 22 to 24 weeks, the baby measures about 20cm in length. The fingers have nails as well as ridges that will become fingerprints. A layer of fine hair called lanugo covers the baby's skin. This hair disappears before birth.

▶ Between 38 and 40 weeks, the baby is ready to be born. It will journey through the vagina and out into the world.

amniotic fluid surrounds the baby

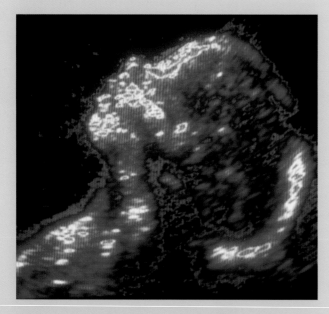

▲ This ultrasound scan shows the head and upper body of a 22-week-old fetus. The baby may move when it hears its mother's voice or her abdomen is touched.

Watching the baby

Although the fetus is hidden away in the womb, a special test, called an ultrasound scan, allows doctors to peer inside the uterus. This test is used to measure the baby, to watch its heart beating, to look out for twins, and to detect any problems.

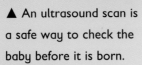

▲ An ultrasound scan is a safe way to check the baby before it is born.

infolab

■ By the end of the pregnancy, there can be up to 1.5 litres of fluid in the bag around the baby.

■ Babies born before 38 weeks can often survive with medical help.

■ After 27 weeks, the fetus may begin to open its eyes and suck a finger or thumb.

■ Pregnant women may want to eat food they do not normally like!

placenta

umbilical cord

Baby fat

Towards the end of pregnancy, the baby has put on a layer of fat which makes it look rounder. After the baby is born, this fat will help to keep it warm and to provide energy. All the organs are now fully developed and the baby is usually in a head down position, ready for birth.

▶ As the baby grows, the surrounding womb increases in size, making the mother's abdomen swell.

cervix

vagina

Birth

About nine months after the egg was fertilized, the baby is ready to be born. The mother will feel powerful movements, called contractions, in her uterus. This is one of the signs that labour has begun. During labour, the baby is pushed out into the world.

▲ The first stage of labour pushes the baby's head into the mother's vagina, or birth canal.

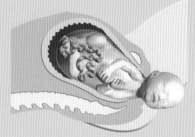

▲ During the second stage, the mother's contractions push the baby out of her body.

▲ After the baby is born, the placenta, with attached umbilical cord, passes through the birth canal.

The journey begins

During the first stage of labour, the muscles of the uterus tighten and begin to squeeze the baby out into the birth canal. At the same time, the cervix, or opening of the uterus, gets wider. The protective bag around the baby may break open, releasing a flood of fluid.

Pushing hard

The second stage of labour begins once the cervix has stretched wide enough to allow the baby to move through the birth canal. With each contraction, the mother usually feels a very strong urge to push the baby out further. At last, the baby is born.

Afterbirth

Once the baby is born, the uterus continues to contract, but much more gently. It still has one more job to do. The placenta, sometimes called the afterbirth, is no longer needed and must also be delivered. This is the third stage of labour.

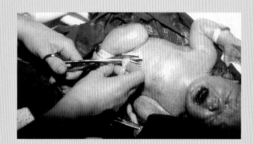

◄ Soon after birth, the baby's umbilical cord is cut.

◄ A newborn baby opens its mouth and cries. This fills the lungs with air.

105

Inheritance

Have you ever wondered why you look the way you do? Genes – the instructions that tell your body how to make itself – have the biggest influence. If you look like your parents or your brother or sister, this is because genes are inherited, or passed on, during reproduction.

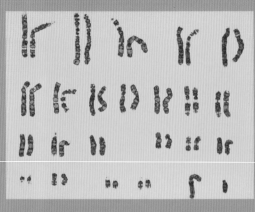

▲ ▼ A cell's nucleus contains 23 pairs of chromosomes. The genes inside each pair control how your body is put together.

cell

nucleus

chromosomes

▼ You can see similar features across four generations of females from the same family.

▲ An egg fertilized by sperm carrying the X chromosome will develop into a girl.

Chromosomes

Your body is made up of trillions of tiny units, or cells. Each cell has a control centre called a nucleus. This is where your genes are stored. The genes are found in string-like strands called chromosomes.

Odd one out

There are 23 pairs of chromosomes inside most cells of your body. But egg and sperm cells are different. Instead of pairs of chromosomes, they only have one of each of the 23 chromosomes.

Joining up

During fertilization, the set of 23 chromosomes from the egg and the set of 23 chromosomes from the sperm join together. This means the new baby has 46 chromosomes altogether and inherits a mixture of genes from both parents.

Boys and girls

A pair of chromosomes called the sex chromosomes controls whether a fetus develops as a boy or a girl. Girls have two of the same type of sex chromosome, called X chromosomes. Boys have two different types of sex chromosomes – one X and one Y chromosome. It is the Y chromosome that makes them boys.

▼ If the sperm that joins with the egg carries the Y chromosome, the fetus will become a boy.

Why we look different

Walk down the street and you will see all kinds of different people – large and small, short and tall, fair and dark. Although we are all built in the same way, there are tiny differences in our genes that help to make each one of us unique.

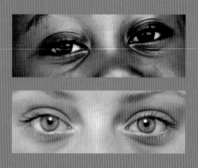

▲ Your genes alone are responsible for the colour of your eyes.

More than your genes

Some features, such as the colour of your hair and eyes, are controlled by genes. But others depend on both your genes and what you experience. So while a person may have inherited the genes to be tall, illness or poor nutrition may stop him or her from reaching full height.

Body shapes

In colder parts of the world, bodies tend to be stocky and ears and feet are small. This helps to prevent heat loss. In very hot climates, people are often tall and thin, with larger ears and noses so that heat can escape quickly.

◀ Each of us looks different, even though we share almost exactly the same genes.

◀ The Masai tribespeople of Kenya have dark skin to protect them from the fierce sun. Long limbs allow heat to escape, keeping them cool.

▶ The Inuit people of northern Canada have stocky bodies. This helps them to stay warm. They still need fur clothing to survive the cold.

You are what you eat

Exercise and a healthy diet can make a difference to your appearance. They help you to build muscles and prevent you from becoming overweight. For some people, lack of exercise and eating junk food have the opposite effect.

▲ Swimmers develop broad shoulders and strong arms to pull themselves through the water.

Life as a baby

▲ A newborn baby can grasp an adult's finger very tightly. This is called a reflex.

A newborn baby knows how to cry! At birth, babies are helpless and completely dependent on others. Crying is the only way to get attention. But by the end of the first year, the infant may be playing simple games, learning a few words and taking his or her first steps.

On the move

At first, the baby's muscles are weak and it cannot lift its head. Slowly, the baby learns how to roll over and to sit up without falling over. By about nine months, the baby can crawl and stand up straight without help.

▼ A strong bond between baby and parents is very important. Lots of eye contact and holding will help the baby develop into a confident and happy child.

Magic milk

Babies are able to feed from their mother's breast or a bottle as soon as they are born. In the first few months, breast milk contains all the ingredients a baby needs to grow, as well as a few extra ones to help fight infections.

First words

At first, babies learn by copying their parents. After a few months, a baby can smile. By nine months, the baby can babble and shout. By one year, a baby can say a few simple words.

▲ After six months, a baby can pick up and move objects.

infolab

- A baby's weight will triple in the first year.

- In New Zealand, the Maori people massage their babies to make them grow strong.

- A baby's first teeth begin to come through after three months.

Lots of sleep

Newborn babies need about 16 hours of sleep every day. They wake up every few hours for feeding. By six months, most babies sleep through the night.

▼ By the end of the first year, a baby may be ready to walk without help.

◄ At nine months, this baby has learned how to crawl.

111

Childhood

Infancy comes to an end after the first year of a person's life. Over the next few years, children become more confident in their movements. They learn how to count and later how to read and write. During childhood, the body continues to grow.

Growth

Different parts of the body grow at different speeds during childhood. In the first year, the head appears very large. From the age of two, the body, including the arms and legs, becomes longer. At this age, there is a thick layer of fat under the skin. This gives a baby-faced look. But from about five, the face loses this layer of fat and the features become much clearer.

Fast learners

By the age of two, children are putting together words to make simple sentences. Two years later, they can have a conversation with another person and begin to use words to express their feelings. Reading and writing start by the age of five years.

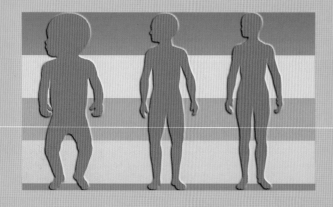

◀ At birth, a baby's head is one-quarter the size of its body. The head reaches its full adult size – one-seventh the length of the body – at 15 years.

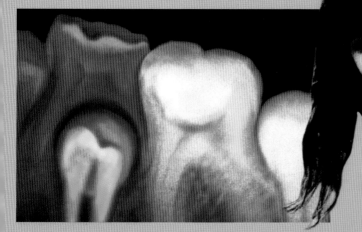

▲ This x-ray picture shows an adult tooth (green) ready to push out a milk tooth just above it. Adult teeth replace milk teeth between the ages of six and 14 years.

Child's play

Playing with other children is a fun and important part of a child's life. Through play, children learn to communicate with others, to practise new skills and to work as part of a team.

▶ Around the age of four, children begin to form friendships. Playing together lets children explore the world in new ways.

◀ Children learn all kinds of skills as they become older. Many of these will be needed for the rest of their lives.

infolab

■ By the age of two, most children have reached half their adult height.

■ By the age of five, a child can draw and describe pictures.

113

Child to adult

Between the ages of 10 and 14, boys and girls notice big changes happening to their bodies. Apart from when we are babies, this time, called puberty, is when we grow most rapidly. Our bodies develop adult features and our reproductive systems begin to work. Feelings and the way we behave also change as childhood is left behind.

▲ Teenage girls and boys are often very aware about their bodies and how they look.

► The time of change when teens become more independent and mature is called adolescence.

Becoming a woman

From the age of 10 or 11, a girl's shape begins to change. As well as growing taller, her breasts develop and her hips become wider. Inside her body, the ovaries and uterus are also growing. By the age of 12 or 13, she has her first menstrual period.

▼ During puberty, the proportions of the body change. Girls become curvier while boys become broader and more muscular.

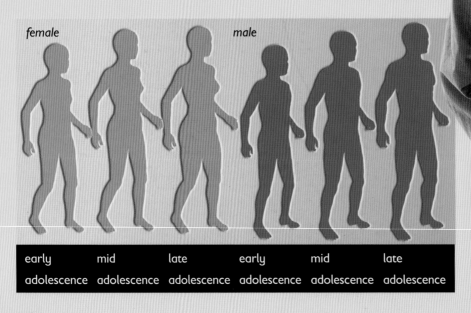

female   male

| early adolescence | mid adolescence | late adolescence | early adolescence | mid adolescence | late adolescence |

▲ Shaving is one new skill teenage boys need to learn! Puberty makes hair on the face grow thicker and faster.

Boy to man

Puberty arrives a little later for a boy than a girl, usually between the ages of 12 and 14. He gains height rapidly and over the next few years his body becomes broader and more muscular. His voice deepens and hair appears on the face.

New challenges

Adolescence is an exciting and challenging time. Teenagers may start a special relationship with a boyfriend or girlfriend. Life often appears to become more complicated as teenagers face important decisions and experience new feelings and mood changes.

Adulthood

Once you become an adult, you stop growing. But the body must continue to look after itself, repairing damage and replacing cells that die or are lost. As the years go by, these repairs do not work quite so well. Some cells die and cannot be replaced. This leads to changes in the body that we call ageing.

▲ During their twenties and thirties, men and women often form lasting relationships and decide to have children.

Being an adult

When you are an adult, you are free to decide how you want to live your life. You can choose a career, travel the world or start your own family. Adulthood also brings important responsibilities, such as looking after children or caring for elderly relatives.

▲ Wrinkles and lines develop as a person grows older, because the skin becomes thinner and less stretchy.

◄ In later years, the bones can weaken and even collapse. This causes the spine to curve, so we lose height, as seen here from left to right.

◀ After the age of 40, many people need to wear glasses for reading.

▼ Although people often become less physically fit as they get older, many continue to lead very active lives.

Signs of ageing

As people get older, their skin becomes wrinkled and their hearing becomes less sensitive. But the ability to solve problems and make difficult decisions can improve with age.

Eyesight

Many adults find that they have to start wearing glasses. The lens in the eye becomes larger with age, and less able to change its shape. This makes it more difficult to focus on nearby objects, such as a book, which will appear blurry.

Glossary

abdomen The central part of the body between the chest and the hips.

Achilles tendon The tendon that connects the muscle at the back of the lower leg to the heel.

adolescence The stage of life during which a child develops into an adult.

adrenaline A hormone that prepares the body to face danger by speeding up the heart, sending more blood to the muscles and releasing sugar for energy.

artery A blood vessel that carries blood from the heart to the body.

bladder A hollow, muscular organ that collects urine from the kidneys and stores it before passing it from the body.

blood vessels Tubes that carry blood around the body – veins, arteries or capillaries, for example.

bone marrow Soft tissue found in the central cavity of long bones and in spongy bone. Yellow bone marrow stores fat, red bone marrow makes blood cells.

brain The part of the nervous system that is enclosed inside the skull. The brain is the control centre of the body.

capillaries The smallest blood vessels in the body. In the capillaries, oxygen moves from the blood into the cells.

carbohydrate A type of nutrient found in food that the body uses as a supply of energy. Potatoes, bread and pasta are rich in carbohydrates.

carbon dioxide A colourless gas made by the cells of the body and breathed out by the lungs.

cartilage A tough but flexible tissue that covers the surface of bones in the joints. Cartilage is also found in the nose, ears and elsewhere in the body.

cell The smallest unit found in any living organism. Every tissue and organ of the human body is made from a collection of cells.

cerebellum The area at the back of the brain that controls balance and co-ordinates movement.

cervix The opening of the uterus, or womb, through which a baby passes during birth.

chromosomes Microscopic threads found in cells. They are made of a chemical called DNA and contain the genes. Each cell has 46 chromosomes.

cochlea Part of the inner ear where sound vibrations are turned into nerve signals and sent to the brain.

cornea A transparent layer at the front of the eye. The cornea works with the lens to focus light onto the retina.

cranium The domed upper part of the skull, which forms a protective casing for the brain.

diaphragm A dome-shaped sheet of muscle below the lungs that plays an important part in breathing.

dislocation When two bones next to each other are knocked out of position or line by a very strong force.

DNA The chemical found in each cell that carries information about how to build and run the body. DNA is stored in the chromosomes.

eardrum A part of the ear that vibrates when sound waves reach it. It separates the middle ear from the outer ear.

egg see **ovum**

endocrine system The system of glands around the body that makes chemical messages called hormones and releases them into the bloodstream.

fertilization The joining together of a female sex cell (egg) and a male sex cell (sperm). A fertilized egg develops into a new baby.

fontanelles Gaps between the bones of the skull in a baby. These gaps, which are covered by a stretchy tissue, slowly close up during the first 18 months.

fracture A break or crack in a bone, which may be caused by an accident.

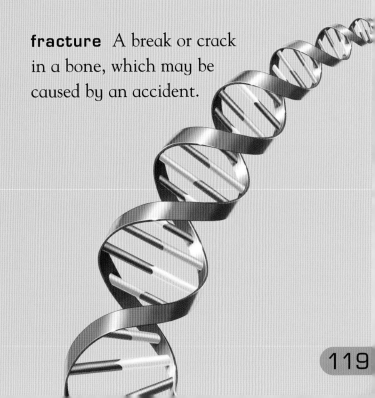

genes The instructions that tell the body how to make and run itself.

hormones Chemicals produced by glands. Hormones pass in the bloodstream to specific areas. They control how other cells or organs work.

immune system The collection of cells in the body that fight disease.

intestines A long tube from the stomach to the end of the digestive system. Here, food is turned into a liquid and nutrients pass into the bloodstream.

iris The coloured ring at the front of the eye. It controls the size of the pupil.

joint A part of the body where two or more bones meet. At most joints, the body can move or bend.

kidney A bean-shaped organ that cleans the blood and makes urine to get rid of waste products and excess fluid.

labour The last stage of pregnancy, during which the womb contracts to push out the baby.

lens A transparent disc in the eye that focuses rays of light onto the retina.

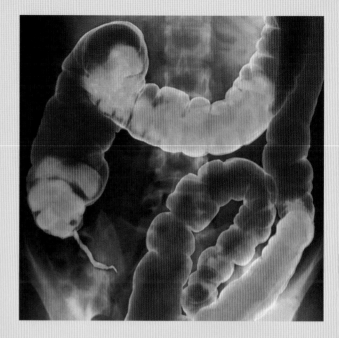

ligament Tough bands of fibre that stretch across or around a joint and hold bones together where they meet.

mandible Also known as the jaw bone, this is the large bone that forms the jaw and contains the lower teeth. It is the only moveable bone in the skull.

micro-organisms Tiny living things that can only be seen under a microscope, such as bacteria, viruses and fungi.

nerve A string-like bundle of nerve cells that carries information between the nervous system and the rest of the body.

nerve fibre The thread-like part of a nerve cell. Electrical signals pass along nerve fibres.

nervous system The network of nerve cells that carries information around the body, and controls many of the body's activities. The brain is the nervous system's headquarters.

neuron A nerve cell that carries signals at high speed around the body.

nucleus The control centre of a cell.

nutrients Substances found in food and drinks that the body needs for energy, growth and repair. Nutrients include protein, carbohydrates and vitamins.

optic nerve A bundle of neurons that carries information from the retina, at the back of the eye, to the brain.

organ A major part of the body, such as the heart or kidney. An organ carries out a particular task.

ovary A small organ in a woman's pelvis that makes and releases eggs, or ova. A woman has two ovaries.

ovulation The release of a female sex cell (an egg, or ovum) from the woman's ovary. This happens once every 28 days.

ovum A female sex cell, also known as an egg, that is made in the ovaries.

oxygen A gas taken from air in the lungs into the bloodstream. It is used to release energy from food and is essential for life.

pelvis A basin-shaped bone that joins the legs to the lower part of the spine and supports the organs of the abdomen.

placenta A spongy disc that grows inside the womb during pregnancy. It supplies the baby with oxygen and food.

puberty The stage of life when the reproductive organs start working. It begins between the ages of 10 and 14.

pupil The circular opening in the centre of the iris, through which light rays pass into the eye.

reflex An automatic reaction, often in response to danger.

retina The eyeball lining. It uses light to form images which are turned into electrical signals and sent to the brain.

saliva Fluid made in the mouth. It moistens food and starts the process of digestion.

sense organ A part of the body, such as the eye, ear or skin, that sends information about the outside world to the brain.

skeleton A hard framework made of bones and covered by the muscles. The skeleton supports the body, gives it shape and protects the internal organs.

sperm Male sex cells. They are made in an organ called the testes.

spinal cord The part of the nervous system packed with neurons that runs from the brain down the backbone.

spine A flexible, strong column of bone, made of 33 bones called vertebrae. It forms a protective tunnel for the spinal cord, and is also known as the spinal column or the backbone.

taste bud A small cluster of sensors that detect taste chemicals in saliva.

tendon A tough cord of tissue that joins muscle firmly onto bone.

testes A pair of oval-shaped organs found in a man. They make sperm and hang outside the body in the scrotum.

tissue A part of the body formed by cells of a similar type. Each sort of tissue, such as muscle or nerve tissue, carries out a particular job.

umbilical cord A thick cord that contains blood vessels. It connects the fetus, or developing baby, to the placenta.

uterus A hollow organ found in a woman's pelvis. An unborn baby grows here during pregnancy.

vagina A tube from a woman's womb to the outside of her body, through which a baby is born.

vein A blood vessel that carries blood from the body back to the heart.

vertebrae The 33 irregular-shaped bones that are piled on top of each other to form the spinal column.

windpipe A long tube, also known as the trachea, that carries air from the back of the throat down into the lungs.

womb see **uterus**

x-ray A type of picture that allows doctors to see inside the body.

Websites

Kidshealth has lots of information on your muscles, bones and joints, your brain and your organs:
www.kidshealth.org/kid

Find cartoons, quizzes and fun facts about health and the body at BrainPop:
www.brainpop.com/health

This site, called 'Your Gross and Cool Body', tells you all about your muscles:
http://yucky.kids.discovery.com/flash/
   body/pg000123.html

...and your skeleton:
http://yucky.kids.discovery.com/flash/
   body/pg000124.html

...and the endocrine system:
http://yucky.kids.discovery.com/
   noflash/body/pg000133.html

...and digestion:
http://yucky.kids.discovery.com/flash/
   body/pg000126.html

Take a grand tour of the human body:
www.vilenski.org/science/humanbody/
   index.html

Play interactive games and learn loads of fun facts at the BBC:
www.bbc.co.uk/science/humanbody/body

For an introduction to cells, genes and DNA, try these two sites:
http://ology.amnh.org/genetics/
   index.html
www.genecrc.org/site/ko/index_ko.htm

Learn all about the food:
www.nutritionexplorations.org/
   kids/main.asp

For more on your senses, explore the Neuroscience for Kids website:
http://faculty.washington.edu/chudler/
   chsense.html

Test your reflexes with the fastball reaction challenge:
www.exploratorium.edu/baseball/
   reactiontime.html

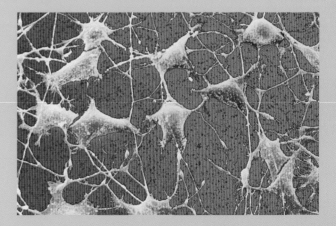

Index

Acknowledgements

The publisher would like to thank the following for permission to reproduce their material. Every care has been taken to trace copyright holders. However, if there have been unintentional omissions or failure to trace copyright holders, we apologize and will, if informed, endeavour to make corrections in any future edition.

Key: b = bottom, c = centre, l = left, r = right, t = top

Cover c Getty Imagebank; bl Corbis; cr Getty; br Corbis; page 1 Getty Imagebank; 2 Digital Vision/Getty; 3 SPL; 4 Corbis; 8bl Corbis; 9 Corbis; 10tl SPL; 10br SPL; 11cr SPL; 12tc SPL; 12tr SPL; 12cc SPL; 12cr SPL; 13 Corbis; 14tl SPL; 14cr Comstock; 14bl SPL; 15tl SPL; 15tr SPL; 15b SPL; 16tl SPL; 16bl SPL; 17tl SPL; 17r SPL; 18tl SPL; 19 Alamy; 20tl SPL; 20bl SPL; 21tl SPL; 21tr Stone/Getty Images; 22 Imagebank/Getty; 23 Imagebank/Getty Images; 24bl SPL; 24l SPL; 27b Digital Vision/Getty; 29cl SPL; 29cr SPL; 31cr SPL; 31b SPL; 32tr Alamy; 32–33 SPL; 32cl Corbis; 33tl SPL; 33br Corbis; 34 Corbis; 36tl Getty Taxi; 36bl Corbis; 36cr Alamy; 37l Getty Rubberball Productions; 37r The Art Archive; 38tl SPL; 38bl Corbis; 39br SPL; 40tr Corbis; 40cl Getty Taxi; 41bl Getty Stone; 41r Getty Imagebank; 42 Getty Photodisc Green; 43 Alamy; 44 SPL; 45c SPL; 45br Getty Stone; 47 Exploratorium; 48cl Getty Stone; 48bl Corbis; 49cr SPL; 49bl Getty Imagebank; 50–51 Alamy; 51tr Getty Stone; 51c SPL; 52cl Corbis; 52b Getty Imagebank; 52–53 Alamy; 53 Corbis; 54 Robert Harding; 55l Getty Stone; 55r Getty Stone; 56tl Corbis; 56cr Alamy; 58tr SPL; 58–59 Corbis; 59 Corbis; 60l Corbis; 60bc Corbis; 61cl Getty Imagebank; 61r Corbis; 64tl Actionplus; 64r Actionplus; 64bl Getty Stone; 65l Actionplus; 65tr SPL; 65cr Actionplus; 65br Getty Stone; 66–67 SPL; 68bl SPL; 68c SPL; 68–69 Getty Imagebank; 69r SPL; 70bl SPL; 70–71 Alamy; 71tr Getty Imagebank; 72bl Corbis; 72bc SPL; 72tr Corbis; 73 SPL; 74tl zefa; 74bl SPL; 75br zefa; 76tl Getty Stone; 76bl SPL; 77c Imaging Body; 77cr Imaging Body; 77br SPL; 78bl Corbis; 78r Alamy; 79b Corbis; 80–81 SPL; 82tl Alamy; 82b SPL; 82–83 Getty Allsport; 83cr Actionplus; 83br SPL; 84tl SPL; 84–85 Getty/Photographer's Choice; 85tr Getty Brand X Pictures; 85cl Medical-On-Line; 86 SPL; 87tr SPL; 87cr Corbis; 88tl Corbis; 88bl zefa; 88–89 Corbis; 89t Getty Photographer's Choice; 89c Getty Allsport; 90–91 SPL; 92t SPL; 92b Corbis; 93t Getty Imagebank; 93c Corbis; 93b Corbis; 94–95 SPL; 95bl SPL; 95br Corbis; 96–97 SPL; 97c Getty Stone; 98–99 SPL; 100–101 SPL; 102t Getty Stone; 102b SPL; 103t SPL; 103b Corbis; 104–105 Getty Imagebank; 105cr Imaging Body; 106 SPL; 107t Getty Photographer's Choice; 107b Getty Photodisc; 108tr Corbis; 108cr SPL; 108b Getty Imagebank; 109 Getty Stone; 110tl Getty Stone; 110bl Getty Imagebank; 110–111 Getty Taxi; 111tl Getty Taxi; 111br Getty Stone; 112tr Getty Imagebank; 112tcr Getty Imagebank; 112bcr Getty Taxi; 112br Getty Imagebank; 113tl SPL; 113r Getty Stone; 114–115 Getty Taxi; 115tl Getty Stone; 116tl Getty Stone; 116cr Getty Taxi; 116bl SPL; 116–117 Getty Taxi; 117tl Getty Taxi; 120 SPL; 123 SPL

VILLAGE CHRISTMAS & THE CHRISTMAS MOUSE

One Christmas Eve a mouse's appearance in an old widow's bedroom leads to a chance encounter with a small boy—a meeting that would be remembered by both of them for a long time, in *The Christmas Mouse*. And in *Village Christmas* the peaceful lives of the Misses Waters are disturbed by the arrival of the noisy, cheerful Emery family in the house across the street. It was only the advent of a Christmas baby that was to thaw the sisters' frosty attitude and cause a warm flowering of seasonal goodwill in Fairacre.

Village Christmas
&
The
Christmas
Mouse

Miss Read

CHIVERS PRESS
BATH

The Christmas Mouse first published 1973
by
Michael Joseph
Village Christmas first published 1966
by
Michael Joseph
This Large Print edition published by
Chivers Press
by arrangement with
Michael Joseph Ltd
1993

ISBN 0 7451 7616 X

British Library Cataloguing in Publication Data available

Village Christmas

❄ ❄ ❄

To
Jill and John
with love

❄

THE DARKNESS throbbed with the clamor of church bells. The six sonorous voices of St. Patrick's peal chased each other, now in regular rhythm, now in staccato clashes, as the bellringers sweated at their Christmas peal practice.

The night was iron-cold. Frost glittered on the hedges and fields of Fairacre although it was not yet eight o'clock. Thatched roofs were furred with white rime beneath a sky brilliant with stars. Smoke rose in unwavering blue wisps from cottage chimneys, for the air was uncannily still.

The sound of the bells carried far in such weather. At Beech Green, three miles away, Miss Clare heard them clearly as she stooped to put her empty milk bottle tidily on her cottage doorstep, and she smiled at the cheerful sound. She knew at least four of those six bellringers, for she had taught them their early lessons long ago at Fairacre school. Arthur Coggs, furtively setting rabbit snares in a copse near Springbourne, heard them as clearly. The shepherd high on the downs above the village and the lonely signalman tending his oil lamps on the branch line which meandered along the Cax valley to the market town, heard them too.

9

Nearer at hand, in the village of Fairacre, the bells caused more positive reactions. The rooks, roosting in the topmost boughs of the elm trees hard by the reverberating belfry, squawked an occasional protest at this disturbance. A fox, slinking towards Mr. Willet's hen run, thought better of it as the bells rang out, and beat a retreat to the woods. Mrs. Pringle, the dour cleaner of Fairacre school, picked up a flake of whitewash with disgust from the spotless floor where it had fluttered from the quaking kitchen wall, and a new baby nearby, woken by the clamor, wailed its alarm.

Miss Margaret Waters and her sister Mary were quietly at work in their cottage in the village street. They sat, one at each side of the big round table in the living room, penning their Christmas cards in meticulous copperplate. Music tinkled from the large old-fashioned wireless set on the dresser by the fireplace, vying with the noise of the bells outside. Mary's gray curls began to nod in time to a waltz, and putting her pen between her teeth, she rose to increase the volume of the music. At that moment an excruciating clashing of St. Patrick's peal informed the world of Fairacre that at least three of the six bellringers were hopelessly awry in their order.

"Switch it off, Mary, do! Them dratted bells drowns anything else. We may as well save the electric!" exclaimed Margaret, looking over the top of her gold-rimmed spectacles.

Mary obeyed, as she always did, and returned to her seat. It would have been nice, she thought

10

privately, to hear "The Merry Widow Waltz" all the way through, but it was not worth upsetting Margaret — especially with Christmas so near. After all, it was the season of good will. She picked up a card from the central pile and surveyed it with affection.

"All right for Uncle Toby?" she queried, her head on one side. "He's partial to a robin."

Her sister looked up from her writing and studied the card earnestly. Sending just the right card to the right person was something which both sisters considered with the utmost care. Their Christmas cards had been chosen from the most modestly priced counter at Bell's, the Caxley stationer's, but even so the amount had been a considerable sum from the weekly pension of the two elderly sisters.

"You don't feel it's a mite spangly? That glitter on the icicles don't look exactly *manly* to me. I'd say the coach and horses myself."

Mary set aside the robin reluctantly, and began to inscribe the card with the coach and horses:

From your affectionate nieces,
Margaret and Mary

The ancient mahogany clock, set foursquare in the middle of the mantelpiece, ticked steadily as it had done throughout their parents' married life and their own single ones. A log hissed on the small open fire, and the black kettle on the trivet began to hum. By bedtime it would be boiling, ready for the sisters' hot-water bottles. It was very peaceful and warm in the cottage and Mary sighed with content as she tucked in the flap of Uncle Toby's envelope. It was the time of day she loved best, when the work was done, the curtains were drawn, and she and Margaret sat snugly and companionably by the fire.

"That seems to be the lot," she observed, putting the envelopes into a neat stack. Margaret added her last one. Three, including the rejected robin, remained unused.

"There's bound to be someone we've forgot," said Margaret. "Put 'em all on the dresser, dear, and we'll post 'em off tomorrow."

The church bells stopped abruptly and the room seemed very quiet. Ponderously and melodiously the old clock chimed half-past eight from the mantelpiece, and Mary began to yawn. At that moment there came a sharp rapping at the door. Mary's mouth closed with a snap.

"Who on earth can that be, at this time of night?" she whispered. Her blue eyes were round with alarm. Margaret, made of sterner stuff, strode to the door and flung it open. There, blinking in the sudden light, stood a little girl.

"Come in, do, out of the cold," begged Mary, who had followed her sister. "Why, Vanessa, you haven't got a coat on! You must be starved with the cold! Come by the fire now!"

The child advanced toward the blaze, plump hands outstretched like pink starfish. She sniffed cheerfully and beamed up at the two sisters who looked down at her with so much concern. The child's two front milk teeth had recently vanished and the gap gave her wide smile a gamin air. She shook the silky fringe from her sparkling eyes. Clearly, Miss Vanessa Emery was very happy to be inside Flint Cottage.

"And what do you want, my dear, so late in the day?" inquired Margaret, unusually gentle.

"Mummy sent me," explained the child. "She said could you lend her some string to tie Grandpa's parcel. *Thick* string, she said, if you could manage it. It's a box of apples, you see, off our tree, and sticky tape won't be strong enough on its own."

"Indeed it won't," agreed Mary, opening the dresser drawer and taking out a square tin. She opened it and placed it on the table for the child to inspect. Inside were neat coils of string, the thickest at the left-hand side, and the finest — some of it as thin as thread — in a tidy row on the right-hand. The child drew in her breath with delight and put a finger among the coils.

"Where did you buy it?" she asked.

"*Buy* it?" echoed Margaret, flabbergasted. "Buy *string?* We've never bought a bit of string in all our borns! This comes off all the parcels that have come here over the years."

"Mum cuts ours off and throws it away," explained the child, unabashed. She picked up a fat gingery coil of hairy twine and examined it closely.

"Could you spare this?" she asked politely.

13

"Of course, of course," said Mary, hurrying to make amends for the horrified outburst from her sister. She tucked it into the pocket on the front of the child's cotton apron.

"And now I'll see you across the road," she added, opening the front door. "It's so late I expect you should be in bed."

The child left the fire reluctantly. One hand gripped the string inside her pocket. The other she held out to Margaret.

"Goodnight, Miss Waters," she said carefully, "and thank you for the string."

"You're welcome," replied Margaret, shaking the cold hand. "Mind the road now."

The two sisters watched the child run across to the cottage opposite. It sat well back from the village street in a little hollow, surrounded by an overgrown garden. Against the night sky its thatched roof and two chimneys gave it the air of a great cat crouched comfortably on its haunches. They heard the gate bang, and turned again to their fire, slamming the door against the bitter cold.

"Well!" exploded Margaret. "Fancy sending a child out at this time of night! And for a bit of string! 'Cuts it off' indeed! Did you ever hear of such wicked waste, Mary?"

"Dreadful!" agreed her sister, but with less vehemence. "And that poor little mite with no coat on!"

"Well, I've always said, there's some people as have no business to be parents and them Emerys belong to 'em. Three under seven and another on the way! It's far too many. I feel downright sorry for that poor unborn. She can't look after the three she's got already!"

Margaret picked up the poker and rapped smartly at a large lump of coal. It split obediently and burst into joyous flame. The kettle purred with increased vigor, and Margaret moved it further back on the trivet.

The two sisters sat down, one at each side of the blaze. From the cupboard under the dresser Mary drew forth a large bundle, unrolled it, and gave one end to Margaret. They were making a hearth rug, a gigantic monster of Turkish design, in crimson and deep blue. Each evening the sisters spent some time thrusting their shining hooks in and out of the canvas as they laboriously added strand after strand of bright wool.

Margaret's end was growing much more quickly than Mary's. Her hook moved more briskly, with sharp staccato jabs, and the wool was tugged fiercely into place. Mary moved more slowly, and she fingered each knotted strand as though she loved it. She would be sorry when the work was finished. Margaret would be glad.

"I must say, they seem happy enough," observed Mary, reverting to the topic of the Emerys. "And very healthy too. They're dear little girls — and so polite. Did you notice the way Vanessa shook hands?"

"It's not the children I'm criticizing," replied Margaret. "It's their parents. There'll be four little

15

mites under that roof soon, and dear knows how many more to come. And they don't seem to have any idea of bringing them up right! Look at their fancy names, for one thing! Vanessa, Francesca, Anna-Louise — I ask you!"

"I rather like them," said Mary with spirit. Margaret snorted and jabbed the canvas energetically.

"And all dressed up in a frilly little apron with a heart-shaped pocket, and no decent warm coat on the child's back," continued Margaret, now in full spate. "It's all on a par with the house. All fancy lamp shades, and knickknacks hanging on the wall, and great holes in the sheets, for all to see, when she hangs 'em on the line. 'Twasn't no surprise to me to hear she cuts up her string and throws it out. We done right, Mary, not to get too familiar with her. She's the sort as would be in here, everlasting borrowing, given half a chance, as I told you at the outset."

"I daresay you're right, dear," responded Mary equably. She usually was, thought Mary, pensively. They worked in silence and Mary looked back to the time when the Emerys had first arrived in Fairacre three months before, and from a vantage point behind the bedroom curtain she had watched their furniture being carried up the brick path.

It was a golden afternoon in late September and Margaret had gone to St. Patrick's to help with the decorations for Harvest Festival. A bilious headache had kept Mary from accompanying her, and she retired to bed with an aspirin and a cup of tea.

She had slept for an hour and the sound of children's voices woke her. At first she thought the schoolchildren must be running home, but it was only three o'clock by the flowered china timepiece on the mantelshelf, and she had gone to the window to investigate.

A dark green pantechnicon almost blocked the village street. The men were staggering to the house opposite with a large and shabby sideboard between them. Two little girls danced excitedly beside them, piping shrilly to each other like demented moorhens. Their mother, cigarette in mouth, watched the proceedings from the side of the doorway.

Mary was a little shocked — not by the cigarette, although she felt smoking was not only a wicked waste of money but also very unhealthy — but at the young woman's attire. She wore black tights, with a good-sized hole in the left leg, and a short scarlet jerkin which ended at mid-thigh. Her black hair was long and straight, and her eyes were heavily made up. To Mary she appeared like an actress about to take part in a play set in the Middle Ages. No one — absolutely no one — dressed like that in Fairacre, and Mary only hoped that the young woman would not hear the remarks which must inevitably come from such village stalwarts as Mrs. Pringle and her own sister if she continued to dress in this manner.

Nevertheless, Mary was glad to see that they had neighbors, and gladder still to see that there were children. The thatched cottage had stood empty all the summer, ever since the old couple who had lived there from the time of their marriage in good Queen Victoria's reign had departed to a daughter's house in Caxley and had moved from thence to Fairacre churchyard. It would be good to see a light winking through the darkness again from the cottage window, and to see the neglected garden put into order once more, thought Mary.

Her headache had gone and she straightened the bed coverlet and made her way down the steep dark staircase. She was pleasantly excited by the activity outside the front door, and tried to hear what the children were saying, but in vain. A thin wailing could be heard and, peeping out from behind the curtain, Mary saw that the woman now had a baby slung over her shoulder and was patting its back vigorously.

"Three!" breathed Mary, with delight. She was devoted to children and thoroughly enjoyed taking her Sunday School class. To be sure, she was often put out when some of the bigger boys were impudent, and she was quite incapable of disciplining them, but small children, and particularly little girls of gentle upbringing, delighted her warm old spinster's heart.

When Margaret returned she told her the good news. Her sister received it with some reserve.

"I'll be as pleased as you are," she assured Mary, "if they behaves themselves. But let's pray they

18

ain't the squalling sort. You can hear too much in that bedroom of ours when the wind's that way."

"I wondered," began Mary timidly, "if it would be a kindness to ask them over for a cup of tea when we makes it."

"If she was alone," replied Margaret after a moment's consideration, "I'd say 'Yes,' but with three children and the removal men too, I reckons we'd be overdone. Best leave it, Mary — but it does you credit to have thought of it."

Mary was about to answer, but Margaret went on. Her expression was cautious.

"We don't want to be too welcoming yet awhile, my dear. Let's see how they turn out. Being neighborly's one thing, but living in each other's pockets is another. Let 'em get settled and then we'll call. Best not to go too fast or we'll find ourselves babysitting every evening."

A thought struck her.

"Seen the man, Mary?"

Mary admitted that she had not.

"Funny!" ruminated her sister. "You'd have thought he'd be on hand."

"Maybe he's clearing things up the other end," suggested Mary.

"Maybe," agreed Margaret. "I only hope and pray she's not a widow woman, or worse still one that's *been left*."

"We'll soon know," replied Mary comfortably, well versed in village ways. Fairacre had a lively grape vine, and there would be no secrets hidden

19

in the cottage opposite, the sisters felt quite sure.

Within a week it was common knowledge that the Emerys had moved from a north London suburb — Enfield, according to Mrs. Pringle, Southgate, by Mr. Willet's reckoning, though the vicar was positive that it was Barnet. Much to Margaret's relief, Mr. Emery had appeared, and her first glimpse of him was as he put out the milk bottles the next morning whilst still clad in dashing crimson pajamas with yellow frogging.

He worked "up the Atomic," as did many other Fairacre residents, but drove there in a shabby old Daimler about nine, instead of going on the bus which collected the other workers at seven-thirty each morning.

"One of the high-ups," commented Mr. Willet. "Had a bit of book-learning in science and that, I don't doubt. Looks scruffy enough to have a degree, to my mind. Wants a new razor blade, by the looks of things, and that duffle coat has seen a few meals down it."

Fairacre was inclined to agree with Mr. Willet's somewhat tart summing-up of Mr. Emery, though the female residents pointed out that he seemed to take his share of looking after the children and, say what you like, he had very attractive thick black hair. It was Mrs. Emery who provided more fodder for gossip.

As Mary had foreseen, her Bohemian garments scandalized the older generation. And then, she was so breathtakingly friendly! She had introduced herself to Mr. Lamb in the post office, and to two venerable residents who were collecting their pensions, shaking hands with them warmly and asking such personal questions as where they lived and what were their names.

"Wonder she didn't ask us how old we be," said one to the other when they escaped into the open air. "She be a baggage, I'll lay. I'll take good care to steer clear of that 'un."

She hailed everyone she met with equal heartiness, and struck horror into every conservative Fairacre heart by announcing her decision to join every possible club and society in the village "to get to know people," and her intention of taking the little girls with her if the times of the meetings proved suitable.

"Terribly important for them to make friends," she told customers and assistants in the village shop one morning. Her wide warm smile embraced them all. She seemed unaware of a certain frostiness in the air as she made her purchases, and bade them all goodbye, with considerable gusto, when she left.

Margaret and Mary viewed their ebullient neighbor with some alarm. Three days after her arrival, when Margaret was already planning the best time to call, Mrs. Emery knocked briefly on the sisters' front door and almost immediately opened it herself.

"Anyone at home?" she chirped blithely. "Can I come in?"

Before the startled sisters could reply, she was in the room, with two beaming little girls following her.

"I'm your new neighbor, as I expect you know," she said, smiling disarmingly. "Diana Emery. This is Vanessa, and this one Francesca. Say 'Hello,' darlings."

"Hello! Hello!" piped the two children.

Mary collected her wits with remarkable composure. She found the Emery family attractive, despite their forward ways.

"There now!" she began kindly. "We were wondering when to call and see you. Won't you take a cup of coffee? Margaret and I usually have some about this time."

"I'll get it," said Margaret swiftly, glad to escape for a moment to take stock of the situation. Mary could see from her expression that she was not pleased by the invasion.

"Lovely!" sighed Mrs. Emery, flinging off a loose jacket of jade green, and settling in Margaret's arm chair. The two little girls collapsed cross-legged on the hearth rug and gazed about them with squirrel-bright eyes beneath their silky fringes.

"What about the baby?" asked Mary, concerned lest it should have been left outside. The morning was chilly.

"Not due until the New Year," replied Mrs. Emery nonchalantly. "And jolly glad I shall be when it's arrived."

There was a gasp from the doorway as Margaret

bore in the tray. She was pink, and obviously put out. Mary hastened to explain.

"I meant the *third* little girl," she said.

"Oh, Anna-Louise! She's fast asleep in the pram. Quite safe, I can assure you."

"We want a brother next time," announced Vanessa, eying the plate of biscuits.

"Three girlth ith three too many," announced Francesca. "Thatth's what my daddy thayth."

"That's a joke," explained Vanessa.

"Sometimes I wonder," their mother said, but her tone was cheerful.

Margaret poured coffee and tried to avert her eyes from Mrs. Emery's striped frock which gaped widely at the waist fastening, displaying an extraordinary undergarment of scarlet silk. Could it *possibly* be a petticoat, Margaret wondered? Were there really petticoats in existence of such a remarkable color?

Mary did her best to make small talk. It was quite apparent that Margaret was suffering from shock, and was of little help.

"Is there anything you want to know about the village? Perhaps you go to church sometimes? The services are at ten-thirty and six-thirty."

"We're not much good at churchgoing," admitted their neighbor. "Though I must say the vicar looks a perfect poppet."

Margaret swallowed a mouthful of coffee too quickly and coughed noisily. This was downright sacrilege.

"Gone down the wrong way," explained

23

Francesca, coming close to Margaret and gazing up anxiously into her scarlet face. Speechless, but touched by the child's solicitude, Margaret nodded her agreement.

"And if you want to go to Caxley," continued Mary, "there is a bus timetable on the wall of 'The Beetle and Wedge.' Is there anything else we can help you with?"

Mrs. Emery put her cup carelessly upon its saucer so that the spoon crashed to the floor. Both children pounced upon it and returned it to the table.

"Well, yes, there is something," said their mother. "Could you possibly change a check for me? I'm absolutely out of money and want to get some cigarettes. Edgar won't be home until eight or after."

There was a chilly silence. The sisters had no banking account, and the idea of lending money, even to their nearest and dearest, was against their principles. To be asked, by a stranger, to advance money was profoundly shocking. Margaret found her tongue suddenly.

"I'm afraid we can't oblige. We keep very little in the house. I suggest that you ask Mr. Lamb. He may be able to help." Her tone was glacial, but Mrs. Emery appeared unperturbed.

"Ah well," she said cheerfully, struggling from the armchair and gaping even more hugely at the waistband, "never mind! I'll try Mr. Lamb, as you suggest. Must have a cigarette now and again with this brood to look after."

24

She picked up the green jacket and smiled warmly upon the sisters.

"Thank you so much for the delicious coffee. Do pop over and see us whenever you like. We'll probably be seeing quite a bit of each other as we're such close neighbors."

And with these ominous words she had made her departure.

Ever since then, thought Mary, busily prodding her hook in the rug, she and Margaret had fought a polite, but quietly desperate, battle against invasion.

"Be friendly to all, but familiar with few," said an old Victorian sampler hanging on their cottage wall. The sisters found its advice timely. The children, they agreed, were adorable, and although they appeared far too often for "a-shilling-for-the-electricity-meter" or "a-box-of-matches-because-the-shop's-shut" and other like errands, the two sisters had not the heart to be annoyed with them. In any case, it was simple to dismiss them when their business was done, with a piece of chocolate to sweeten their departure.

Mrs. Emery, growing weekly more bulky, was more difficult to manage, and the two sisters grew adept at making excuses. Once inside, she was apt to stay over an hour, seriously throwing out the working of the sisters' day. She certainly was an embarrassment as a neighbor.

Mary's eyes strayed to the table, and the rejected Christmas card with the gay robin among his spangles. A thought struck her, and she put down her hook.

"Margaret," she said suddenly, "what about sending that robin to the Emery children?"

Margaret began to look doubtful.

"Well, my dear, you know what a mite of trouble we've had with that woman! I just wonder —"

"Oh, do now!" pressed Mary, her face flushed. " 'Tis Christmas! No time for hard thoughts, sister, and them children would just love it. I could slip over with it after dark on Christmas Eve and pop it through the letter box."

Margaret's face relaxed into a smile.

"We'll do it, Mary, that we will!"

She began to roll up the rug briskly, as the church clock struck ten. Mary gave a happy sigh, and lifted the singing kettle from the trivet.

"Time for bed," she said, taking two hot-water bottles from the bottom of the dresser cupboard "Think of it, Margaret! Only three more days until Christmas!"

The next three days were busy ones for the ladies at Flint Cottage. Red-berried holly, pale mistletoe, and glossy ivy were collected and used to decorate the living room. Two red candles stood one at each end of the mantlepiece, and a holly garland hung from the brass knocker on the front door.

The cake was iced, the pudding fetched down from the top shelf in the pantry, the mincemeat jar stood ready for the pies, and a trifle was made. One of Mrs. Pringle's chickens arrived ready for the table, and sausage meat came from the butcher.

Margaret crept away privately while Mary was bringing in logs from the woodshed, and wrapped two pairs of sensible lisle stockings which she had bought in Caxley for her sister's present. Mary took advantage of Margaret's absence at the post office and swiftly wrapped up a pair of stout leather gloves and hid them in the second drawer of the bedroom chest.

All Fairacre was abustle. Margaret and Mary helped to set up the Christmas crib in the chancel of St. Patrick's church. The figures of Joseph, Mary and the Child, the shepherds, and the wise men reappeared every year, standing in the straw provided by Mr. Roberts, the farmer, and lit with somber beauty by discreetly placed electric lights. The children came in on their way from school to see this perennial scene, and never tired of looking.

The sisters helped to decorate the church too. There were Christmas roses on the altar, their pearly beauty set off by sprigs of dark yew amidst the gleaming silverware.

On Christmas Eve the carol singers set out on their annual pilgrimage round the village. Mr. Annett, the choir master, was in charge of the church choir and any other willing chorister who volunteered to join the party. This year, the new-comer Mr. Emery was among them, for word had soon gone round that he sang well and Mr. Annett had invited him to join the carol singers. Clad in the duffle coat which Mr. Willet thought of so poorly, he strode cheerfully along the frosty lanes of Fairacre, swinging a hurricane lamp as though he had lived in the village all his life, and rattling away to his companions with the same friendly foreign loquacity as his wife's.

One of their stopping places was outside "The Beetle and Wedge," strategically placed in the village street. Margaret and Mary opened their window and watched the singers at their work. Their breath rose in silver clouds in the light of the lanterns. The white music sheets fluttered in the icy wind which spoke of future snow to the weather-wise of Fairacre. Some of the lamps were hung on tall stout ash sticks, and these swayed above the ruffled hair of the men and the hooded heads of the women.

Mr. Annett conducted vigorously and the singing was controlled as well as robust. As country voices caroled the eternal story of joyous birth, Mary felt that she had never been so happy. Across the road she could see the upstairs light in the bedroom of the Emery children, and against the glowing pane were silhouetted two dark heads.

How excited they must be, thought Mary! The stockings would be hanging limply over the bed rail, just as her own and Margaret's used to hang so many years ago. There was nothing to touch the exquisite anticipation of Christmas Eve.

"Hark the herald angels sing,
Glory to the newborn King,"

fluted the choir boys, their eyes on Mr. Annett,
their mouths like dark O's in the lamp light. And
the sound of their singing rose like incense to the
thousands of stars above.

On Christmas morning Margaret and Mary
were up early and went to eight o'clock service.
A feeling of night still hung about the quiet village,
although the sun was staining the eastern sky and
giving promise of a fine day ahead.

The lighted crib glowed in the shadowy chancel
like the star of Bethlehem itself, and the aromatic
smell of the evergreens added to the spirit of
Christmas. Later, the bells would ring out and the
winter sunshine would touch the flowers and silver
on the altar with brightness. All would be glory
and rejoicing, but there was something particularly
lovely and holy about these quiet early morning
devotions, and the two sisters preferred to attend
then, knowing that the rest of the morning would
be taken up with the cheerful ritual of Christmas
Day cooking.

They unwrapped their few parcels after breakfast, exclaiming with genuine pleasure at the
modest calendars and handkerchiefs, the unaccustomed luxury of richly perfumed soap or choc-
olates which friends and relatives had sent.

Margaret thanked Mary warmly for the gloves.
Mary was equally delighted with her stockings.

They exchanged rare kisses and told each other how lucky they were.

"There's not many," said Margaret, "as can say they live as contented as we do here. And under our own roof, thank God, and nothing owing to any man!"

"We've a lot to be thankful for," agreed Mary, folding up the bright wrappings neatly. "Best of all each other — and next best, our health and strength, sister."

"Now I'm off to stuff the bird," announced Margaret, rising with energy. "I'll put on the pudding too while I'm in the kitchen. Must have that properly hotted up by midday."

She bustled off and Mary began to make up the fire and sweep the hearth. The two red candles looked brave and gay, standing like sentinels on each side of the Christmas cards arranged along the mantelpiece. She wondered if the Emery children had liked the fat robin. She could see them now, in imagination, surrounded by new Christmas presents, flushed and excited at the joy of receiving and of giving.

At that moment a rapping came at the front door and she rose from her sweeping to open it. Vanessa stood there, looking far from flushed and excited. The child's eyes were large with alarm her face pale with cold and fright.

"What is it, my love? Come in quickly," cried Mary.

"It's Mummy. She said could you come over, please. She's ill."

"Is Daddy with her?" asked Margaret, appearing in the doorway with her fingers pink and sticky with sausage meat.

"No. He's had to go to Grandma's. Grandpa rang up last night after we'd gone to bed. Grandma's being stroked."

"Had a stroke," corrected Margaret automatically. "Dear me, that's bad news! We'll be over as soon as we've put the dinner in."

The child's eyes grew more enormous than ever. She looked imploringly at Mary.

"But it's the baby coming! You must come this minute. Please, please!"

Without a word Margaret began to take off her kitchen apron.

"Go over, Mary," she said quietly. "I'll follow you."

Indescribable chaos greeted Mary's eyes when she stepped into the Emerys' kitchen. It was a large square room with a brick floor, and comfortably warmed by an Esse cooker appallingly streaked with grime. Quantities of anthracite dust were plentifully sprinkled on the floor at its base, and had been liberally trodden about the room.

The debris of breakfast littered the table, and colored paper, tags, and string garnished sticky cereal bowls and mugs. A ginger cat lapped up some milk, which dripped from an overturned jug, and the confusion was made more acute by Francesca, who stood proudly holding a new scarlet

31

scooter, ringing the shiny bell without cessation.

"Give over, do!" begged Mary, peremptory in her flurry. The child obeyed, still beaming. Nothing could quench her Christmas bliss, and Mary was immediately glad to see that this was so. The sound of Anna-Louise's wailing became apparent, and Mary opened the door of the box staircase and began to mount. The two little girls started to follow her.

"You stop here, there's dears," said Mary, much agitated. Who knows what terrors might be aloft? "Pick up the paper and make it nice and tidy."

To her relief they fell upon the muddle joyously, and she creaked her way above. Mrs. Emery's voice greeted her. She sounded as boisterous as ever, and Mary's fears grew less. At least she was conscious!

"You are a darling! You really are!" cried Mrs. Emery. She was standing by the window, a vast figure in a red satin dressing gown embroidered on the back with a fierce dragon. Mary suddenly realized how very young she looked, and her heart went out to her.

"We were so sorry to hear about your mother-in-law," began Mary, a little primly.

"Poor sweet," said Mrs. Emery. "It would have to happen now. Edgar went off as soon as he came back from carol singing. And then, this! *Much* too early. I suppose I've got the dates wrong again. Ah well!"

She sighed, and suddenly clutched the front of the dressing gown again. Mary felt panic rising.

"Do get into bed, there's a love," she begged, turning back the rumpled bed clothes invitingly. The bottom sheet had a tear in it six inches long, and a very dirty rag doll was also revealed. Poor Mary was appalled. She must put something clean on the bed! Suppose the baby was born in that unhygienic spot! She looked for help towards Mrs. Emery, who was bowed before the chest of drawers and gasping in an alarming way.

"You must have clean sheets," announced Mary with an authoritative ring in her voice which wholly surprised her.

"Cupboard," gasped Mrs. Emery, nodding toward the next room.

An unpleasant smell was the first thing that Mary noticed about the adjoining bedroom. Anna-Louise was standing in a cot. Her nightgown and the bedding were ominously stained, but her cries had ceased and she threw Mary a ravishing smile.

"You pretty thing," cried Mary, quite entranced. "Aunt Mary'll see to you in just a minute."

She swiftly ransacked the cupboard. She found a roll of mackintosh sheeting and two clean linen ones. Bustling back to the bedroom she set about making the bed with vigorous speed. Mrs. Emery was upright again, leaning her damp forehead against the cool windowpane. She consented to be led to the bed, unprotesting, and let Mary remove the flamboyant dressing gown.

"There, there!" soothed Mary, tucking her in as though she were a child. "I'll bring you a drink."

"I'm all right now," whispered the girl, and at that moment Margaret appeared.

"Does Nurse know?" was her first remark. Mary felt suddenly guilty. Of course it was the first thing she should have found out. Trust Margaret to know exactly what to do!

"Yes," replied Mrs. Emery. "At least, someone at her house does. Nurse was out on another baby case. They were sending word."

"What about Doctor Martin?" continued Margaret.

"Nurse will get him, if need be," said the girl. She sank back on the pillow and suddenly looked deathly tired. "It won't come for hours," she told them. "It's just that I was worried about the children."

"I know, I know," said Margaret gently. "We'll look after them all right. Leave it all to us."

"Anna-Louise needs a wash," said Mary, retiring to the next room. She beckoned Margaret to follow her, and closed the door between the two rooms.

"What on earth shall we do?" she implored Margaret. Margaret, for once, looked flummoxed.

"Dear knows, and that's the honest truth," admitted her sister. "Let's hope nature knows best and Nurse comes pretty smartly. This is foreign stuff to us, Mary, but we must just hold the fort till help comes."

She turned to survey Anna-Louise, who was jumping rhythmically up and down in the cot with dire results.

"Land's sake, Mary! That child wants dumping in the bath — and the bedding too!"

"I'll do her," said Mary swiftly. "And then I can keep an eye on Mrs. Emery up here. You see to things downstairs."

"Won't do no harm to give Nurse another ring," observed Margaret, turning to the door. She looked back at her sister.

"Who'd 'a' thought we'd 'a' been spending Christmas like this?"

She vanished downstairs and Mary went to turn on the bath for her charge.

Anna-Louise, well soaped, was absolutely adorable. Fat and pink, with a skin like satin, she made Mary a willing slave. She patted the water vigorously, sending up showers of spray, and drenching Mary kneeling beside the bath. Mary could have stayed there all day, murmuring endearments and righting the celluloid duck time and time again. But the water cooled rapidly, and there was much to do. She gathered the naked child into a grubby bath towel, and dried her on her lap.

"She hasn't had her breakfast yet," Mrs. Emery said drowsily when the child was dressed. She looked at her daughter with amusement.

"That's Francesca's jumper," she observed, "but no matter. Tie a bib on the poor lamb. She's a filthy feeder."

Below stairs, all was amazingly quiet. The table had been cleared and the two little girls were blissfully engaged in filling in their new Christmas drawing books with glossy long crayons as yet unbroken. Margaret was busy sweeping the floor with a broom from which most of the bristles had long vanished.

"Has the baby come yet?" asked Vanessa, without looking up from the mad oscillation of her crayoning.

"Not yet," replied Mary, threading Anna-Louise's fat legs through her high chair. She stood back and surveyed the baby anxiously. "And what does Anna-Louise like for breakfast?"

Francesca put down her crayon and gazed earnestly at her younger sister.

"She liketh bacon rindth betht," she told Mary.

"Well, we've no time to cook bacon," said Margaret flatly, still wielding the broom.

"Egg," said Vanessa briefly. "All horrible and runny. That's what she likes."

The sisters exchanged questioning glances.

"Sounds reasonable," muttered Margaret, "if you can find the egg saucepan."

"It's the milk one as well," volunteered Vanessa, making for a cupboard. "Here you are." She produced a battered saucepan with a wobbly handle, and returned to the drawing book.

"Did you get through to Nurse?" asked Mary agitatedly, as she filled the saucepan.

"Still out. Message supposed to have been passed on. I reckons we ought to get her husband back. It's his business after all." Margaret spoke with some asperity.

"I'll go and ask Mrs. Emery," said Mary, "while the egg boils."

She returned to the bedroom to find Mrs. Emery humped under the bedclothes with her head in the pillow. She was groaning with such awful intensity that Mary's first impulse was to fly for Margaret, but she controlled it. She patted the humped back consolingly and waited for the spasm to pass. Somewhere, far away it seemed, the bells of St. Patrick's began to peal for morning service. A vivid picture of the peaceful nave, the holly and the Christmas roses, the fragrance of the cypress and yew came clearly to Mary, standing helplessly there watching her neighbor in labor. How long ago, it seemed since she and Margaret knelt in the church! Yet only three or four hours had gone by.

The spasm passed and Diana Emery's face appeared again.

"Better," she said. "Can I have that drink now? Coffee, please — no milk. Any sign of that confounded nurse?"

"She's on her way," said Mary. "And we thought we ought to phone your husband."

"His parents aren't on the telephone," said Mrs. Emery.

"We could ring the police," suggested Mary with sudden inspiration. Mrs. Emery laughed with such unaffected gaiety that Mary could hardly believe that she had so recently been in such pain.

"It's not *that* serious. Nurse will be along any

minute now, and think how wonderful it will be to present Edgar with a fine new baby!"

She sounded so matter-of-fact and cheerful that Mary gazed at her open-mouthed. Was child-bearing really undertaken so lightly? She remembered Margaret's tart comments on people who had large families with such apparent fecklessness. How many more would there be in this casual household, Mary wondered? Then she remembered the sight of Anna-Louise in the bath and hoped suddenly, and irrationally, that there would be more — lots more — and that she would be able to enjoy them.

"I'll get your coffee, my love," she said warmly and went below.

Returning with the steaming black brew, she remembered something.

"Shouldn't we put the baby's things ready for nurse?" she asked.

"There's not a great deal," confessed the girl, warming her hands round the cup. "I intended to do most of the shopping after Christmas in Caxley. So many people about, I just couldn't face it."

"But you must have *some* things," persisted Mary, aghast.

"In the bottom drawer," said the girl vaguely. "And there are lots of Anna-Louise's things that will do in the airing cupboard."

Mary was shocked at such a slapdash approach to an important event, and her face must have shown it for Mrs. Emery laughed.

"After the first you don't bother quite so much," she confessed. "You can get by with all the odds and ends the others had."

Mary found six new diapers in the drawer, and a bundle of small undershirts, some tiny nightgowns yellow with much washing, and a shawl or two in the airing cupboard.

"And what shall we put the baby in?" she inquired.

"Anna-Louise's carry-cot. It's in her room. It probably wants clean things in it." The girl had slipped down into the bed again and closed her eyes. She looked desperately tired, thought Mary, with a pang.

The carry-cot held two dolls, a headless teddy bear, and a shoe, all carefully tucked up in a checked tablecloth. Mary took the carry-cot downstairs to wash it out and dry it ready for the new occupant.

"If that dratted nurse don't come soon," said Margaret, "I'll fetch Doctor Martin myself, that I will! I'll just slip over home, Mary, and turn that bird and add a mite of hot water to the pudding."

"We'll never have a chance to eat dinner, sister," cried Mary. "Not as things are!"

"There's them three to think of," replied Margaret, nodding at the children. "We've got them to feed, don't forget."

She lifted the latch and hurried across to their cottage, while Mary dried the carry-cot and took stock. One or two parishioners, in their Sunday best, were making their way to church. Mary saw Mr. and Mrs. Willet stop to speak to her sister as she stood with one hand on their doorknob. There was much head-shaking, and Mrs. Willet looked across at the Emerys' house with some alarm.

"The news will soon be round Fairacre," thought Mary, as she dried the carry-cot.

It was clean and peaceful now in the kitchen, and she noticed the paper chains festooned against the ceiling, and the Christmas cards pinned along the rafters. Her own fat robin was there, and she glowed with pleasure. Vanessa and Francesca were still engrossed in their artistic efforts, and Anna-Louise wiped her eggy plate with her fingers and sucked them happily. What dear good children they were, thought Mary!

At that moment she heard their mother calling from overhead. Her voice sounded shrill and desperate. Mary took the stairs at a run. The girl was sitting up in bed, clenching and unclenching her hands on the coverlet.

"You *must* get that nurse — or the doctor, or someone. I can't stick this now. It's coming pretty fast."

"I'll ring again," promised Mary, thoroughly frightened by the urgency of the girl's pleas. "Just lie down again. I'm sure it's better. Can I do anything? Rub your back, say, or bring you a hot-water bottle?"

She did her best to appear calm, but inwardly terror gripped her. Supposing the baby came this

40

minute? What on earth did you do with a newborn baby? Wasn't there something about cutting a cord? And if so, where did you cut it? And how did you tie it up afterwards? Hadn't she heard once that mothers bled to death if the cord wasn't tied properly? And that wretched carry-cot wouldn't be anywhere near aired, let alone made up with clean bedding, if the baby arrived now! Mary found herself shaking with panic, and praying desperately. Don't let it come yet, please, dear Lord! Not until Nurse arrives, please God!

"There, my love —" she began, when she stopped abruptly. The door of the staircase had opened and someone was mounting.

"Margaret!" she cried. "Quickly, Margaret!"

A sturdy figure appeared in the doorway.

"Nurse! Thank God!" cried Mary, and began to weep.

"You go and make us all a cup of tea," said Nurse Thomas with gruff kindness. And Mary fled.

An hour later, Margaret and Mary sat at their own table, serving three excited little girls with Christmas dinner. Nurse's car still stood outside the cottage opposite, but Doctor Martin's was not to be seen. Evidently all was going well, and Nurse had everything well in hand.

Mary found herself as excited as the children. What a relief it was to be at home again, and to know that Mrs. Emery was being properly nursed! It was impossible to eat amidst such momentous happenings, and she was glad to neglect her own plate and to have the pleasant task of guiding Anna-Louise's teaspoon in the right direction.

In the afternoon the youngest child slept soundly in Mary's own bed. St. Patrick's clock chimed three, and still no message came from the house across the road.

A few Fairacre folk began to go by, taking an afternoon stroll for the sake of their digestions between Christmas dinner and the further challenge of iced cake for tea. They noted Nurse's car and the light in the upstairs window, and fell to wondering.

Margaret was reading "The Tale of Two Bad Mice" from a new glossy copy which the children had received that morning when a tapping came at the door. Mrs. Lamb from the post office stood outside with a bouquet of anemones in her hand. She caught sight of the two little girls inside and spoke in a whisper.

"For their mother, my dear. Hope all's going well. We heard about it after church. You're going over again, I expect?"

"Yes, indeed," answered Margaret, accepting the bright bunch. "She'll be pleased with these. Nurse is still there, as you see."

She nodded toward the car.

"Give Mrs. Emery our best wishes," said Mrs. Lamb. "Poor soul, without her husband too! She's got everyone's sympathy, that's a fact."

She set off homeward, and Margaret returned to the fireside. It began to grow dark, for the af-

42

ternoon was overcast, and Mary took a taper and lit the bright red candles. The flames stretched and dwindled in the draft and the little girls gazed at them starry-eyed.

"Do you always have candles?" asked Vanessa. "Or just at Christmas?"

"Just at Christmas," said Margaret.

She put down the book and gazed at the bright flames with the children. The waiting seemed endless, and suddenly she felt desperately tired. How much longer, she wondered, before they knew?

Just then they heard the sound of a gate shutting and footsteps coming to their door. Margaret and Mary exchanged swift glances. Could it be — ?

Mary opened the door and there stood the nurse, smiling.

"Come in," said Mary.

"I daren't. I'm late now," said the nurse, "but all's well."

Margaret and the children gathered at the door.

"A boy," Nurse announced proudly. "Seven pounds and bonny. And Mrs. Emery's asleep. Can one of you go over?"

"You go," said Margaret to Mary. "I'll bring the children over later."

"We want to see him," pleaded Vanessa.

"*Now!*" added Francesca stubbornly.

"Now!" echoed Anna-Louise, not understanding the situation, but glad to try a new word.

"Later on," responded Nurse firmly. "Your mummy's tired."

She turned to go and then looked back.

"Mr. Emery rang up. I've told him the news and he'll be back very soon."

She waved and made her way across the road to the car.

"Tell Mrs. Emery I'll be in in the morning," she called, and drove off in a cloud of smoke.

As if by magic, two heads popped out from the doorway of "The Beetle and Wedge." They belonged to the landlord and his wife.

"Couldn't help seeing Nurse go off," he said to Mary. "What is it?"

"A boy," said Mary, smiling.

"Now, ain't that good news?" beamed his wife. "You tell her we'll be wetting the baby's head in here tonight."

"Ah, she's a grand little mother, for all her funny ways," declared her husband. "Tell her it'll be nice to have another young 'un in the village."

Mary tiptoed into the silent cottage. Everything seemed to slumber. The cat slept on a chair by the stove. Nothing moved. She left the door of the staircase ajar so that she could hear the slightest sound from above, and sat down at the table.

In the domestic stillness which enveloped her, after the stress of the day, old and lovely words came into her mind. *And she brought forth her first-born son; and she wrapped him in swaddling clothes, and laid him in a manger . . .*

She slipped off her stout country shoes and tiptoed up the stairs. It was very quiet in the bedroom. Mrs. Emery, looking pathetically young and pale, slept deeply. Beside the bed, on two

44

chairs, was the carry-cot.

Mary leant over and gazed in wonder. Swaddled tightly, in the shawl she had found for him in the airing cupboard, was the newborn baby, as oblivious of the world about him as his sleeping mother. Full of joy she crept below once more.

There was a sound outside, and she looked up from lacing her shoes. There stood Mr. Emery, his face alight.

"Where is she?" he asked.

"They're both upstairs," whispered Mary, and opened the staircase door so that he could go aloft and see his son.

Late that night, the two sisters sat at each side of the hearth, working at their rug.

"D'you know what Vanessa said when her father fetched her?" asked Margaret. "She said: 'This is the loveliest Christmas we've ever had!' 'Twas good of the child to say it, I thought, after such a muddling old day. It touched me very much."

"She spoke the truth," replied Mary slowly. "Not only for herself, but for all of us here in Fairacre. 'Tis a funny thing, sister, but when I crept up the stairs to take a first look at that new babe the thought came to me: 'Ah! You're a true Fairacre child, just as I was once, born here, and most likely to be bred up here, the Lord willing!' And then another thought came: 'You've warmed up us cold old Fairacre folk quicker'n the sun melts frost.' You know, Margaret, them Emerys have put us all to shame, many a time, with their friendly ways, and been snubbed too, often as not. It took a Christmas baby to kindle some proper Christmas good will in Fairacre."

" 'Tis true," admitted Margaret, putting down the rug hook, and gazing into the dying fire. Into her tired mind there floated irrelevant memories ... Mrs. Emery's scarlet petticoat, a ginger kitten lapping milk, Anna-Louise fumbling with her egg spoon while her sisters watched her with squirrel-bright eyes laughing at her antics ... all adding up to color and warmth and gentle loving-kindness.

"Now this has happened," she said soberly, "it won't stop at *Christmas* good will, sister. The Emerys are part and parcel of this village for good. There's room for all sorts in Fairacre, Mary, but it took a newborn babe to show us."

She began to roll up the rug briskly.

"Come, sister. Time we was abed."

The Christmas Mouse

FOR
Elizabeth Ann Green
WHO STARTED THE STORY

Contents

❄

Chapter One

The rain set early in tonight . . .
            —Robert Browning

THE RAIN began at noon.

At first it fell lightly, making little noise. Only the darkening of the thatched roofs, and the sheen on the damp flagstones made people aware of the rain. It was dismissed as "only a mizzle." Certainly it did not warrant bringing in the tea towels from the line. Midday meals were taken in the confident belief that the shower would soon blow over. Why, the weathermen had predicted a calm spell, hadn't they, only that morning?

But by two o'clock it was apparent that something was radically wrong with the weather forecast. The wind had swung round to the northwest, and the drizzle had turned to a downpour. It hissed among the dripping trees, pattered upon the cabbages in cottage gardens and drummed the bare soil with pock marks.

Mrs. Berry, at her kitchen window, watched the clouds of rain drifting across the fields, obscuring

53

the distant wood and veiling the whole country-side. A vicious gust of wind flung a spatter of rain-drops against the pane with so much force that it might have been a handful of gravel hurled in the old lady's face. She did not flinch, but instead raised her voice against the mounting fury of the storm.

"What a day," said Mrs. Berry, "for Christmas Eve!"

Behind her, kneeling on the rush matting, her daughter Mary was busy buttoning her two little girls into their mackintoshes.

"Hold still," she said impatiently, "hold still, do! We'll never catch the bus at this rate."

They were fidgeting with excitement. Their cheeks were flushed, their eyes sparkling. It was as much as they could do to lift their chins for their mother to fasten the stiff top buttons of their new red mackintoshes. But the reminder that the bus might go without them checked their excitement. Only two afternoon buses a week ran past the cottage, one on market day, and one on Saturday. To miss it meant missing the last-minute shopping expedition for the really important Christmas presents — those for their mother and grandmother. The idea of being deprived of this joy brought the little girls to partial submission.

Mary, her fingers busy with the buttons, was thinking of more mundane shopping — Brussels sprouts, some salad, a little pot of cranberry jelly for the turkey, a few more oranges if they were

54

not too expensive, a lemon or two. And a potted plant for Mum. A cyclamen perhaps? Or a heather, if the cyclamen proved to be beyond her purse. It was mean the way these florists put up the prices so cruelly at Christmas. But there, she told herself, scrambling to her feet, the poor souls had to live the same as she did, she supposed, and with everything costing so much they would have to look after themselves like anyone else.

"You wait here quietly with Gran for a minute," she adjured the pair, "while I run and get my coat on, and fetch the baskets. Got your money and your hankies? Don't want no sniffing on the bus now!"

She whisked upstairs and the children could hear her hurrying to and fro above the beamed ceiling of the kitchen.

Old Mrs. Berry was opening her brown leather purse. There were not many coins in it, and no notes, but she took out two silver fivepenny pieces.

"To go towards your shopping," said the old lady. "Hold out your hands."

Two small hands, encased in woollen gloves knitted by Mrs. Berry herself, were eagerly outstretched.

"Jane first," said Mrs. Berry, putting the coin into the older girl's hand. "And now Frances."

"Thank you, Gran, thank you," they chorused, throwing their arms round her comfortable bulk, pressing wet kisses upon her.

"No need to tell your mum," said Mrs. Berry. "It's a little secret between us three. Here she comes."

The three hurried to the cottage door. The rain was coming down in sheets, and Mary struggled with an umbrella on the threshold.

"Dratted thing" — she puffed — "but can't do without it today. I'll wager I forget it in some shop, but there it is. Come on now, you girls. Keep close to me, and run for it!"

Mrs. Berry watched them vanish into the swirling rain. Then she shut the door upon the weather, and returned to the peaceful kitchen.

She put her wrinkled hand upon the teapot. Good, it was still hot. She would have another cup before she washed up.

Sitting in the wooden armchair that had been

her husband's, Mrs. Berry surveyed the kitchen with pleasure. It had been decorated a few years before and young Bertie, Mary's husband, had made a good job of it. The walls were white, the curtains cherry-red cotton, and the tiles round the sink were blue and white. Bertie, who had set them so neatly, said they came from a fireplace over in Oxfordshire and were from Holland originally. The builder, a friend of his, was about to throw them out but Bertie had rescued them.

A clever boy with his hands, thought Mrs. Berry, stirring her tea, though she could never understand what poor Mary saw in him, with that sandy hair and those white eyelashes. Still, it did no good to think ill of the dead, and he had made a good husband and father for the few short years he and Mary had been married. This would be the third Christmas without him — a sad time for Mary, poor soul.

Mrs. Berry had once wondered if this youngest daughter of hers would ever marry. The two older girls were barely twenty when they wed. One was a farmer's wife near Taunton. The other had married an American, and Mrs. Berry had only seen her twice since.

Mary, the prettiest of the three girls, had never been one for the boys. After she left school, she worked in the village post office at Springbourne, cycling to work in all weather and seeming content to read and knit or tend the garden when she returned at night.

Mrs. Berry was glad of her daughter's company.

She had been widowed in 1953, after over thirty years of tranquil marriage to dear Stanley. He had been a stonemason, attached to an old-established firm in Caxley, and he too cycled daily to work, his tools strapped securely on the carrier with his midday sandwiches. On a day as wild and wet as this Christmas Eve, he had arrived home soaked through. That night he tossed in a fever, muttering in delirium, and within a week he was dead — the victim of a particularly virulent form of influenza.

In the weeks of shock and mourning that followed, Mary was a tower of strength to her mother. Once the funeral was over, and replies had been sent to all the friends and relatives who had written in sympathy, the two women took stock of their situation. Thank God, the cottage was her own, Mrs. Berry said. It had taken the savings of a lifetime to buy when it came on the market, but now they had a roof over their heads and no weekly rent to find. There was a tiny pension from Stanley's firm, a few pounds in the post office savings bank, and Mary's weekly wage. Two mornings of housework every week at the Manor Farm brought in a few more shillings for Mrs. Berry. And the farmer's wife, knowing her circumstances, offered her more work, which she gladly accepted. It was a happy household, and Mrs. Berry was as grateful for the cheerful company she found there as for the extra money.

Mother and daughter fell into a comfortable routine during the next few years. They breakfasted together before the younger woman set off on her bicycle, and Mrs. Berry tidied up before going off to her morning's work at the farmhouse. In the afternoon, she did her own housework, washed and ironed, gardened, or knitted and sewed. She frugally made jams and jellies, chutneys and pickles for the store cupboard, and it was generally acknowledged by her neighbors that Mrs. Berry could stretch a shilling twice as far as most. The house was bright and attractive, and the door stood open for visitors. No one left Mrs. Berry without feeling all the better for her company. Her good sense, her kindness and her courage brought many people to her door.

Mary had been almost thirty when she met Bertie Fuller. He was the nephew of the old lady who kept the Springbourne post office and had come to lodge with her when he took a job at the Caxley printing works.

Even those romantically inclined had to admit that nothing as fantastic as love at first sight engulfed Mary and Bertie. She had never been one to show her feelings and now, at her age, was unlikely to be swept off her feet. Bertie was five years her senior and had been married before. There were no children of this first marriage, and his wife had married again.

The two were attracted to each other and were engaged within three months of their first meeting.

"Well, my dear, you're old enough to know your own mind," said Mrs. Berry, "and he seems a decent, kindly sort of man, with a steady job. If you'd like to have two rooms here while you look for a house you're both welcome."

No, the villagers agreed, as they gossiped among themselves, Mary Berry hadn't exactly caught "a regular heart-throb," but what could you expect at thirty? She was lucky really to have found anyone, and they did say this Bertie fellow was safe at the printing works, and no doubt was of an age to have sown all the wild oats he wanted.

The wedding was as modest as befitted the circumstances, and the pair were married at Caxley registry office, spent their brief honeymoon at Torquay, and returned to share the cottage with old Mrs. Berry. It was October 1963 and the autumn was one of the most golden and serene that anyone could recall.

Their first child was due to arrive the following September. Mary gave up her job at the post office in June.

The summer was full of promise. The cottage garden flowered as never before, and Mary, resting in a deck chair, gazed dreamily at the madonna lilies and golden roses, and dwelt on the happy lot of the future baby. They had all set their hearts on a boy, and Mary was convinced that it would be a son. Blue predominated in the layette that she and Mrs. Berry so lovingly prepared.

When her time came she was taken to the maternity wing of the local cottage hospital, and gave birth to a boy, fair and blue eyed like his father. She held him in her arms for a moment before returning him to the nurse's care. In her joy she did not notice the anxious looks the doctor and nurse exchanged. Nor did she realize that her child had been taken from her bed straight to an oxygen tent.

In the morning, they broke the news to her that the boy had died. Mary never forgot the utter desolation that gripped her for weeks after this terrible loss. Her husband and mother together nursed her back to health, but always, throughout her whole life, Mary remembered that longed-for boy with the blue gaze, and mourned in secret.

A daughter, Jane, was born in the spring of 1966, and another, Frances, in 1968. The two little girls were a lively pair, and when the younger one was beginning to toddle, Bertie and Mary set about finding a cottage of their own. Until that time, Mrs. Berry had been glad to have them with her. Mary's illness, then her second pregnancy, made her husband and mother particularly anxious. Now, it seemed, the time had come for the young family to look for their own home. Mrs. Berry's cottage was becoming overcrowded.

The search was difficult. They wanted to rent a house to begin with, but this proved to be almost impossible. The search was still on when the annual printing-house outing, called the wayz-goose, took place. Two buses set off for Weymouth carrying the workers and their wives. Mary decided not to go on the day's outing. Frances had a summer cold and was restless, and her mother had promised to go to a Women's Institute meeting in the afternoon. So Bertie went alone.

It was a cloudless July day, warm from the sun's rising until its setting. Mary, pushing the pram along a leafy lane, thought enviously of Bertie and his companions sitting on the beach or swimming in the freshness of the sea. She knew Weymouth from earlier outings and loved its great curved bay. Today it would be looking its finest.

The evening dragged after the children had gone to bed. Usually, the adults retired at ten, for all rose early. On this evening, however, Mrs. Berry went upstairs alone, leaving Mary to await Bertie's coming. Eleven o'clock struck, then twelve. Yawning, bemused with the long day's heat, Mary began to lock up.

She was about to lock the front door when she heard a car draw up. Someone rapped upon the door, and when Mary opened it, to her surprise she saw Mr. Partridge, the vicar, standing there. His kind old face was drawn with anxiety.

"I'm sorry to appear so late, my dear Mrs. Fuller, but a telephone message has just come to the vicarage."

"Yes?" questioned Mary. The vicar looked about him in agitation.

"Do you think we might sit down for a moment?"

Mary remembered her manners.

"Of course; I'm so sorry. Come in."

She led the way into the sitting room, still bewildered.

"It's about Bertie," began the vicar. "There's

been an accident, I fear. Somewhere south of
Caxley. When things were sorted out, someone
asked me to let you know that Bertie wouldn't
be home tonight."

"What's happened? Is he badly hurt? Is he dead?
Where is he?"

Mary sprang to her feet, her eyes wild. The vicar
spoke soothingly.

"He's in Caxley hospital, and being cared for.
I know no more, my dear, but I thought you would
like to go there straight away and see him."

Without a word Mary lifted an old coat from
the back of the kitchen door. The vicar eyed her
anxiously.

"Would it not be best to tell Mrs. Berry?" he
suggested.

She shook her head.

"I'll leave a note."

He waited while she scribbled briefly upon a piece of paper, and watched her put it in the middle of the kitchen table.

"No point in waking her," she said, closing the front door softly behind her.

The two set off in silence, too worried to make conversation. The air was heavy with the scent of honeysuckle. Moths glimmered in the beams of the headlights, and fell to their death.

How easily, Mary thought — fear clutching her heart — death comes to living things. The memory of her little son filled her mind as they drove through the night to meet what might be another tragedy.

At the hospital they were taken to a small waiting room. Within a minute, a doctor came to them. There was no need for him to speak. His face told Mary all. Bertie had gone.

The wayzgoose, begun so gaily, had ended in tragedy. The two buses had drawn up a few miles from Caxley to allow the passengers to have a last drink before closing time. They had to cross a busy road to enter the old coaching inn, famed for its hospitality. Returning to the bus, Bertie and a friend waited some time for a lull in the traffic. It was a busy road, leading to the coast, and despite the late hour the traffic was heavy. At last they made a dash for it, not realizing that a second car was overtaking the one they could see. The latter slowed down to let the two men cross, but the second car could not stop in time. Both men were hurled to the ground, Bertie being dragged some yards before the car stopped.

Despite appalling injuries, he was alive when admitted to hospital, but died within the hour. The organizer of the outing, knowing that Mary was not on the telephone, decided to let the local vicar break the news of the accident.

Mr. Partridge and poor Mary returned along the dark lanes to the darker cottage, where he aroused Mrs. Berry, told her the terrible story and left her trying to comfort the young widow.

If anyone can succeed, Mr. Partridge thought as he drove sadly to his vicarage, she can. But oh, the waste of it all! The wicked waste!

Chapter Two

This being Christmas Eve I had my Parlour
Windows dressed of as usual with Hulver-
boughs well seeded with red-Berries.
                    —*Parson Woodforde, December 24, 1788*

OLD MRS. BERRY, remembering that dreadful night,
shook her head sadly as she washed up her cup
and saucer at the sink. The rain still fell in torrents,
and a wild wind buffeted the bushes in the garden,
sending the leaves tumbling across the grass.

In Caxley it would not be so rough, she hoped.
Most of the time her family would be under cover
in the shops. But out here, at Shepherds Cross,
they always caught the full violence of the weather.

Mrs. Berry's cottage was the third one spaced
along the road that led to Springbourne. All three
cottages were roomy, with large gardens containing gnarled old apple and plum trees. Each cottage
possessed ancient hawthorn hedges, supplying
sanctuary to dozens of little birds.

An old drovers' path ran at right angles to the
cottages, crossing the road by Mrs. Berry's house.
This gave the hamlet its name, although it was
many years since sheep had been driven along that

green lane to the great sheep fair at the downland village ten miles distant.

Some thought it a lonely spot, and declared that they "would go melancholy mad, that they would!" But Mrs. Berry, used to remote houses since childhood, was not affected.

She had been brought up in a gamekeeper's cottage in a woodland ride. As a small child she rarely saw anyone strange, except on Sundays, when she attended church with her parents.

She had loved that church, relishing its loftiness, its glowing stained-glass windows and the flowers on the altar. She paid attention to the exhortations of the vicar too, a holy man who truly ministered to his neighbors. From him, as much as from the example of her parents, she learned early to appreciate modesty, courage, and generosity.

When she was old enough to read she deciphered a plaque upon the chancel floor extolling the virtues of a local benefactor, a man of modest means who nevertheless *was hospitable and charitable all his Days"* and who, at his end, left *"the interest of Forty Pounds to the Poor of the parish forever."*

It was the next line or two which the girl never forgot, and which influenced her own life. They read:

Such were the good effects of
Virtue and Oeconomy.
Read, Grandeur, and Blush

Certainly, goodness and thrift, combined with a horror of ostentation and boasting, were qualities

67

which Mrs. Berry embodied all the days of her life, and her daughters profited by her example.

Mrs. Berry left the kitchen and went to sit by the fire in the living room. It was already growing dark, for the sky was thick with storm clouds, and the rain showed no sign of abating.

Water bubbled in the crack of the window frame, and Mrs. Berry sighed. It was at times like this one needed a man about the place. Unobtrusively, without complaint, Stanley and then Bertie had attended to such things as drafty windows, wobbly door knobs, squeaking floorboards and the like. Now the women had to cope as best they could, and an old house, about two hundred years of age, certainly needed constant attention to keep it in trim.

Nevertheless, it looked pretty and gay. The Christmas tree, dressed the night before by Jane and Frances — with many squeals of delight — stood on the side table. This table, spangled with stars and tinsel, displayed the Victorian fairy doll, three inches high, which had once adorned the Christmas trees of Mrs. Berry's childhood. The doll's tiny wax face was brown with age but still bore that sweet expression which the child had imagined was an angel's.

Sprigs of holly were tucked behind the picture frames, and a spray of mistletoe hung where the oil lamp had once swung from the central beam over the dining table.

Mrs. Berry leaned back in her chair and surveyed it all with satisfaction. It looked splendid

and there was very little more to be done to the preparations in the kitchen. The turkey was stuffed, the potatoes peeled. The Christmas pudding had been made in November and stood ready on the shelf to be plunged into the steamer tomorrow morning. Mince pies waited in the tin, and a splendid Christmas cake, iced and decorated with robins and holly by Mrs. Berry herself, would grace the tea table tomorrow.

There would also be a small Madeira cake, with a delicious sliver of green angelica tucked into its top. The old lady had made that for those who, like herself, could not tackle Christmas cake until three or four hours after Christmas pudding. It had turned out beautifully light, Mrs. Berry remembered.

She closed her eyes contentedly, and before long, drifted into a light sleep.

Mrs. Berry awoke as the children burst into the room. A cold breeze set the Christmas tree ornaments tinkling and rustled the paper chain, which swung above the door.

The little girls' faces were pink and wet, their bangs stuck to their foreheads and glistened with dampness. Drops fell from the scarlet mackintoshes and their woolly gloves were soaked. But nothing could damp their spirits on this wonderful day, and Mrs. Berry forbore to scold them for the mess they were making on the rug.

Mary, struggling with the shopping, called from the kitchen.

"Come out here, you two, and get off those wet things! What a day, Gran! You've never seen anything like Caxley High Street. Worse than Michaelmas Fair! Traffic jams all up the road, and queues in all the shops. The Caxley traders will have a bumper Christmas, mark my words!"

Mrs. Berry stirred herself and followed the children into the kitchen to help them undress. Mary was unloading her baskets and carrier bags, rescuing nuts and Brussels sprouts which burst from wet paper bags on to the floor, and trying to take off her own sodden coat and headscarf all at the same time.

"I seem to have spent a mint of money," she said apologetically, "and dear knows where it's all gone. We'll have a reckon-up later on, but we were that pushed and hurried about I'll be hard put to it to remember all the prices."

"No point in worrying," said Mrs. Berry calmly. "If 'tis gone, 'tis gone. You won't have wasted it, I know that, my girl. Here, let's put on the kettle and make a cup of tea. You must be exhausted."

"Ah! It's rough out," agreed Mary, sounding relieved now that she had confessed to forgetting the cost of some of her purchases. "But it's the rush that takes it out of you. If only that ol' bus came back half an hour later 'twould help. As it is, you have to keep one eye on the town clock all the time you're shopping."

The little girls were delving into the bags, searching for their own secret shopping.

"Now mind what you're at," said Mary sharply. "Take your treasures and put 'em upstairs, and I'll help you pack 'em up when we've had a cup of tea."

"Don't tell," wailed Jane. "It's a secret!"

"A secret!" echoed Frances.

"It still is," retorted their mother. "Up you go then, and take the things up carefully. And put on your slippers," she shouted after them, as they clambered upstairs clutching several small packets against their chests.

"Mad as hatters, they are," Mary confided to her mother. "Barmy as March hares — and all because of Christmas!"

"All children are the same," replied Mrs. Berry, pouring boiling water into the teapot, and peering

71

through the silvery steam to make sure it was not overfull. "You three were as wild as they are, I well remember." She carried the tray into the living room. "Could you eat anything?" she asked.

"Not a thing," said Mary, flopping down, exhausted, into the armchair by the fire, "and a biscuit will be enough for the girls. They're so excited they won't sleep if they have too much before bedtime."

"We'll get them upstairs early tonight," said her mother. "There are still some presents to pack."

"We'll be lucky if they go to sleep before nine," prophesied Mary. "I heard Jane say she was going to stay awake to see if Father Christmas really does come. She doesn't believe it anymore, you know. I'm positive about that, but she don't let on in case he doesn't come!"

"She's seven," observed Mrs. Berry. "Can't expect her to believe fairy tales all her life."

"They've been telling her at school," said Mary. "Once they start school they lose all their pretty ways. Frances has only had six months there, but she's too knowing by half."

The women sipped their tea, listening to the children moving about above them and relishing a few quiet moments on their own.

"They can have a good long time in the bath tonight," said Mary, thinking ahead, "then they'll be in trim to go to church with you tomorrow."

"But wouldn't you like to go?"

"No, Mum. I'll see to the turkey while you're out. The service means more to you than me.

Somehow church doesn't seem the same since Bertie went. Pointless, somehow."

Mrs. Berry was too taken aback to comment on this disclosure, and the entry of the children saved her from further conversation on the matter.

Her thoughts were in turmoil as she poured milk into the children's mugs and opened the biscuit tin for their probing fingers.

That unguarded remark of Mary's had confirmed her suspicions. She had watched Mary's growing casualness to religious matters and her increasing absences at church services with real concern. When Stanley died, she had found her greatest consolation in prayer and the teachings of the church. "Thy Will Be Done," it said on the arch above the chancel steps, and for old Mrs. Berry those words had been both succor, support and reason.

But, with the death of Bertie, Mary had grown hard, and had rejected a God Who allowed such suffering to occur. Mrs. Berry could understand the change of heart, but it did not lessen her grief for this daughter who turned her face from the comfort of religious beliefs. Without submission to a divine will, who could be happy? We were too frail to stand and fight alone, but that's what Mary was doing, and why she secretly was so unhappy.

Mrs. Berry thrust these thoughts to the back of her mind. It was Christmas Eve, the time for good will to all men, the time to rejoice in the children's pleasure, and to hope that, somehow, the warmth and love of the festival would thaw the frost in Mary's heart.

"Bags not the tap end!" Mrs. Berry heard Jane shout an hour later, as the little girls capered naked about the bathroom.

"Mum, she *always* makes me sit the tap end!" complained Frances. "And the cold tap drips down my back. It's not fair!"

"No grizzling now on Christmas Eve," said Mary briskly. "You start the tap end, Frances, and you can change over at halftime. That's fair. You're going to have a nice long bathtime tonight while I'm helping Gran. Plenty of soap, don't forget, and I'll look at your ears when I come back."

Mrs. Berry heard the bath door close, and then open again.

"And stop sucking your facecloth, Frances," scolded her mother. "Anyone'd think you're a little baby, instead of a great girl of five."

The door closed again, and Mary reappeared, smiling.

"They'll be happy for twenty minutes. Just listen to them!"

Two young treble voices, wildly flat, were bellowing "Away in a manger, no crib for a bed," to a background of splashes and squeals.

"Did you manage to find some slippers for them?" asked Mrs. Berry.

"Yes, Tom's Christine had put them by for me, and I had a quick look while the girls were watching someone try on shoes. There's a lot to be said for knowing people in the shops. They help you out on occasions like this."

She was rummaging in a deep oilcloth bag as she spoke, and now drew out two boxes. Inside were the slippers. Both were designed to look like rabbits, with shiny black beads for eyes, and silky white whiskers. Jane's pair were blue, and Frances' red. They were Mrs. Berry's present to her grandchildren and she nodded her approval at Mary's choice.

"Very nice, dear, very nice. I'll just tuck a little chocolate bar into each one —"

"There's no need, Mum. This is plenty. You spoil them," broke in Mary.

"Maybe, but they're going to have the chocolate. Something to wear is a pretty dull Christmas present for a child. I well remember my Aunt Maud — God rest her, poor soul. What a dance she led my Uncle Hubert! She used to give us girls a starched white pinafore every Christmas, and very miserable we thought them."

She shook her head.

"Ungrateful, weren't we? Now I can see it was a very generous present, as well as being useful; but my old grandad gave us two sugar mice, one pink and one white with long string tails, and they were much more welcome, believe me."

"Like the tangerine and toffees you and Dad used to tuck in the toe of our stockings." Mary smiled. "We always rushed for those first before unpacking the rest. Funny how hungry you are at five in the morning when you're a child!"

"Get me some wrapping paper," said Mrs. Berry briskly, "and I'll tie them up while those two rascals are safe for ten minutes. They've eyes in the backs of their heads at Christmastime."

Mary left her mother making two neat parcels. Her wrinkled hands, dappled with brown age spots, were as deft as ever. Spectacles on the end of her nose, the old lady folded the paper this way and that, and tied everything firmly with bright red string.

Mary took the opportunity to smuggle a beautiful pink cyclamen into her own bedroom and hide it behind the curtain on the windowsill. It had cost more than she could really afford, but she had decided to forego a new pair of winter gloves. The old ones could be mended, and who was to notice the much sewn seams in a little place like Shepherds Cross?

She drew the curtains across to hide the plant and to keep out the draft, which was whistling through the cracks of the ancient lattice-paned window. Outside, the wind roared in the branches; a flurry of dead wet leaves flew this way and that as the eddies caught them. The rain slanted down pitilessly, and as a car drove past, the beams of its headlights lit up the shining road where the raindrops spun like silver coins.

She took out from a drawer her own presents for the children. There were two small boxes and two larger ones, and she opened them to have one last look before they were wrapped. In each of the smaller boxes a string of little imitation pearls nestled against a red mock-velvet background. How pretty they would look on the girls' best frocks! Simple, but good, Mary told herself, with satisfaction. As Mum had said, children wanted something more than everyday presents at Christmas, and the two larger boxes *were* rather dull perhaps.

They held seven handkerchiefs, one for each day of the week, with the appropriate name embroidered in the corner. Sensible, and would teach them how to spell too, thought Mary, putting back the lids.

She was just in time, for at that moment the door burst open and she only had a second in which to thrust the boxes back into the drawer, when two naked cherubs skipped in, still wet with bath water.

"What d' you think —" she began, but was cut short by two vociferous voices in unison.

"The water's all gone. Frances pushed out the plug —"

"I never then!"

"Yes, you did! You know you did! Mum, she wriggled it out with her bottom —"

"Well, she never changed ends, like you said. I only wriggled 'cos the cold tap dripped down my back. I couldn't help it!"

"She done it a-purpose."

"I never. I told you —"

Mary cut short their protestations.

"You'll catch your deaths. Get on back to the

bathroom and start to rub dry. Look at your wet foot marks on the floor! What'll Gran say?"

They began to giggle, eying each other.

"Let's go down and frighten her, all bare," cried Jane.

"Don't you dare now!" said their mother, her voice sharpened by the thought of the slippers being wrapped below.

A little chastened by her tone, the two romped out of the room, jostling together like puppies. Mary heard their squeals of laughter from behind the bathroom door, and smiled at her reflection in the glass.

" 'Christmas comes but once a year,' " she quoted aloud. "Perhaps it's as well!"

She followed her rowdy offspring into the bathroom.

Twenty minutes later the two girls sat barefoot on their wooden stools, one at each side of the fire. On their laps they held steaming bowls of bread and milk, plentifully sprinkled with brown sugar.

"You said we could hang up pillow slips tonight," remarked Jane, "instead of stockings."

"I haven't forgotten. There are two waiting on the banisters for you to put at the end of your bed."

"Will Father Christmas know?" asked Frances anxiously, her eyes wide with apprehension.

"Of course he will," said their grandmother robustly. "He's got plenty of sense. Been doing the job long enough to know what's what."

Mary glanced at the clock.

"Finish up now. Don't hang it out, you girls. Gran and I've got a lot to do this evening, so you get off to sleep as quick as you can."

"I'm staying awake till he comes," said Jane firmly.

"Me too," echoed Frances, scooping the last drop of milk from the bowl.

They went to kiss their grandmother. She held their soft faces against hers, relishing the sweet smell of soap and milk. How dear these two small mortals were!

"The sooner you get to sleep, the sooner the morning will come," she told them.

She watched them as, followed by Mary, they tumbled up the staircase that opened from the room.

"I *shall* stay awake!" protested Jane. "I shan't close my eyes, not for *one minute!* I promise you!"

Mrs. Berry smiled to herself as she put another log on the fire. She had heard that tale many times before. If she were a betting woman she would lay a wager that those two would be fast asleep within the hour!

But, for once, Mrs. Berry was wrong.

Chapter Three

There was a roaring in the wind all night;
The rain came heavily and fell in floods.
                    —*William Wordsworth*

UPSTAIRS, in the double bed, the two little girls pulled the clothes to their chins and continued their day-long conversation.

A nightlight, secure in a saucer on the dressing table, sent great shadows bowing and bending across the sloping ceiling, for the room was criss-crossed with drafts on this wild night from the ill-fitting window and door. Sometimes the brave little flame bent in a sudden blow from the cold air, as a crocus does in a gust of wind, but always it righted itself, continuing to give out its comforting light to the young children.

"Shall I tell you why I'm going to stay awake all night?" asked Jane.

"Yes."

"Promise to do what I tell you?"

"Yes."

"Promise *faithfully?* See my finger wet and dry? Cross your heart? *Everything?*"

"Everything," agreed Frances equably. Her eye lids were beginning to droop already. Left alone, free from the vehemence of her sister, she would have fallen asleep within a minute.

"Then eat your pillow," demanded Jane.

Frances was hauled back roughly from the rocking sea of sleep.

"You know I can't!" she protested.

"You promised," said Jane.

"Well, I unpromise," declared Frances. "I can't eat a pillow, and anyway what would Mum say?"

"Then I shan't tell you what I was going to."

"I don't care," replied Frances untruthfully.

Jane, enraged by such lack of response and such wanton breaking of solemn vows, bounced over onto her side, her back to Frances.

"It was about Father Christmas," she said hotly, "but I'm not telling you now."

"He'll come," said Frances drowsily.

This confidence annoyed Jane still further.

"Maybe he won't then! Tom Williams says there isn't a Father Christmas. That's why I'm going to stay awake. To see. So there!"

Through the veils of sleep which were fast enmeshing her, Frances pondered upon this new problem. Tom Williams was a big boy, ten years old at least. What's more, he was a sort of cousin. He should know what he was talking about. Nevertheless . . .

"Tom Williams don't always speak the truth," answered Frances. In some ways, she was a wiser child than her sister.

Jane gave an impatient snort.

"Besides," said Frances, following up her point, "our teacher said he'd come. She don't tell lies. Nor Mum, nor Gran."

These were powerful allies, and Jane was conscious that Frances had some support.

"Grownups hang together," said Jane darkly. "Don't forget we saw *two* Father Christmases this afternoon in Caxley. What about that then?"

"They was men dressed up," replied Frances stolidly. "Only *pretend* Father Christmases. It don't mean there isn't a real one as 'll come tonight."

A huge yawn caught her unawares.

"You stay awake if you want to," she murmured,

turning her head into the delicious warmth of the uneaten pillow. "I'm going to sleep."

Secure in her faith, she was asleep in five minutes, but Jane, full of doubts and resentful of her sister's serenity, threw her arms above her head, and, gripping the rails of the brass bedstead, grimly began her vigil. Tonight she would learn the truth!

Downstairs, the two women assembled the last few presents that needed wrapping on the big table.

They made a motley collection. There were three or four pieces of basketwork made by Mary, who was neat with her fingers, and these she eyed doubtfully.

"Can't see myself ever making a tidy parcel of these flower holders," she remarked. "D' you think just a Christmas tag tied on would be all right?"

Mrs. Berry surveyed the hanging baskets thoughtfully.

"Well, it always looks a bit slapdash, I feel, to hand over something unwrapped. Looks as though you can't be bothered —"

"I can't," said Mary laconically.

"But I see your point. We'd make a proper pig's ear of the wrapping paper trying to cover those. You're right, my girl. Just a tag."

Mary sat down thankfully and drew the packet of tags towards her. The presents were destined for neighbors, and the tags seemed remarkably juvenile for the elderly couples who were going to receive the baskets. Father Christmas waved from a chimney pot, a golliwog danced a jig, two pixies bore a Christmas tree, and a cat carried a Christmas pudding. Only two tags measured up to Mary's requirements, a row of bells on one and a red candle on the other. Ah well, she told herself, someone must make do with the pixies or the cat, and when you came to think of it the tags would be on the back of the fire this time tomorrow, so why worry? She wrote diligently.

Outside the wind still screamed, rattling the window, and making the back door thump in its frame. The curtains stirred in the onslaught, and now and again a little puff of smoke came into the room from the log fire, as the wind eddied round the chimney pot.

Mrs. Berry looked up from the jar of honey she was wrapping.

"I'll go and see if the rain's blowing in under that door at the back."

She went out, causing a draft that rustled the wrapping paper and blew two of Mary's tags to the floor. Mrs. Berry was gone for some minutes, and returned red-faced from stooping.

"A puddle a good yard wide," she puffed. "I've left that old towel stuffed up against the crack. We'll have to get a new sill put on that threshold, Mary. It's times like this we miss our menfolk."

Mary nodded, not trusting herself to speak. Hot tears pricked her eyes, but she bent lower to her task, so that her mother should not see them. How was it, she wondered, that she could keep calm and talk about her loss, quite in control of her feelings, for nine tenths of the time, and yet a chance remark, like this one, pierced her armor so cruelly? Poor Gran! If only she knew! Better, of course, that she did not. She would never forgive herself if she thought she had caused pain.

Unaware of the turmoil in her daughter's mind, Mrs. Berry turned her attention to a round tin of shortbread.

" 'Pon my word," she remarked. "I never learn! After all these years, you'd think I'd know better than to pick a round tin instead of a square 'un. I'll let you tackle this, Mary. It's for Margaret and Mary Waters. They're good to us all through the year, taking messages and traipsing round with the parish magazine in all weathers."

Mary reached across for the tin, then checked. The eyes of the two women met questioningly. Above the sound of the gale outside they had heard the metallic clink of their letter box.

"I'll go," said Mary.

An envelope lay on the damp mat. She opened the door, letting in a rush of wind and rain and a few sodden leaves. There was no one to be seen, but in the distance Mary thought she could see the bobbing light of a flashlight. To shout would have been useless. To follow, in her slippers, idiotic. She pushed the door shut against the onslaught, and returned to the light with the envelope.

"For you, Mum," she said, handing over the glistening packet.

Mrs. Berry withdrew a Christmas card, bright with robins and frosted leaves, and two embroidered white handkerchiefs.

"From Mrs. Burton," said Mrs. Berry wonderingly. "Now, who'd have thought it? Never exchanged presents before, have we? What makes her do a thing like this, I wonder? And turning out too, on such a night. Dear soul, she shouldn't have done it. She's little enough to spare as it is."

"You did feed her cat and chickens for her while she was away last summer," said Mary. "Perhaps that's why."

"That's only acting neighborly," protested Mrs.

Berry. "No call for her to spend money on us."

"Given her pleasure, I don't doubt," answered Mary. "The thing is, do we give her something back? And, if so, what?"

It was a knotty problem. Their eyes ranged over the presents before them, already allotted.

"We'll have to find *something*," said Mrs. Berry firmly. "What about that box of soap upstairs?"

"People are funny about soap," said Mary. "Might think it's a hint, you know. She's none too fond of washing, nice old thing though she is."

They racked their brains in silence.

"Half a pound of tea?" suggested Mrs. Berry at last.

"Looks like charity," replied Mary.

"Well, I wouldn't say no to a nice packet of tea," said Mrs. Berry with spirit. "What about one of our new tea towels then?"

"Cost too much," said Mary. "She'd mind about that."

"I give up then," said Mrs. Berry. "You think of something. I must say these last-minute surprises are all very fine, but they do put you to some thinking."

She tied a final knot round the honey pot and rose to her feet again.

"Talking of tea, what about a cup?"

"Lovely," said Mary.

"Shall I cut us a sandwich?"

"Not for me. Just a cup of tea."

The old lady went out, and Mary could hear

the clattering of cups and saucers, and the welcome tinkle of teaspoons. Suddenly, she felt inexpressibly tired. She longed to put her head down among the litter on the table and fall asleep. Sometimes she thought Christmas was more trouble than it was worth. All the fuss and flurry, then an empty purse just as the January bills came in. If only she had her mother's outlook! She still truly loved Christmas. She truly celebrated the birth of that God who walked beside her every hour of the day. She truly loved her neighbor — even that dratted Mrs. Burton, who was innocently putting them to such trouble.

Mrs. Berry returned with the round tin tray bearing the cups and saucers and the homely brown tea-pot clad in a knitted tea cosy. Her face had a triumphant smile.

"I've thought of something. A bottle of my black-currant wine. How's that? She can use it for her cough, if she don't like it for anything better. What say?"

"Perfect!" said Mary. In agreement at last, they sipped their tea thankfully.

Still awake upstairs, Jane heard the chinking of china and the voices of her mother and grandmother. Beside her, Frances snored lightly, her pink mouth slightly ajar, her lashes making dark crescents against her rosy cheeks.

Jane's vigil seemed lonelier and bleaker every minute. What's more, she was hungry, she discovered. The thought of the blue biscuit tin, no doubt standing by the teacups below, caused her stomach to rumble. Cautiously, she slid her skinny legs out of bed, took a swift glance at the two empty pillowcases draped expectantly one each end of the brass bed rail, and crept to the door.

The wind was making so much noise that no one heard the latch click, or the footsteps on the stairs. The child opened the bottom door, which led directly into the living room, and stood blinking in the light like a little owl caught in the sunshine.

"Mercy me!" gasped Mrs. Berry, putting down her cup with a clatter. "What a start you gave me, child!"

"Jane!" cried her mother. "What on earth are you doing down here?" Her voice was unusually sharp. Surprised and startled, she could have shaken the child in her exasperation.

"I'm hungry," whispered Jane, conscious of her unpopularity.

"You had a good supper," said Mary shortly. "Time you was asleep."

"Let her come by the fire for a minute," pleaded Mrs. Berry. "Shut that door, my dear. The draft fairly cuts through us. Want a cup of tea, and a biscuit?"

The child's face lit up.

"Shall I fetch a cup?"

"Not with those bare feet," said Mary. "I'll get your mug, and then you go straight back to bed as soon as you're finished. Your gran's too good to you."

She hurried kitchenwards, and the child sat on the rag rug smiling at the flames licking the log. It was snug down here. It was always snug with Gran.

She put a hand on the old lady's knee.

"Mum's cross," she whispered.

"She's tired. Done a lot today, and you know you should really be abed, giving her a break."

They always hang together, these grownups, thought Jane rebelliously; but she took the mug of weak tea gratefully, and the top biscuit from the tin when it was offered, even though it was a Rich Tea and she knew there were Ginger Nuts further down.

"Is Frances asleep?" asked Mary.

"Yes. I couldn't get off."

"You told me you didn't intend to," replied her mother. "Trying to see Father Christmas, silly girl. As though he'll come if you're awake! The sooner you're asleep the sooner he'll come!"

Torn with doubts, the child looked swiftly up into her grandmother's face. It told her nothing. The familiar kind smile played around the lips. The eyes looked down at her as comfortingly as ever.

"Your mother's right. Drink up your tea, and then snuggle back into bed. I'll come and tuck you up this time."

Jane tilted her mug, put the last fragment of biscuit into her mouth, and scrambled to her feet.

"Whose presents are those?" she said, suddenly aware of the parcels on the table.

"Not yours," said Mary.

"Neighbors'," said her grandmother in the same breath. "You shall take some round for us tomorrow. And I want you to carry a bottle of wine very carefully to Mrs. Burton. Can you do it, do you think?"

The child nodded, hesitated before her mother, then kissed her warmly on the cheek.

"You hussy!" said Mary, but her voice was soft, and the child saw that she was forgiven. Content at last, she followed her grandmother's bulk up the narrow stairs.

The flame of the night light was burning low in the little hollow of its wax. The shadows wavered about the room as the old woman and the child moved towards the bed.

"Now, no staying awake, mind," whispered Gran, in a voice that brooked no argument. "I don't know who's been stuffing your head with nonsense, but you can forget it. Get off to sleep, like Frances there. You'll see Father Christmas has been, as soon as you wake up."

She kissed the child, and tucked in the bedclothes tightly.

Jane listened to her grandmother's footsteps descending the creaking stairs, sighed for her lost intentions, and fell, almost instantly, into a deep sleep.

Chapter Four

Mice and rats and such small deer . . .
                              —William Shakespeare

"MY! That was a lucky escape," said Mrs. Berry. "Good thing we hadn't got out those pillow-cases!"

Two pillowcases, identical to those hanging limply upstairs, had been hidden behind the couch in the cottage parlor for the last two days. Most of the presents were already in them. There were a doll for each, beautifully dressed in handsewn clothes, joint presents from Mary and her mother; a game of Ludo for Frances and Snakes and Ladders for Jane; and a jigsaw puzzle apiece. All should provide plenty of future pleasure.

The American aunt had sent two little cardigans, pale pink and edged with silver trimming — far more glamorous than anything to be found in the Caxley shops. The less well-off aunt at Taunton had sent bath salts for both, which, Mary knew, would enchant the little girls. There were also gifts from kind neighbors — a box of beads, a toy shop

92

(complete with tiny metal scales), and several tins of sweets, mint humbugs and homemade toffee among them.

A stocking, waiting to be filled with small knicknacks, lay across each pillowcase. As soon as the children were safely asleep, the plan had been to substitute the full pillowcases for the empty ones.

"I thought she might reappear," admitted Mary. "She's twigged, you know, about Father Christmas. Some of the children at school have let it out."

"She won't come down again, I'm certain," replied Mrs. Berry comfortingly. "Let's fill up the stockings, shall we? We can put the last-minute odds and ends in when we carry up the pillowcases."

Mary nodded agreement and went to the parlor, returning with the limp stockings. They were a pair of red and white striped woollen ones, once the property of the vicar's aunt, and reputedly kept for skating and skiing in her young days. Mary had bought them at a jumble sale, and each Christmas since they had appeared to delight the little girls.

From the dresser drawer, Mrs. Berry collected the store of small treasures that had been hidden there for the last week or so. A few wrapped sweets, a curly stick of barley sugar, a comb, a tiny pencil and pad, a brooch and a handkerchief followed the tangerines that stuffed the toe of each stocking. Then, almost guiltily, Mrs. Berry produced the final touch — two small wooden Dutch dolls.

"Saw them in the market at Caxley," she said, "and couldn't resist them, Mary. They reminded me of a family of Dutch dolls I had at their age. They can amuse themselves dressing them up."

The dolls were tucked at the top, their shiny black heads and stiff wooden arms sticking out attractively. The two women gazed at their handiwork with satisfaction.

"Well, that's that!" said Mrs. Berry. "I'm just going to clear away this tray and tidy up in the kitchen, and I shan't be long out of bed."

"I'll wait till I'm sure those two scallywags are really asleep," answered Mary. "I wouldn't put it past our Jane to pretend, you know. She's stubborn when she wants to be, and she's real set on finding out who brings the presents."

The hands of the clock on the mantelpiece stood at ten o'clock. How the evening had flown! Mary tidied the table, listening to the gale outside, and the sound of her mother singing in the kitchen.

She suddenly remembered her own small presents upstairs still unwrapped and crept aloft to fetch them. The door of the girls' room was ajar. She tiptoed in and looked down upon the sleeping pair. It seemed impossible that either of them could be feigning sleep, so rhythmically were they breathing. What angels they looked!

She made her way downstairs and swiftly wrapped up the necklaces and handkerchiefs. The very last, she thought thankfully! Just a tag for Mum's cyclamen, and I can write that and tie it on when I go to bed.

She selected the prettiest tag she could find, and slipped it into her skirt pocket to take up-stairs.

Mrs. Berry reappeared, carrying the glass of water that she took to her bedroom every night.

"I'll be off then, my dear. Don't stay up too long. You must be tired."

She bent to kiss her daughter.

"The girls have gone off, I think, but I'll give them another ten minutes to make sure."

"See you in the morning, then, Mary," said the old lady, mounting the stairs.

Mary raked the hot ashes from the fire and swept up the hearth. She fetched the two bulging pillowcases and put the stockings on top of them. Then she sat in the old armchair and let exhaustion flood through her. Bone-tired, she confessed to herself. Bone-tired!

Above her she could hear the creaking of the floorboards as her mother moved about, then a cry and hasty footsteps coming down the stairs.

The door flew open and Mrs. Berry, clad in her flannel nightgown, stood, wild eyed, on the threshold.

"Mum, what's the matter?" cried Mary, starting to her feet.

"A mouse!" gasped Mrs. Berry, shuddering un-controllably. "There's a mouse in my bedroom!"

The two women gazed at each other, horror

struck. Mary's heart sank rapidly, but she spoke decisively.

"Here, you come by the fire, and let's shut that door. The girls will be waking up."

She pushed up the armchair she had just vacated and Mrs. Berry, still shuddering, sat down thankfully.

"You'll catch your death," said Mary, raking a few bright embers together and dropping one or two shreds of dry bark from the hearth onto the dying fire. "You ought to have put on your dressing gown."

"I'm not going up there to fetch it!" stated Mrs. Berry flatly. "I know I'm a fool, but I just can't abide mice."

"I'll fetch it," said Mary, "and I'll set the mouse-trap too while I'm there. Where did it go?"

96

Mrs. Berry shivered afresh.

"It ran under the bed, horrible little thing! You should've seen its tail, Mary! A good three inches long! It made me cry out, seeing it skedaddle like that."

"I heard you," said Mary, making for the kitchen to get the mousetrap.

Mrs. Berry drew nearer to the fire, tucking her voluminous nightgown round her bare legs. A cruel draft whistled in from the passage, but nothing would draw her from the safety of the armchair.

Who knows how many more mice might be at large on a night like this?

Mary, her mouth set in a determined line, reappeared with the mousetrap and went quietly upstairs. She returned in a moment, carrying her mother's dressing gown and slippers.

"Now you wrap up," she said coaxingly, as if she were addressing one of her little daughters. "We'll soon catch that old mouse for you."

"I'm ashamed to be so afeared of a little creature," confessed Mrs. Berry, "but there it is. They give me the horrors, mice do, and rats even worse. Don't ask me why!"

Mary knew from experience this terror of her mother's. She confronted other hazards of country life with calm courage. Spiders, caterpillars, bulls in fields, adders on the heath, any animals in pain or fury found old Mrs. Berry completely undaunted. Mary could clearly remember her mother dealing with a dog that had been run over and writhed, demented with pain, not far from their cottage door. It had savaged two would-be helpers, and a few distressed onlookers were wondering what to do next when Mrs. Berry approached and calmed the animal in a way that had seemed miraculous. But a mouse sent her flying, and Mary knew, as she found some wood to replenish the fire, that nothing would persuade her mother back to the bedroom until the intruder had been dispatched.

She settled herself in the other armchair, resigned to another twenty minutes or more of waiting. She longed desperately for her bed, but could not relax until her mother was comfortably settled. She listened for sounds from above — the click of the mousetrap that would release her from her vigil, or the noise of the children waking and rummaging for the pillowcases, wailing at the nonappearance of Father Christmas.

But above the noise of the storm outside, it was difficult to hear anything clearly upstairs. She pushed the two telltale pillowcases under the table, so that they were hidden from the eyes of any child who might enter unannounced, and leaned back with her eyes closed.

Invariably, Bertie's dear face drifted before her when she closed her eyes, but now, to her surprise and shame, another man's face smiled at her. It was the face of one of Bertie's workmates. He too had been one of the party on that tragic wayzgoose, and had written to Mary and her mother soon after the accident. She had known him from childhood. Rather a milksop, most people said of Ray Bullen, but Mary liked his gentle ways and thought none the less of him because he had remained a bachelor.

"Some are the marrying sort, and some aren't," she had replied once to the village gossip who had been speculating upon Ray's future. Mary was all too conscious of the desire of busybodies to find her a husband in the months after Bertie's death. They got short shrift from Mary, and interest waned before long.

"Too sharp tongued by half," said those who had been lashed by it. "No man in his senses would take her on, with them two girls too."

Here they were wrong. One or two men had paid attention to Mary, and would have welcomed some advances on her side. But none were forthcoming. Truth to tell, Mary was in such a state of numbed shock for so long that very little affected her.

But Ray's letter of condolence had been kept. There was something unusually warm and comforting in the simple words. Here was true sympathy. It was the only letter that had caused Mary to weep and, weeping, to find relief.

She saw Ray very seldom, for their ways did not cross. But that afternoon in Caxley he had been at the bus stop when she arrived laden with baskets and anxious about the little girls amidst the Christmas traffic. He had taken charge of them all so easily and naturally — seeing them onto the bus, disposing of the parcels, smiling at the children and wishing them all well at Christmas — that it was not until she was halfway to Shepherds Cross that Mary realized that he had somehow contrived to give the little girls a shilling each. Also, she realized with a pang, he must have missed his own bus, which went out about the same time as theirs.

She supposed, leaning back now in the armchair, that her extreme tiredness had brought his face before her tonight. It was not a handsome face, to be sure, but it was kind and gentle, and, from all she heard, Ray Bullen had both those qualities as well as strong principles. He was a Quaker, she knew, and she remembered a little passage about Quakers from the library book she was reading. Something about them "making the best chocolate and being very thoughtful and wealthy and good." It had amused her at the time, and though Ray Bullen could never be said to be wealthy, he was certainly thoughtful and good.

She became conscious of her mother's voice, garrulous in her nervousness.

"It's funny how you can sense them when you're frightened of them. Not that I had any premonition tonight, I was too busy thinking about getting those pillowcases safely upstairs. But I well remember helping my aunt clear out her scullery when I was a child. No older than Frances, I was then, and she asked me to lift a little old keg she kept her flour in. And, do you know, I began to tremble, and I told her I just couldn't do it. 'There's a mouse in there!' I told her.

"She was so wild. 'Rubbish!' she stormed. She was a quick-tempered woman, red haired and plump, and couldn't bear to be crossed. 'Pick it up at once!'

"And so I did. And when I looked inside, there *was* a mouse, dead as a doornail and smelling to high heaven! I dropped that double quick, you can be sure, and it rolled against a bottle of cider and smashed it to smithereens. Not that I waited to see it happen. I was down at the end of the garden, in the privy with the door bolted. She couldn't get at me there!"

Mary had heard the tale many times, but would not have dreamed of reminding her mother of the fact. It was her mother's way, she realized, of apologizing for the trouble she was causing.

Mrs. Berry hated to be a nuisance, and now, with Mary so near to complete exhaustion, she was being the biggest nuisance possible, the old lady told herself guiltily. Why must that dratted mouse arrive in her bedroom on Christmas Eve?

In the silence that had fallen there was the unmistakable click of a mousetrap. Mary leaped to her feet.

"Thank God!" said Mrs. Berry in all seriousness. Panic seized her once more. "Don't let me see it, Mary, will you? I can't bear to see their tails hanging down."

"I'll bring the whole thing down in the wastepaper basket," promised Mary.

But when she returned to the apprehensive

old lady waiting below, she had nothing in her hand.

"He took a nibble and then got away," she said. "We'll have to wait a bit longer. I've set it a mite finer this time."

"I wish you had a braver mother," said Mrs. Berry forlornly. Mary smiled at her, and her mother's heart turned over. The girl looked ten years younger when she smiled. She didn't smile enough, that was the trouble. Time she got over Bertie's loss. There was a time for grieving, and a time to stop grieving. After all, she was still young and, smiling as she was now, very pretty too.

Conversation lapsed, and the two tired women listened to the little intimate domestic noises of the house, the whispering of the flames, the hiss of a damp log, the rattle of the loose-fitting window. Outside, the rain fell down pitilessly. Mrs. Berry wondered if the rolled-up towel was stemming the flood at the back door but was too tired to go and see.

She must have dozed, for when she looked at the clock it was almost eleven. Mary was sitting forward in her chair, eyes fixed dreamily on the fire, miles away from Shepherds Cross.

She stirred as her mother sat up.

"I'll go and see if we've had any luck."

Up the stairs she tiptoed once more, and returned almost immediately. She looked deathly pale with tiredness, and Mrs. Berry's heart was moved.

"Still empty. He's a fly one, that mouse. What shall we do?"

Mrs. Berry took charge with a flash of her old energy and spirit.

"You're going to bed, my girl. You're about done in, I can see. I'll stay down here for the night, for go up to that bedroom I simply cannot do!"

"But, Mum, it's such a beast of a night! You'd be better off in bed. Just wake me if the trap springs and I'll come and see to it. It's no bother, honest."

"No, Mary, you've done more than enough, and tomorrow's a busy day. I'll be all right here in the armchair. 'Tisn't the first time I've slept downstairs, and the storm don't trouble me."

Mary looked doubtfully at the old lady but could see that her mind was made up.

"All right then, Mum. I'll go and fetch your eiderdown and pillow, and see you've got enough firing handy."

Yet again she mounted the stairs, while Mrs. Berry made up the fire and bravely went to have a quick look at the towel by the back door. No more water had seeped in, so presumably the defenses were doing their work satisfactorily. She returned to the snug living room to find Mary plumping up the pillow.

"Now, you're sure you're all right?" she asked anxiously. "If I hear that trap go off before I get to sleep, shall I call you?"

"No, my dear. You'll be asleep as soon as your

head hits the pillow tonight. I can see that. I shall settle here and be perfectly happy."

Mary retrieved the pillowcases, kissed her mother's forehead, and went to the staircase for the last time that night.

"Sleep well," she said, smiling at her mother, who by now was wrapped in the eiderdown. "You look as snug as a bug in a rug, as the children say."

"Good night, Mary. You're a good girl," said her mother, watching the door close behind her daughter.

Nearly half-past eleven, thought Mrs. Berry. What a time to go to bed! Ten o'clock was considered quite late enough for the early risers of Shepherds Cross.

She struggled from her wrappings to turn off the light, and to put a little small coal on the back of the fire. The room was very pretty and cosy by the flickering firelight. There was no sound from upstairs. All three of them, thought Mrs. Berry, would be asleep by now, and that wretched mouse still making free in her own bedroom, no doubt.

Ah well, she was safe enough down here, and there was something very companionable about a fire in the room when you were settling down for the night.

She turned her head into the feather-filled pillow. Outside the storm still raged and she could hear the rain drumming relentlessly upon the roof and the road. It made her own comfort doubly satisfying.

God pity all poor travelers on a night like this, thought Mrs. Berry, pulling up the eiderdown. "There's one thing: I shan't be awake long, storm or no storm."

She sighed contentedly and composed herself for slumber.

Chapter Five

Christmas Eve and twelve of the clock . . .
                              —*Thomas Hardy*

BUT, tired though she was, Mrs. Berry could not get to sleep. Perhaps it was the horrid shock of the mouse, or the unusual bustle of Christmas that had overtired her. Whatever the reason, the old lady found herself gazing at the rosy reflection of the fire on the ceiling, her mind drifting from one inconsequent subject to the next.

The bubbling of rain forcing its way through the crack of the window reminded her of the more ominous threat at the back door. Well, she told herself, that towel was standing up to the onslaught when she looked a short while ago. It must just take its chance. In weather like this, usual precautions were not enough. Stanley would have known what to do. A rolled-up towel wouldn't have been good enough for him! Some sturdy carpentry would have made sure that the back door was completely weatherproof.

Mrs. Berry sighed and thought wistfully of their

manless state. Two good husbands gone, and no sons growing up to take their place in the household! It seemed hard, but the ways of God were inscrutable and who was to say why He had taken them first?

She thought of her first meeting with Stanley, when she was nineteen and he two years older. She had been in service then at the vicarage. Her employer was a predecessor of Mr. Partridge's, a bachelor who held the living of Fairacre for many years. He was a vague, saintly man, a great Hebrew scholar who had written a number of learned commentaries on the minor prophets of the Old Testament. His parishioners were proud of his scholarship but, between themselves, admitted that he was "only nine-pence in the shilling" when it came to practical affairs.

Nevertheless, the vicarage was well run by a motherly old body who had once been nurse to a large family living in a castle in the next county. This training stood her in good stead when she took over the post of housekeeper to the vicar of Fairacre. She was methodical, energetic and abundantly kind. When a vacancy occurred for a young maid at the vicarage, Mrs. Berry's parents thought she would be extremely lucky to start work in such pleasant surroundings. They applied for the post for their daughter, then aged thirteen.

Despite her lonely upbringing in the gamekeeper's cottage, Amelia Scott, as she was then, was a friendly child, anxious to help and blessed with plenty of common sense. The housekeeper realized her worth, and trained her well, letting her help in the kitchen as well as learning the secrets of keeping the rest of the establishment sweet and clean.

She thrived under the old lady's tuition, and learned by her example to respect the sterling qualities of her employer. He was always ready to help his neighbors, putting aside his papers to assist anyone in trouble, and welcoming all — even the malodorous vagrants who "took advantage of him," according to the housekeeper — into his study to give them refreshment of body and spirit.

One bright June morning, when the dew sparkled on the roses, Amelia heard the chinking of metal on stone, and leaned out of the bedroom window to see two men at work on one of the buttresses of St. Patrick's church. The noise continued all the morning, and as the sun rose in the blue arc of a cloudless sky, she wondered if the master would send her across with a jug of cider to wash down the men's dinners, as he so often did. Then she remembered that he was out visiting at the other end of the parish. The housekeeper too was out on an errand. She was choosing the two plumpest young fowls, now running about in a neighbor's chicken run, for the Sunday meal.

Amelia was helping Bertha, the senior housemaid, to clean out the attics when they heard the ringing of the back-door bell.

"You run and see to that," said Bertha, her arms full of derelict pillows. "I'll carry on here."

Amelia sped downstairs through the shadows

and sunlight that streaked the faded blue carpet, and opened the back door.

A young man, with thick brown hair and very bright dark eyes, smiled at her apologetically.

He held his left hand, which was heavily swathed in a red spotted handkerchief, in his right one, and dark stains showed that he was bleeding profusely.

"Been a bit clumsy," he said. "My tool slipped."

"Come in," said Amelia, very conscious that she was alone to cope with this emergency. She led the way to the scullery and directed the young man to the shallow slate sink.

"Put your hand in that bowl," she told him, "and I'll pump some water. It's very pure. We've got one of the deepest wells in the parish."

It was certainly a nasty gash, and the pure water,

so warmly recommended by Amelia, was soon cloudy with blood.

"Keep swilling it around," directed Amelia, quite enjoying her command of the situation, "while I get a bit of rag to bandage it."

"There's no need, miss," protested the young man. "It's stopping. Look!"

He held out the finger, but even as he did so, the blood began to well again. Amelia took one look and went to the bandage drawer in the kitchen dresser. Here, old pieces of linen sheeting were kept for just such an emergency, and the housekeeper's pot of homemade salve stood permanently on the shelf above.

No one quite knew what the ingredients of this cure-all were, for the recipe's secret was jealously guarded, but goose grease played a large part in it, along with certain herbs that the old lady gathered from the hedgerows. During the few years of Amelia's residence at the vicarage she had seen this salve used for a variety of ailments, from chilblains to the vicar's shaving rash, and always with good results.

She returned now with the linen and the pot of ointment. The young man still smiled, and Amelia smiled back.

"Let me wrap it up," she said. "Let's put some of this stuff on first."

"What's in it?"

"Nothin' to hurt you," Amelia assured him. "It's good for everything. Cured some spots I had on my chin quicker 'n lightning."

"I don't believe you ever had spots," said the young man gallantly. He held out the wounded finger, and Amelia twisted the strip round and round deftly, cutting the end in two to make a neat bow.

"There," she said with pride, "now you'll be more comfortable."

"Thank you, miss. You've been very kind."

He picked up the bloodied handkerchief.

"Leave that here," said Amelia, "and I'll wash it for you."

"No call to trouble you with that," said the young man. "My ma will wash it when I get back."

"Blood stains need soaking in cold water," Amelia told him, "and the sooner the better. I'll put it to soak now, then wash it out."

"Well, thank you. We're working on the church for the rest of the week. Can I call in tomorrow to get it?"

Amelia felt a glow of pleasure at the thought of seeing him again so soon. She liked his thick hair, his quick eyes, and his well-tanned skin — a proper nut-brown man, and polite too. Amelia looked at him with approval.

"I'll be here," she promised.

"My name's Berry," said the young man. "Stanley Berry. What's yours?"

"Amelia Scott."

"Well, thank you, Amelia, for a real good job. I must be getting back to work or I'll get sacked."

She watched him cross the garden in the shim-

111

mering heat, the white bandage vivid against the brown background of his skin and clothes. He paused in the gateway leading to the churchyard, waving to her.

Delighted, she waved back.

"You've taken your time," grumbled Bertha, when she returned to the attic. She looked at Amelia's radiant face shrewdly.

"Who'd you see down there? Prince Charming?"

Amelia forbore to answer, but thought that Bertha seemed to have guessed correctly.

The next morning the young man called to collect his handkerchief. Amelia had washed and ironed it with extreme care, and had put it carefully on the corner of the dresser to await its owner.

He carried a bunch of pink roses, and at the sight of them Amelia felt suddenly shy.

"You shouldn't have bothered," she began, but the young man hastily put her at ease.

"My ma sent them, to thank you for what you did, and for washing the handkerchief. She said you're quite right. She'd have had the devil's own job to get out the stain if I'd left it till evening."

Amelia took the bunch and smelled them rapturously.

"Please to thank her for them. They're lovely. I'll put them in my room."

Stanley gave her a devastating smile again.

"I picked them," he said gently.

"Then, thank you too," said Amelia, handing over the handkerchief.

112

They stood in silence for a moment, gazing at each other, loath to break the spell of this magic moment.

"Best be going," said Stanley, at length. He gave a gusty sigh, which raised Amelia's spirits considerably, and set off, stuffing the handkerchief in his pocket. He had not gone more than a few steps when he halted and turned.

"Can I come again, Amelia?"

"*Please*," said Amelia, with rather more fervor than a well-bred young lady should have shown. But then Amelia always spoke her mind.

There was no looking back, no hesitation, no lovers' quarrels. From that first meeting they trod a smooth, blissfully happy path of courtship. They were both even-tempered, considerate people, having much the same background and, most important of all, the same sense of fun. There were no family difficulties, and the wedding took place on a spring day as sunny as that on which they had first met.

They lived for the first few years at Beech Green, in a small cottage thatched by Dolly Clare's father, who was one of their neighbors. The first two girls were born there, and then the house at Shepherds Cross was advertised to let. It was considerably bigger than their first house, and although it meant a longer cycle ride for Stanley, this did not deter him.

Here Mary was born. They had hoped for a boy this time, but the baby was so pretty and good that the accident of her sex was speedily forgotten.

Amelia and Stanley were true homemakers. Amelia's early training at the vicarage had given her many skills. She could make frocks for the children, curtains, bedspreads, and rag rugs as competently as she could make a cottage pie or a round of shortbread. The house always looked as bright as a new pin, and Stanley saw to it that any stonework or woodwork was in good repair. They shared the gardening, and it was Mrs. Berry's pride that they never needed to buy a vegetable.

The longing for a son had never left Amelia. She liked a man about the place, and it was doubly grievous when Stanley died so suddenly. She lost not only her lover and husband, but the comfort of all that a shared life meant.

Mary's Bertie brought back to the cottage the feeling of comfort and reliability. The birth of her grandson had meant more to Mrs. Berry than she cared to admit. It was the continuance of male protection that subconsciously she needed. The baby's early death was something she mourned as deeply as Mary and Bertie had.

A piece of wood fell from the fire, and Mrs. Berry stirred herself to reach for the tongs and replace it. Not yet midnight! She seemed to have been lying there for hours, dreaming of times passed.

Poor Stanley, poor Bertie, poor baby! But what a blessing the two little girls were! Mary knew how to bring up children. Plenty of fun, but no nonsense when it came to doing as they were told. Say what you will, thought old Mrs. Berry, it didn't do people any harm to have a little discipline. You could cosset them too much, and give in to their every whim, and what happiness did that bring?

She remembered neighbors in the early days of her marriage at Beech Green. They were an elderly pair when their first child arrived, a pale sickly little fellow called, much to the ribaldry of some of the Beech Green folk, Clarence.

The baby was only put out into the garden on the warmest days, and then he was so swaddled in clothes that his normally waxen complexion was beaded with perspiration. The doctor harangued the doting mother; friends and neighbors, genuinely concerned for the child's health, proffered advice. Nothing was of any avail. Clarence continued to be smothered with love.

Not surprisingly, he was late in walking and talking. When he was at the toddling stage, his mother knitted him a long pair of reins in scarlet wool, and these were used in all his walks abroad. Mrs. Berry herself had seen the child tethered by these same red reins to the fence near the back door, so that his mother could keep an eye on him as she worked.

He was a docile child, too languid to protest against his restrictions and, never having known freedom, he accepted his lot with a sweet meekness that the other mothers found pathetic.

Clarence reached the age of six, still cosseted,

still adored, still forbidden the company of rough playmates who might harm him. But one bleak December day he fell ill with some childish infection that a normal boy would have thrown off in a day or two. Clarence drooped and died within the week, and the grief of the parents was terrible to see.

Poor Clarence and his red reins! thought Mrs. Berry, looking back over the years. She thought of him as "the sweet dove" that died, in Keats' poem. Long, long ago she had learned it, chanting with the other children at the village school, and still, seventy years on, she could remember it.

I had a dove, and the sweet dove died;
And I have thought it died of grieving:
Oh, what could it grieve for? Its feet were tied
With a silken thread of my own hand's weaving;
Sweet little red feet! Why should you die —
Why should you leave me, sweet bird, why?
You lived alone in the forest tree,
Why, pretty thing, would you not live with me?
I kissed you oft and gave you white peas;
Why not live sweetly, as in the green trees?

Yes, that was Clarence! "Tied with a silken thread" of his poor mother's weaving. The stricken parents had moved away soon after the tragedy, and very little was heard of them, although someone once said that the mother had been taken to the madhouse, years later, and was never fit to be released.

Thank God, thought Mrs. Berry, turning her pillow, that children were brought up more sensibly these days. She thought of Mary's two vivacious daughters, their glossy hair and round pink cheeks, their exuberance, their inexhaustible energy. Well, they were quiet enough at the moment, though no doubt they would wake early and fill the house with their excitement.

Mrs. Berry rearranged the eiderdown, turned her cheek into the pillow, and, thanking God for the blessing of a family, fell asleep at last.

Chapter Six

Wee, sleekit, cow'rin' tim'rous beastie!
O what a panic's in thy breastie!
—*Robert Burns*

AN UNACCUSTOMED SOUND woke the old lady within an hour. She slept lightly these days, and the stirring of one of her granddaughters or the mewing of a cat was enough to make her instantly alert.

She lay listening for the sound again. The wind still moaned and roared outside, the rain pattered fitfully against the windowpane, and the fire whispered as the wood ash fell through the bars of the grate.

It was a metallic noise that had roused her. What could it be? It might possibly be caused by part of the metal trellis which she and Mary had erected against the front porch to aid the growth of a new rose. Could it have blown loose?

But she could have sworn that the sound was nearer at hand, somewhere inside the house. It was not the welcome click of the mousetrap at its work. Something downstairs . . .

She sat upright in the chair. The fire had burned very low, and she leaned forward to put a little more wood on it, taking care to make no noise. Her ears strained for a repetition of the sound.

Now she thought she could hear a slight scuffling noise. A bird? Another mouse? Her heart began to beat quickly. And then the tinny sound again, as though a lid were being lifted from a light saucepan, or a cake tin. Without doubt, someone was in the kitchen!

Mrs. Berry sat very still for a minute. She felt no fear, but she was cautious. She certainly did not intend to rouse the sleeping family above. Whoever it was, Mrs. Berry felt quite capable of coping with him. Some rough old tramp probably, seeking a dry billet from the storm and, if left alone, on his way before the house stirred at daybreak. Mrs. Berry began to feel justifiable annoyance at the thought of some wastrel making free with her accommodation, and, what was more to the point, rifling the larder.

She bent to pick up the poker from the hearth. There was only one chance in ten that she would need to use it, but it was as well to be armed. It gave her extra confidence, and should the man be so silly as to show fight, then she would lay about her with energy and leave him marked.

Tightening her dressing-gown cord round her ample waist, Mrs. Berry, poker in hand, moved silently to the door of the living room. This door, then a short passage, and then the kitchen door needed to be negotiated before she came face to face with her adversary. Mrs. Berry determined to take the obstacles at a rush, catching the intruder before he had a chance to make his escape.

For one brief moment, before she turned the doorknob, the battered face of an old woman swam into Mrs. Berry's mind. The photograph had been given pride of place in the local paper only that week, and showed the victim of some young hooligans who had broken into her pathetic home to take what they could. Well, Mrs. Berry told herself sturdily, such things might happen in a town. It wouldn't occur in a little homely place like Shepherds Cross! She had dealt with plenty of scoundrels in her day, and knew that a stout heart was the best defense against bullies. Right would always triumph in the end, and no good ever came of showing fear!

She took a deep breath, a firmer grip on the poker, and flung open the door. Four quick determined steps took her to the kitchen door. She twisted the knob, and pushed the door open with her foot.

There was a stifled sound, something between a sob and a scream, a scuffle, and an unholy clattering as a large tin fell upon the tiles of the kitchen floor.

Mrs. Berry switched on the light with her left hand, raised the poker menacingly in her right, and advanced upon her adversary.

Upstairs, Jane stirred. She lay still for a minute or two, relishing the warmth of her sister's back against hers, and the deliciously warm hollow in which her cheek rested.

Then she remembered, and sat up. It was just light enough to see that the two empty pillowcases had vanished. She crept carefully out of bed, and went to the foot. There on the floor stood two beautiful knobbly pillowcases, and across each lay an equally beautiful striped stocking.

He had been! Father Christmas had been! Wild excitement was followed by a wave of shame. And she had not seen him! She had fallen asleep, after all her resolutions! It would be a whole year now before she could put Tom Williams' assertions to the test again. She shivered in the cold draft that blew under the door.

Her hands stroked the bulging stocking lovingly. There was the tangerine, there were the sweets, and this must be a dear little doll at the top. If only morning would come! She did not intend to undo the presents now. She would wait until Frances woke.

She crept back to bed, shivering with cold and excitement. She thrust her head into the hollow of her pillow again, leaned back comfortably against her sister, sighed rapturously at the thought of joys to come, and fell asleep again within a minute.

Mrs. Berry's stern gaze, which had been directed to a point about six feet from the ground, at a height where her enemy's head should reasonably have been, now fell almost two feet to rest upon

a pale, wretched urchin dressed in a streaming wet raincoat.

At his feet lay Mrs. Berry's cake tin, luckily right way up, with her cherished Madeira cake exposed to the night air. The lid of the cake tin lay two yards away, where it had crashed in the turmoil.

"*Pick that up!*" said Mrs. Berry in a terrible voice, pointing imperiously with the poker.

Sniveling, the child did as he was told, and put it on the table.

"*Now the lid!*" said Mrs. Berry with awful emphasis. The boy sidled nervously towards it, his eyes fixed fearfully upon the menacing poker. He retrieved it and replaced it fumblingly, Mrs. Berry watching the while.

The floor was wet with footmarks. The sodden towel had been pushed aside by the opening door. Mrs. Berry remembered with a guilty pang that she had forgotten to lock the door amidst the general excitement of Christmas Eve.

She looked disapprovingly at the child's feet, which had played such havoc upon the kitchen tiles. They were small, not much bigger than Jane's, and clad in a pair of sneakers that squelched with water every time the boy moved. He had no socks, and his legs were mauve with cold and covered with goose pimples.

Mrs. Berry's motherly heart was smitten, but no sign of softening showed in her stern face. This boy was nothing more than a common housebreaker and thief. A minute more and her beautiful Madeira cake, with its artistic swirl of angelica across the top, would have been demolished — gulped down by this filthy ragamuffin.

Nevertheless, one's Christian duty must be done.

"Take off those shoes and your coat," commanded Mrs. Berry, "and bring them in by the fire. I want to know more about you, my boy."

He struggled out of them, and picked them up in a bundle in his arms. His head hung down and little droplets of water ran from his bangs down his cheeks.

Mrs. Berry unhooked the substantial striped roller towel from the back of the door and motioned to the boy to precede her to the living room.

"And don't you dare to make a sound," said Mrs. Berry in a fierce whisper. "I'm not having everyone woken up by a rapscallion like you."

She prodded him in the back with the poker and followed her reluctant victim to the fireside.

He was obviously completely exhausted and was about to sink into one of the armchairs, but Mrs. Berry stopped him.

"Oh, no you don't, my lad! Dripping wet, as you are! You towel yourself dry before you mess up my furniture."

The boy took the towel and rubbed his soaking hair and wet face. Mrs. Berry studied him closely. Now that she had time to look at him, she saw that the child was soaked to the skin. He was dressed in a T-shirt and gray flannel shorts, both dark with rainwater.

"Here, strip off," commanded Mrs. Berry.

"Eh?" said the boy, alarmed.

"You heard what I said. Take off those wet clothes. Everything you've got on."

The child's face began to pucker. He was near to tears.

"Lord, boy," said Mrs. Berry testily, "I shan't look at you. In any case, I've seen plenty of bare boys in my time. Do as you're told, and I'll get you an old coat to put on while your things dry."

She stood a chair near the fire and hung the child's sodden coat across the back of it. His small sneakers were placed on the hearth, on their sides, to dry.

The boy slowly divested himself of his wet

clothing, modestly turning his back towards the old lady.

She thrust more wood upon the fire, looking at the blaze with satisfaction.

"Don't you dare move till I get back," warned Mrs. Berry, making for the kitchen again. An old duffel coat of Jane's hung there. It should fit this skinny shrimp well enough. Somewhere too, she remembered, a pair of shabby slippers, destined for the next jumble sale, were tucked away.

She found them in the bottom of the shoe cupboard and returned to the boy with her arms full. He was standing shivering by the fire, naked but for the damp towel round his loins.

He was pathetically thin. His shoulder blades stuck out like little wings, and every rib showed. His arms were like sticks, his legs no sturdier, and they were still, Mrs. Berry noticed, glistening with water.

"Sit down, child," she said, more gently, "and give me that towel. Seems you don't know how to look after yourself."

He sat down gingerly on the very edge of the armchair, and Mrs. Berry knelt before him rubbing energetically at the skinny legs. Apart from superficial mud, Mrs. Berry could see that the boy was basically well cared for. His toe nails were trimmed, and his scarred knees were no worse than most little boys'.

She looked up into the child's face. He was pale with fatigue and fright, his features sharp, the nose prominent; his small mouth, weakly open, disclosed two slightly projecting front teeth. Mouselike, thought Mrs. Berry, with an inward shudder, and those great ears each side of the narrow pointed face added to the effect.

"There!" said Mrs. Berry. "Now you're dry. Put your feet in these slippers and get this coat on you."

The child did as he was told in silence, fumbling awkwardly with the wooden toggle fastenings of the coat.

"Here, let me," said Mrs. Berry, with some exasperation. Deft herself, she could not abide awkwardness in others. The boy submitted to her ministrations, holding up his head meekly, and gazing at her from great dark eyes as she swiftly fastened the top toggles.

"Now pull that chair up close to the fire, and stop shivering," said Mrs. Berry briskly. "We've got a lot to talk about."

The boy did as he was bidden, and sat with his hands held out to the blaze. By the light of the fire, Mrs. Berry observed the dark rings under the child's eyes and the open drooping mouth.

"Close your mouth and breathe through your nose," Mrs. Berry told him. "Don't want to get adenoids, do you?"

He closed his mouth, swallowed noisily, and gave the most appallingly wet sniff. Mrs. Berry made a sound of disgust, and struggled from her chair to the dresser.

"Blow your nose, for pity's sake!" she said, offering him several paper handkerchiefs. He blew noisily, and then sat, seemingly exhausted by the effort, clutching the damp tissue in his skinny claw.

"Throw it on the back of the fire, child," begged Mrs. Berry. "Where on earth have you been brought up?"

He looked at her dumbly and, after a minute, tossed the handkerchief towards the fire. He missed and it rolled into the hearth by the steaming sneakers. Mrs. Berry suddenly realized that she was bone tired, it would soon be one o'clock, and that she wished the wretched child had chosen some other house to visit at such an hour. Nevertheless, duty beckoned, and she girded herself to the task.

"You know what you are, don't you?" she began. The boy shook his head uncomprehendingly.

"You are a burglar and a thief," Mrs. Berry told him. "If I handed you over to the police, you'd get what you deserve."

At this the child's dark eyes widened in horror.

"Yes, you may well look frightened," said Mrs. Berry, pressing home the attack. "People who break into other people's homes and take their things are nothing more than common criminals and have to be punished."

"I never took nothin'," whispered the boy. With a shock, Mrs. Berry realized that these were the first words that she had heard him utter.

"If I hadn't caught you when I did," replied Mrs. Berry severely, "you would have eaten that

cake of mine double quick! Now wouldn't you?
Admit it. Tell the truth."

"I was hungry," said the child. He put his two
hands on his bare knees and bent his head. A
tear splashed down upon the back of one hand,
glittering in the firelight.

"And I suppose you are still hungry?" observed
Mrs. Berry, her eyes upon the tear that was now
joined by another.

"It's no good piping your eye," she said
bracingly, "though I'm glad to see you're sorry.
But whether 'tis for what you've done, or simply
being sorry for yourself, I just don't know."

She leaned forward and patted the tear-wet
hand.

"Here," she said, more gently, "blow your nose

again and cheer up. I'll go and get you something to eat, although you know full well you don't deserve it." She struggled from her chair again.

"It won't be cake, I can tell you that," she told him flatly. "That's for tea tomorrow — today, I suppose I should say. Do you realize, young man, that it's Christmas Day?"

The boy, snuffling into his handkerchief, looked bewildered but made no comment.

"Well, what about bread and milk?"

A vision of her two little granddaughters spooning up their supper — days ago, it seemed, although it was only a few hours — rose before her eyes. Simple and nourishing, and warming for this poor, silly, frightened child!

"Thank you," said the boy. "I likes bread and milk."

She left him, still sniffing, but with the second paper handkerchief deposited on the back of the fire as instructed.

"Not a sound now," warned Mrs. Berry, as she departed. "There's two little girls asleep up there. And their ma. All tired out and need their sleep. Same as I do, for that matter."

She cut a thick slice of bread in the cold kitchen. The wind had not abated, although the rain seemed less violent, Mrs. Berry thought, as she waited for the milk to heat. She tidied the cake tin away, wondering whether she would fancy the cake at teatime after all its vicissitudes. Had those grubby paws touched it, she wondered?

She poured the steaming milk over the bread

cubes, sprinkled it well with brown sugar and carried the bowl to the child.

He was lying back in the chair with his eyes shut, and for a moment Mrs. Berry thought he was asleep. He looked so defenseless, so young, and so meekly mouselike, lying there with his pink-tipped pointed nose in the air, that Mrs. Berry's first instinct was to tuck him up in her dressing gown and be thankful that he was at rest.

But the child struggled upright, and held out his skinny hands for the bowl and spoon. For the first time he smiled, and although it was a poor, wan thing as smiles go, it lit up the boy's face and made him seem fleetingly attractive.

Mrs. Berry sat down and watched him attack the meal. It was obvious that he was ravenously hungry.

"I never had no tea," said the child, conscious of Mrs. Berry's eyes upon him.

"Why not?"

The boy shrugged his shoulders. "Dunno."

"Been naughty?"

"No."

"Had too much dinner then?"

The child gave a short laugh.

"Never get too much dinner."

"Was your mother out then?"

"No."

The boy fell silent, intent upon spooning the last delicious morsels from the bottom of the bowl.

"I don't live with my mother," he said at last.

"With your gran?"

"No. A foster mother."

Mrs. Berry nodded, her eyes never moving from the child's face. What was behind this escapade?

"Where have you come from?" she asked.

The boy put the empty bowl carefully in the corner of the hearth.

"Tupps Hill," he answered.

Tupps Hill! A good two or three miles away! What a journey the child must have made, and in such a storm!

"Why d' you want to know?" said the boy, in a sudden panic. "You going to send the police there? They don't know nothin' about me runnin' off. Honest! Don't let on, madam, please, madam!"

The "madam" amused and touched Mrs. Berry. Was this how he had been told to address someone in charge of an institution, or perhaps a lady magistrate at some court proceedings? This child had an unhappy background, that seemed certain. But why was he so scared of the police?

"If you behave yourself and show some sense," said Mrs. Berry, "the police will not be told anything at all. But I want to know more about you, young man."

She picked up the bowl.

"Would you like some more?"

"Can I?" said the child eagerly.

"Of course," said Mrs. Berry, resting the bowl on one hip and looking down at the boy.

"What's your name?"

"Stephen."

"Stephen what?"

"It's not my foster mother's name," said the boy evasively.

"So I imagine. What is it though?"

"It's Amonetti. Stephen Amonetti."

Mrs. Berry nodded slowly, as things began to fall into place.

"So you're Stephen Amonetti, are you? I think I knew your dad some years ago."

She walked slowly from the room, sorting out a rag bag of memories, as she made her way thoughtfully towards the kitchen.

Chapter Seven

Some brittle sticks of thorn and briar
Make me a fire
Close by whose living coal I sit
And glow like it . . .

—*Robert Herrick*

AMONETTI!

Pepe Amonetti! She could see him now, as he had first appeared in Beech Green during the final months of the last war. He was a very young Italian prisoner of war, barely twenty, and his dark curls and sweeping black eyelashes soon had all the village girls talking.

He was the youngest of a band of Italian prisoners allotted to Jesse Miller, who then farmed a large area at Beech Green. He was quite irrepressible, bubbling over with the joy of living — doubling relishing life, perhaps, because of his short time on active service.

As he drove the tractor, or cleared a ditch, or slashed back a hedge, he sang at the top of his voice, or chattered in his pidgin English to any passer-by.

The girls, of course, did not pass by. The string of compliments, the flashing glances, the expressive hands, slowed their steps. Pepe, with his foreign beauty, stood out from the local village boys like some exotic orchid among a bunch of cottage flowers. In theory, he had little spare time for such dalliance. In practice, he managed very well, with a dozen or more willing partners.

The young lady most in demand at Beech Green at that time was a blonde beauty called Gloria Jarvis.

The Jarvises were a respectable couple with a string of flighty daughters. Gloria was one of the youngest, and had learned a great deal from her older sisters. The fact that the air base nearby housed several hundred eager young Americans generous with candy, cigarettes and nylon stockings had hastened Gloria's progress in the art of making herself charming.

As was to be expected, "them Jarvis girls" were considered by the upright members of the community to be "a fair scandal, and a disgrace to honest parents." Any man, however ill-favored or decrepit, was reckoned to be in danger from their wiles, and as soon as Pepe arrived at Beech Green it was a foregone conclusion that he would fall prey to one of the Jarvis harpies.

"Not that he'll put up much of a fight," observed one middle-aged lady to her neighbor. "Got a roving eye himself, that lad."

"Well," replied her companion indulgently, "you knows what these foreigners are! Hot blooded. It's all that everlasting sun!"

"My Albert was down with bronchitis and chilblains all though the Italian campaign," retorted the first lady. "No, you can't blame the climate for their goings-on. It's just that they're made that way, and them Jarvis girls won't cool their blood, that's for sure."

It was not long before Pepe's exploits, much magnified in conversations among scandalized matrons, were common knowledge in the neighborhood, and it was Gloria Jarvis who was named as being the chief object of his attentions.

Gloria may have lost her heart to Pepe's Latin charms, but she did not lose her head. An Italian prisoner of war had little money to spend on a girl, and Gloria continued to see a great deal of her American admirers who spent more freely. Those of them who knew about Pepe dismissed the affair good-naturedly. Gloria was a good-time girl, wasn't she? So what?

Pepe, on the other hand, resented the other men's attentions, and became more and more possessive as time went by. He certainly had more hold over the wayward Gloria than his rivals, and though she tossed her blond Edwardian coiffure and pretended indifference, Gloria was secretly a little afraid of Pepe's passion.

The war ended in 1945, a few months after their first meeting, and Pepe elected to stay on in England as a farm worker. By this time, a child was on the way, and Gloria and Pepe were married at the registry office in Caxley.

Their first child, a girl, had Pepe's dark good looks. A blond boy, the image of his mother, appeared a year later, and the family began to be accepted in Beech Green. Pepe continued to work for Jesse Miller and to occupy one of his cottages.

For a few years all went well, and then Pepe vanished. Gloria and the two children had a hard time of it, although Jesse Miller kindheartedly allowed them to continue to live in the cottage. It was during these difficult days that Mrs. Berry had got to know Gloria better.

She was vain, stupid and a slattern, but she was also abandoned and in despair. Mrs. Berry helped her to find some work at a local big house, and now and again looked after the children to enable Gloria to go shopping or to visit the doctor. The old Jarvises were dead, by now, and the older sisters were little help.

Mrs. Berry showed Gloria how to make simple garments for the children, taught her how to knit and, more useful still, how to choose the cheap cuts of meat and cook them so that a shilling would stretch to its farthest limit.

Happily married herself, Mrs. Berry urged Gloria to find Pepe and make it up, if only for the sake of the family. But it was two years before the errant husband was traced, and another fifteen months before he could be persuaded to return.

He had found work in Nottingham, and came back to Beech Green just long enough to collect Gloria and the children, their few poor sticks of furniture and their clothes. They left for Nottingham one gray December day, but Pepe had found

time to call at Mrs. Berry's and to thank her for all she had done.

Handsomer than ever, Pepe had stood on her doorstep, refusing to come in, his eyes shy, his smile completely disarming. No one, least of all Mrs. Berry, could have remained hostile to this winning charmer with his foreign good manners.

"I did nothing — no more than any other neighbor," Mrs. Berry told him. "But now it's your concern, Pepe. You see you treat her right and make a fresh start."

"Indeed, yes. I do mean to do that," said Pepe earnestly. He thrust his hand down inside his greatcoat and produced a ruffled black kitten, which he held out to Mrs. Berry with a courtly bow.

"Would you please to accept? A thank you from the Amonettis?"

Mrs. Berry was taken aback but rallied bravely. She knew quite well that the kitten was their own, and that they could not be bothered to take it with them to their new home. But who could resist such a gesture? And who would look after the poor little waif if she did not adopt it?

She took the warm furry scrap and held it against her face.

"Thank you, Pepe. I shall treasure it as a reminder of you all. Good luck now, and mind my words."

For some time after this Mrs. Berry heard nothing of the Amonettis. The kitten, named Pepe after its donor, grew up to be a formidable mouser and was much loved by the Berry family. Years later, someone in Caxley told Mrs. Berry that Pepe had vanished yet again, and that Gloria had returned to live with a sister in the county seat twenty miles away. Whilst there, she had had one last brief reconciliation with Pepe, but within a week there had been recriminations, violence and police action. After this, Pepe had vanished for good, and it was generally believed that this time he had returned to Italy.

The outcome of that short reunion must be Stephen, Mrs. Berry thought to herself, as she stood in her drafty kitchen preparing the boy's meal. Gloria's present circumstances she knew from hearsay. She continued to live in one room of her sister's house and was what Mrs. Berry still thought of as "a woman of the streets." No wonder that the boy had been taken into the care of the local authority. His mother, though to be pitied in some ways, Mrs. Berry told herself charitably, was no fit person to bring up the boy, and heaven above knows what the conditions of the sister's house might be! Those Jarvis girls had all been first-class sluts, and no mistake!

Mrs. Berry picked up the tray and carried it back to the fireside.

The child's smile was stronger this time.

"You are very kind," he said, with a touch of his father's grace, reaching hungrily for the food.

She sat back in the armchair and watched the boy. Now that he had eaten and was getting warm, the pinched look, which sharpened his mouselike features, had lessened. His cheeks glowed pink and his lustrous dark eyes glanced about the room as he became more relaxed. Given time, thought Mrs. Berry, this boy could become as bewitching as his father. But, at the moment, he was unhappy. What could have sent the child out into such a night as this? And furthermore, what was to be done about it?

Mrs. Berry bided her time until the second bowl-ful had vanished, then took up the poker. The boy looked apprehensive, but Mrs. Berry, ignoring him, set the poker about its legitimate business of stirring the fire into a blaze, and then replaced it quietly.

"Now," she said, in a businesslike tone, "you can just explain what brings you into my house

139

at this time of night, my boy."

There was a long pause. In the silence, the clock on the mantel shelf struck two and a cinder clinked into the hearth. The wind seemed to have shifted its quarter slightly, for now it had found a crevice by the window and moaned there as if craving for admittance.

"I'm waiting," said Mrs. Berry ominously. The boy's thin fingers fidgeted nervously with the toggle fastenings. His eyes were downcast.

"Not much to tell," he said at last, in a husky whisper.

"There must be plenty," replied Mrs. Berry, "to bring you out from a warm bed on Christmas Eve."

The child shook his head unhappily. Tears welled up again in the dark eyes.

"Now, that's enough of that!" said the old lady. "We've had enough waterworks for one night. If you won't tell me yourself, you can just answer a few questions. And I want the truth, mind!"

The boy nodded, and wiped his nose on the back of his hand. Mrs. Berry pointed in silence to the paper hankies beside him. Meekly, he took one and dried his eyes.

"You say you live at Tupps Hill?"

The child nodded.

"Who with?"

A look of fear crept over the mouselike face.

"You tellin' the police?"

"Not if you tell me the truth."

"I live at Number Three. With Mrs. Rose."

"Betty Rose? And her husband's Dick Rose, the roadman?"

"That's right."

Mrs. Berry digested this information, whilst the child took advantage of the lull in the interrogation to turn his shoes in the hearth. They were drying nicely.

Mrs. Berry tried to remember all she knew about the Roses. They had been married some time before her own girls, she seemed to recall, and Betty's mother had been in good service at Caxley. Other than that, she knew little about them, except that they were known to be a respectable honest pair and regular churchgoers. Dick Rose was a slow methodical fellow, who would never rise above his present job of road sweeper in Caxley, from what Mrs. Berry had heard.

"Any children?" she asked.

"Two!" replied the boy. He looked sulky. Was this the clue? Was the child jealous for some reason?

"How old?"

"Jim's eleven, two years older 'n me. Patsy's eight, nearly nine. A bit younger 'n me."

That would be about right, thought Mrs. Berry, trying to piece the past together from her haphazard memories, and the child's reluctant disclosures.

"You're lucky to live with the Roses," observed the old lady, "and to have the two children for company."

141

The boy gave a sniff, but whether in disgust or from natural causes it was impossible to say.

"You get on all right?"

"Sometimes. Patsy tags on too much. Girls is soppy."

"They've usually got more sense than boys," retorted Mrs. Berry, standing up for her own sex. "You notice it isn't Patsy who's run out into a storm and got into trouble."

The child stuck out his lower lip mutinously but said nothing. The drenched raincoat was now steaming steadily, and Mrs. Berry turned it on the back of the chair. The boy's thin T-shirt, which had been hanging over the fire screen, was now dry, and Mrs. Berry smoothed it neatly into shape on her knee before folding it.

"Patsy's got a watch," said the boy suddenly.

"Has she now?"

"So's Jim. They both got watches. Patsy and Jim."

"For Christmas, do you mean?"

"No, no!" said the child impatiently. "Patsy had hers in the summer, for her birthday. Jim had his on his birthday. Last month it was."

"They were lucky."

She waited for further comment, but silence fell again. The boy was clearly upset about something, some injustice connected with the watches, some grievance that still rankled. His fingers plucked nervously at a piece of loose cotton on the hem of the duffel coat. His face was thunderous. Pepe's Latin blood was apparent as his son sat there

142

brooding by the fire.

"They're their own kids, see?" said the boy, at length. "So they give 'em watches. I reckon my real mum'd give me one — just like that, if I asked her."

Light began to break through the dark puzzle in Mrs. Berry's mind.

"Do you know where she is?"

The child looked up, wide eyed with amazement.

"Course I do! She's with me auntie. I sees her once a month. She says she'll have me back, soon as she's got a place of her own. Ain't no room at auntie's, see?"

Mrs. Berry did see.

"I want to know more about these watches. When is your birthday?"

"Second of February."

"Well, you might be lucky too, and get a watch then."

"That's what *they* say!" said the boy with infinite scorn in his voice. His head was up now, his eyes flashing. The mouse had become a lion.

"If they means it," he went on fiercely, "why don't they let me have it for Christmas? That's what I asked 'em."

"And what did they say?"

"Said as there was too much to buy anyway at Christmas. Couldn't expect a big present like a watch. I'd 'ave to wait and see."

"Fair enough," commented Mrs. Berry. The Roses had obviously done their best to explain matters to the disappointed child.

"No, it ain't fair enough!" the child burst out. "Dad Rose, 'e gets extra money Christmastime — a bonus they calls it. *And* all his usual pay. They could easy afford one little watch. The other two 've got theirs. Why should I have to wait? I'll tell you why!"

He leaned forward menacingly. Mrs. Berry could see why Pepe had had such a hold over poor stupid Gloria Jarvis. Those dark eyes could be very intimidating when they flashed fire.

"Because I'm only the foster kid, that's why! They gets paid for havin' me with 'em, but they won't give me a watch, same as their own kids 've got. They don't care about me, that's the truth of it!"

The tears began to flow again, and Mrs. Berry handed him a paper hanky in silence. It was coming out now — the whole, sad, silly, simple little story. Soon she would know it all.

"I thought about it when I got to bed," sniffed Stephen Amonetti, mopping his eyes. "Soon as Jim was asleep, I crept out. They never heard me go. They was watching the telly. Never heard nothing. I knows the way."

"Where to?"

"Me mum, of course. She'd understand. I bet she'd give me a watch for Christmas, *and* let me stay with her too, if she knowed how I was feeling. Anyway, you wants your own folk at Christmas-time. I fair hates the Roses just now."

He blew his nose violently, threw the hanky to

the back of the fire as instructed, and flopped back in the chair, with a colossal shuddering sigh. The duffel coat fell apart, displaying his skinny bare legs. His hands drooped from the arms of the chair.

Mrs. Berry stooped to put another log on the fire, before beginning her lecture. That done, she settled back in the armchair.

"As far as I can see," she began severely, "you are a thoroughly silly, spoiled little boy."

She glanced across at her visitor and saw that she was wasting her breath.

Utterly exhausted, his pink mouse nose pointing towards the ceiling and pink mouse mouth ajar, Mrs. Berry's captive was deep in slumber.

Chapter Eight

For life, with all its yields of joy and woe,
And hope and fear . . .
    believe the aged friend . . .
Is just a chance o' the price
    of learning love . . .

—Robert Browning

UPSTAIRS in her drafty bedroom Mary stirred. Some faint noise had penetrated the thick folds of sleep that wrapped her closely. Too tired to open her eyes or to sit up, she tried bemusedly to collect her thoughts.

Could she have heard voices? She remembered that her mother was below. Perhaps she had turned on the little radio set for company, she told herself vaguely.

Should she go and inspect the mousetrap? The bed was seductively warm, her limbs heavy with sleep. To stir outside was impossible. Besides, she might wake the children as well as her mother.

Exhausted, she turned over, relishing the comfort of her surroundings after the bustle of the day. She began to slip back into unconsciousness, and her last remembrance of Christmas Eve was the sight of Ray Bullen's smile as he hoisted young Frances on to the bus.

146

With a feeling of warm contentment, Mary drifted back to sleep.

Old Mrs. Berry rearranged the eiderdown and put her tired head against the back of the chair. Through half-closed eyes she surveyed her visitor.

He was snoring slightly, and Mrs. Berry's maternal instinct made her want to approach the boy and quietly close his mouth. It was shameful the way some people let their children grow up to be mouth breathers — leading the way to all sorts of infections in later life, besides encouraging snoring, an unnecessary complication to a shared bedroom. Why, Mrs. Berry could recall, from when she was in service, many a shocking case among the gentry of couples agreeing to separate bedrooms simply on account of snoring!

However, on this present occasion, Mrs. Berry proposed to let sleeping dogs lie. The child was not her permanent responsibility. But Betty Rose ought to look into the matter herself, and quickly, before the habit grew worse.

Her thoughts hovered round the events that had led to the boy's presence under her roof. As far as she could judge, the boy was sensibly cared for by the Roses, who seemed to have tackled the child's grievance sympathetically.

There was no doubt in Mrs. Berry's mind that the child was far better off where he was than with that fly-by-night mother of his. As for thinking that she would have him back permanently to live with her — well, that was just wishful thinking on the child's part. The local authority would not allow that, especially in the sordid circumstances in which Gloria now appeared to live and work.

Stephen Amonetti! Mrs. Berry mused, her eyes still on her visitor. He would not be an easy child to bring up, with Pepe and Gloria as parents. She pitied the Roses, and commended them for having the pluck to take on this pathetic outcome of a mixed marriage. He would need a firm hand, and plenty of affection too, to right the wrongs the world had done him. It could not be easy for the Roses, trying to be fair to their own two and to fit this changeling into their family.

She remembered Pepe's quick jealousy of Gloria's earlier rivals. Plainly, this child was as quick to resentment as his father had been. She remembered the fury in those dark eyes as the boy spoke of the watches. That smouldering jealousy was a legacy from his Latin father. The thoughtlessness, culminating in the flight from home, careless of the feelings of others, was a legacy from his casual mother.

This boy was going to be a handful, unless someone pulled him to his senses, thought Mrs. Berry. The Roses, respectable people though they were, might well be too gentle with the child, too ineffectual, although they apparently were doing their best to cope with this cuckoo in their nest. After all, Dick Rose left home early in the morning and was late back at night. It would fall upon Betty's shoulders, this responsibility, and with two children of her own to look after the task might be too great for her.

The child had been thinking on the wrong lines for too long, Mrs. Berry told herself. He had harbored grievances, resented authority, and indulged in self-pity. The old lady, with the strong principles instilled by her Victorian upbringing, condemned such wrong-headedness roundly. That the child was the victim, to a certain extent, of his circumstances, she was ready to concede, but the matter did not end there. She was heartily sick of the modern theories that condoned wrongdoing on the grounds that the wrongdoers were to be pitied and not blamed.

Every individual, she firmly believed, had the freedom of choice between good and evil. If one were so wicked, or thoughtless, or plain stupid enough to choose to do evil, then one must be prepared to take the consequences. Children, naturally, had to be trained and helped to resist temptation and to choose the right path, but to consider them as always in the right, as so many people nowadays seemed to do, was to do them a disservice, thought old Mrs. Berry.

Her own children had been brought up with clear standards. Little Amelia Scott had learned the virtues early, from the plaque in the church extolling modesty and economy, from her upright parents, and from the strict but kindly teachings of the village schoolteachers, the Scriptures and the vicar of the parish. These stood her in good stead when she became a mother.

She had also been told of the things which were evil: lying, boasting, stealing, cruelty and loose living and thinking. It seemed to Mrs. Berry that in these days evil was ignored. Did modern parents and teachers think that by burying their heads in the sand, evil would vanish? It had to be faced today, as bravely as it always had been in the past. It was there, plain for all to see, in the deplorable accounts of murder, bloodshed, violence and exploitation appearing in newspapers and shown on every television screen. The trouble was, thought Mrs. Berry, that too often it was shrugged off as "an aspect of modern living," when it should have been fought with the sword of righteousness, as she and her generation had been taught to do.

It was a great pity that the seven deadly sins were not explained to the young these days. There, asleep in the chair, was the victim of one of them — Envy. Had he been brought up to recognize his enemies in time, young Stephen might have been safely asleep in his own bed, instead of lying there caught in a web of his own weaving.

For, one had to face it, Mrs. Berry told herself, this self-indulgence in envy and self-pity had led the boy to positive wrongdoing. He was, in the eyes of the law and all right-thinking people, a burglar and a would-be thief.

He was also guilty of disloyalty to the Roses, who were doing their best to bring him up. And he had completely disregarded the unhappiness this flight might cause them.

All this she intended to make clear to the child as soon as he awoke. But there was a further problem — a practical one. How could she get the child home again without involving her own family or the Roses?

Would they have missed him yet? Would they have rung the police? As soon as the child woke, she would try and find out the usual practice at night in the Roses' house. Would they on Christmas Eve have put the children's presents on their beds, as she and Mary had done? If so, would they have noticed that the boy was missing from their son's side?

All this must be discovered. Meanwhile, it was enough that the boy was resting. She too would close her eyes for a catnap. They both needed strength to face what was before them.

She dropped, thankfully, into a light doze.

The boy woke first. Bending to feel his drying shoes, he knocked the poker into the hearth. This small clatter roused the old lady.

She was alert at once, as she always was when she woke up, despite her age.

The clock stood at twenty minutes past three, and although the wind still moaned at the window, there seemed to be no sound of rain pattering on the pane. The worst of the storm appeared to be over.

Mrs. Berry felt the raincoat. It was practically dry. She carefully turned the sleeves inside out and rearranged the garment so that it had the full benefit of the fire's heat.

It was very cosy in the room. Refreshed by her nap, the old lady looked with approval at the two red candles on the mantelpiece waiting to be lit at teatime — today, Christmas Day, the day they had prepared for, for so long.

The Christmas tree sparkled on the side table. The paper chains, made by the little girls' nimble fingers, swayed overhead and the holly berries glimmered as brightly as the fire itself.

"Merry Christmas!" said Mrs. Berry to the boy.

"Thank you. Merry Christmas," he responded. "It don't seem like Christmas, somehow."

"I'm not surprised. You haven't made a very good start with it, have you?"

Stephen shook his head dismally.

"What's more," continued the old lady, "you've put your poor foster parents, and me, to a mint of worry and trouble, by being such a wicked, thoughtless boy."

"I'm sorry," said the child. There was something perfunctory about the apology which roused Mrs. Berry's ire.

"You *say* it," she said explosively, "but do you *mean* it? Do you realize that all this trouble stems from your selfishness? You've been given a good home, food, warmth, clothes, comfort, taken into a decent family, and how do you repay the Roses? You ask for something you know full well is too expensive for them to give you, and then you sulk because it's not forthcoming!"

The boy opened his mouth as though to protest

against this harangue, but Mrs. Berry swept on.

"You're a thoroughly nasty, mean-spirited little boy, eaten up with envy and jealousy, and if you don't fight against those things you're going to turn into a real criminal. You understand what I say?"

"Yes, but I never —"

"No excuses," continued Mrs. Berry briskly. "You see what your sulking and envy led you to — breaking into my house and helping yourself to my Madeira cake. Those are crimes in themselves. If you were a few years older, you could be sent to prison for doing that."

The child suddenly bent forward and put his head in his hands. She could see that he was fighting tears, and remained silent, watching him closely, and hoping that some of her words of wisdom had hit their mark.

"Have you ever had a spanking?" she asked suddenly.

"Only from me real mum. She give me a clout now and again. The Roses don't hit none of us."

"They're good people, better than you deserve, I suspect. I warrant if you'd been my little boy, you'd have had a few smacks by now, to show you the difference between right and wrong."

There was a sniffing from the hidden face, but no comment. Mrs. Berry's tone softened.

"What you've got to do, my child, is to start afresh. You've seen tonight where wickedness and self-pity lead you. For all we know, Mr. and Mrs. Rose are distracted — their Christmas spoiled —

just because you must have your own way. And if they've told the police, then that's more people upset by your thoughtlessness.

"No, it's time you thought about other people instead of yourself. Time you counted your blessings, instead of making yourself miserable about things you covet. No selfish person is ever happy. Remember that."

The boy nodded, and lifted his head from his hands. His cheeks were wet, and his expression was genuinely penitent.

"What we've got to do now," said Mrs. Berry, "is to put things right as quickly and quietly as we can. Tell me, do you think the Roses will have missed you?"

The child looked bewildered.

"They don't never look in once they've tucked us up. They calls out, softlike, 'Good night,' when they goes to bed but don't open the door."

"Not even on Christmas Eve?" asked Mrs. Berry, broaching the subject delicately. Did the child still believe in Father Christmas? He had had enough to put up with this night, without any further painful disclosures.

"We has our presents on the breakfast table," said Stephen, catching her meaning at once. "And our stockings at teatime, when we light the candles on the Christmas tree."

"So they may not know you left home?"

"I don't see how they can know till morning."

"I see."

Mrs. Berry fell silent, turning over this fact in

her mind. There seemed to be every hope that the child was right. If so, the sooner he returned, and crept back to bed, the better. It seemed proper in her straightforward mind, that having done wrong the boy himself should put it right. She discounted the wrong done against herself and her own property, although she sincerely hoped that the child had learned his lesson. It was his attitude to his foster parents, and to all others with whom he must work and live, that must be altered.

"Do you go to church?" asked Mrs. Berry.

"To Sunday school. Sometimes we go to Evensong."

"Then you've heard about loving your neighbor."

The child looked perplexed.

"Is it a commandment? We had to learn ten of those once, off of the church wall, at Sunday school."

"It's another commandment: 'Love thy neighbor as thyself.' Do you understand what it means?"

The child shook his head dumbly.

"Well, it sums up what I've been telling you. Think about other people and their feelings. Consider them as much as you consider yourself. Put yourself in your foster parents' place, for instance. How would you feel if the boy you looked after was so discontented that he ran away, making you feel that you had let him down, when all the time you had been doing your level best to make him happy?"

The boy looked at his hands, and said nothing.

"You're going to go back, Stephen, and get into that house as quietly as you can, and get into bed. Can you do it?"

"Of course. The larder window's never shut. I've been in and out dozens of times."

"And you say nothing at all about what has happened tonight. It's a secret between you and me. Understand?"

"Yes," he whispered.

"There's no need for anyone to be upset by this, except you. I hope you'll have learned your lesson well enough to be cheerful and grateful for all that you are given, and all that's done for you, on Christmas Day. Do you promise that?"

The boy nodded. Then his eyes grew round, as he looked at Mrs. Berry in alarm.

"But s'pose they've found out?"

"I was coming to that," said the old lady calmly. "You tell them the truth, make a clean breast of it, and say you'll never do it again — and mean it, what's more!"

The child's eyes grew terrified.

"Tell them about coming in here?"

"Of course. And tell them I should like to see them, to explain matters."

"And the police?"

"If the police have been troubled, then you apologize to them too. You know what I told you. You must face the consequences whatever they are. This night should make you think in future, my boy, and a very good thing too."

156

She stood up, and moved to the window. Outside, the rain had stopped, but a stiff wind blew the ragged clouds swiftly across a watery moon, and ruffled the surface of the puddles.

It was a good step to Tupps Hill, but Stephen must be on his way shortly. Mrs. Berry was not blind to the dangers of the night for a young child walking the lanes alone, but it was a risk that had to be taken. At least the weather was kinder, the child's clothing was dry, and he had eaten and slept. He had got himself into this situation, and it would do him no harm, thought Mrs. Berry sturdily, to get himself out of it. In any case, the chance of meeting anyone abroad at half-past three on Christmas morning was remote.

"Put your clothes on," directed the old lady, "while I make us both a cup of coffee."

She left him struggling with the toggle fastenings as she went into the kitchen. When she returned with the steaming cups of coffee, the boy was lacing his shoes. He looked up, smiling. He was so like Pepe, in that fleeting moment, that the years vanished for old Mrs. Berry.

"Lovely and warm," Stephen said approvingly, holding up his feet.

Mrs. Berry handed him his cup, and offered the biscuit tin. As he nibbled his Ginger Nut with his prominent front teeth, Stephen's resemblance to a mouse was more marked than ever.

The old lady shuddered. Was her own little horror, the mouse, still at large above? Mrs. Berry craved for her bed. She was suddenly stiff and

bone-tired, and longed for oblivion. What a night it had been! Would the boy ever remember anything that she had tried to teach him? She had her doubts, but one could only try. Who knows? Something might stick in that scatterbrained head.

She motioned to the child to fetch his coat, turned the sleeves the right way out, and helped to button it to the neck. His chin was smooth and warm against her wrinkled hand, and reminded her with sudden poignancy of her own sleeping grandchildren.

She held him by the lapels of his raincoat, and looked searchingly into his dark eyes.

"You remember the promise? Say nothing, if they know nothing. Speak the truth if they do. And in future, do what's right and not what's wrong."

The child nodded solemnly.

She kissed him on the cheek, gently and without smiling. They went to the front door together, Mrs. Berry lifting a bar of chocolate from the Christmas tree as she passed.

"Put it in your pocket. You've a long way to go and may get hungry. Straight home, mind, and into bed. Promise?"

"Promise."

She opened the door quietly. It was fairly light, the moon partially visible through fast-scudding clouds. The wind lifted her hair and rustled dead leaves in the road.

"Good-bye then, Stephen. Don't forget what I've told you," she whispered.

"Good-bye," he whispered back.

He stood motionless for a second, as if wondering how to make his farewell, then turned suddenly and began the long trudge home.

Mrs. Berry watched him go, waiting for him to turn, perhaps, and wave. But the child did not look back, and she watched him walking steadily — left, right, left, right — until the bend in the lane hid him from her sight.

Chapter Nine

Two fieldmice, in a scale, weighed down just one copper halfpenny . . . so that I suppose they are the smallest quadrupeds in this island.

—Gilbert White

BACK IN THE WARM LIVING ROOM Mrs. Berry found herself swaying on her feet with exhaustion. She steadied herself by holding on to the back of the armchair that had been her refuge for the night.

It was years since she had felt such utter tiredness. It reminded her of the days when, as a young girl, she had helped with the mounds of washing at the vicarage. She had spent an hour or more at a time turning the heavy mangle — a monster of cast iron and solid wood — in the steamy atmosphere of the washhouse.

She looked now at her downy nest of feather pillow and eiderdown, and knew that if she sat down sleep would engulf her. She would be stiff when she awoke for every nerve and sinew in her old body craved for the comfort of her bed, with room to stretch her heavy limbs.

She would brave that dratted mouse! Ten chances to one it had made its way home again, and, in any case, she was so tired she would see and hear nothing once she was abed.

She glanced round the room. The fire must be raked through, and the two telltale coffee cups washed and put away. Mrs. Berry had no intention of telling Mary and the little girls about her visitor.

She put all to rights, moving slowly, her limbs leaden, her eyes half-closed with fatigue. She drew back the curtains, ready for the daylight, and scanned the stormy sky.

The moon was high now. Ragged clouds skimmed across its face, so that the glimpses of the wet trees and shining road were intermittent. The boy should be well on his way by now. She hoped that he had avoided the great puddles that silvered his path. Those shoes would be useless in this weather.

The old lady sighed, and turned back to the arm-chair, folding the eiderdown neatly and putting the plump pillow across it. Gathering up her bundle, she took one last look at the scene of her encounter with young Stephen. Then, shouldering her burden, she opened the door to the staircase and went, very slowly, to her bedroom.

Exhaustion dulled the terror that stirred her at the thought of the mouse still at large. Nevertheless, the old lady's heart beat faster as she quietly opened the bedroom door. The great double bed was as welcome a sight as a snug harbor to a storm-battered boat.

Mary had turned down the bedclothes. They

gleamed, smooth and white as a snowdrift, in the faint light of the moon.

The room was still and cool after the living room. Mrs. Berry stood motionless, listening for any scuffle or scratching that might betray her enemy. But all was silent.

She switched on the bedside lamp, which had been Mary's last year's Christmas present. It had a deep pink shade that sent a rosy glow into the room. The old lady replaced her pillow and spread out the eider down, then, nerving herself, she bent down stiffly to look under the bed and see if the intruder was still there.

All was as it should be. She scanned the rest of the floor, and saw the mousetrap. It was empty, and the second piece of cheese was still untouched.

Mrs. Berry's spirits rose a little. Surely, this might mean that the mouse had returned to his own home? He would either have been caught, or the cheese would have been eaten, as before. But the trap must not be left there, a danger to the grandchildren, who would come running in barefoot, all too soon, to show their tired grandmother the things that Father Christmas had brought.

Mrs. Berry took a shoe from the floor and tapped the trap smartly. The crack of the spring snapping made her jump but now all was safe. She could not bring herself to touch the horrid thing with her bare fingers, but prodded it to safety, under the dressing table, with her shoe.

Sighing with relief, the old lady climbed into

bed, drew up the bedclothes and stretched lux-
uriously.

How soon, she wondered, before Stephen
Amonetti would be enjoying his bed, as she did
now?

At the rate he was stepping out, thought Mrs.
Berry drowsily, he must be descending the long
slope that led to the fold in the downs at the foot
of Tupps Hill.

She knew that road well. The meadows on that
southern slope had been full of cowslips when little
Amelia Scott and her friends were children. She
could smell them now, warm and sweet in the
May sunshine. She loved the way the pale green
stalks grew from the flat rosettes of leaves, so like
living pen wipers, soft and fleshy, half hidden in
the springy grass of the downland.

The children made cowslip balls as well as bunches to carry home. Some of the mothers made cowslip wine, and secretly young Amelia grieved to see the beautiful flowers torn from their stalks and tossed hugger-mugger into a basket. They were too precious for such rough treatment, the child felt, though she relished a sip of the wine when it was made, and now tasted it again on her tongue, the very essence of a sunny May day.

On those same slopes, in wintertime, she had tobogganed with those same friends. She remembered a childhood sweetheart, a black-haired charmer called Ned, who always led the way on his homemade sled and feared nothing. He scorned gloves, hats, and all the other winter comforts in which loving mothers wrapped their offspring, but rushed bare-headed down the slope, his eyes sparkling, cheeks red, and the breath blowing behind him in streamers.

Poor Ned, so full of life and courage! He had gone to a water-filled grave in Flanders' mud before he was twenty years old. But the memory of that vivacious child remained with old Mrs. Berry as freshly as if it were yesterday that they had swept down the snowy slope together.

In those days a tumbledown shack had stood by a small rivulet at the bottom of the slope. It was inhabited by a poor, silly, old man, called locally Dirty Dick. He did not seem to have any steady occupation, although he sometimes did a little field work in the summer months, singling turnips, picking the wild oats from the farmers' standing corn, or making himself useful when the time came round for picking apples or plums in the local orchards.

The children were warned not to speak to him. Years before, it seemed, he had been taken to court in Caxley for some indecent conduct, and this was never forgotten. The rougher children shouted names after him and threw stones. The more gently nurtured, such as little Amelia, simply hurried by.

"You're not to take any notice of him," her mother had said warningly.

"Why not?"

A look of the utmost primness swept over her mother's countenance.

"He is sometimes a very *rude* old man," she said, in a shocked voice.

Amelia inquired no further.

His end had been tragic, she remembered. He had been found, face downwards, in the little brook, a saucepan in his clenched hand as he had dipped water to boil for his morning tea. The doctor had said his heart must have failed suddenly. The old man had toppled into the stream and drowned in less than eight inches of spring flood water.

Young Amelia had heard of his death with mingled horror and relief. Now she need never fear to pass that hut, dreading the meeting with "a very *rude* old man," whose death, nevertheless, seemed unnecessarily cruel to the soft-hearted child.

Well, Stephen Amonetti would have no Dirty

Dick to fear on his homeward way, but he would have the avenue to traverse, a frightening tunnel of dark trees lining the road for a matter of a hundred yards across the valley. Even on the hottest day, the air blew chill in those deep shadows. On a night like this, Mrs. Berry knew well, the wind would clatter the branches and whistle eerily. Stephen would need to keep a stout heart to hold the bogies at bay as he ran the gauntlet of those age-old trees.

But by then he would be within half a mile of his home, up the steep short hill that overlooked the valley. A small estate of council houses had been built at Tupps Hill, some thirty years ago, and though the architecture was grimly functional and the concrete paths gave an institutional look to the area, yet most of the tenants — countrymen all — had softened the bleakness with climbing wall plants and plenty of bright annuals in the borders.

The hillside position too, was enviable. The houses commanded wide views over agricultural land, the gardens were large and, with unusual forethought, the council had provided a row of garages for their tenants, so that unsightly, old shabby cars were screened from view. Those lucky enough to get a Tupps Hill house were envied by their brethren.

If only Stephen could get in unobserved! Mrs. Berry stirred restlessly, considering her visitor's chances of escaping detection. Poor little mouse! Poor little Christmas mouse! Dear God, please let him creep into his home safely!

And then she froze. Somewhere, in the darkness close at hand, something rustled.

Her first instinct was to snatch the eiderdown from the bed, and bolt. She would fly downstairs again to the safety of the armchair, and there await the dawn and Mary's coming to her rescue.

But several things kept her quaking in the warm bed. Extreme tiredness was one. Her fear that she would rouse the sleeping household was another. The day ahead would be a busy one, and Mary needed all the rest she could get. This was something she must face alone.

Mrs. Berry tried to pinpoint the position of the rustling. A faint squeaking noise made her flesh prickle. What could it be? It did not sound like the squeak of a mouse. The noise came from the right, by the window. Could the wretched creature be on the windowsill? Could it be scrabbling, with its tiny claws, on the glass of the windowpane, in its efforts to escape?

Mrs. Berry shuddered at the very thought of confronting it, of seeing its dreadful stringy tail, its beady eyes, and its more than likely darting to cover into some inaccessible spot in the bedroom.

All her old terrors came flying back, like a flock of evil black birds, to harass her. There was that ghastly dead mouse in her aunt's flour keg, the next one with all those pink hairless babies in her father's toolbox, the one that the boys killed in the school lobby, the pair that set up home once under the kitchen sink, and all those numberless little horrors that Pepe the cat used to bring in, alive and dead, to scare her out of her wits.

But somehow, there had always been someone to cope with them. Dear Stanley, or Bertie, or brave Mary, or some good neighbor would come to her aid. Now, in the darkness, she must manage alone.

She took a deep breath and cautiously edged her tired old legs out of bed. She must switch on the bedside lamp again, and risk the fact that it might stampede the mouse into flight.

Her fingers shook as she groped for the switch. Once more, rosy light bathed the room. Sitting on the side of the bed, Mrs. Berry turned round to face the direction of the rustling, fear drying her throat.

There was no sound now. Even the wind seemed to have dropped. Silence engulfed the room. Could she have been mistaken? Could the squeaking noise have been caused by the thorns of the rosebush growing against the wall? Hope rose. Immediately it fell again.

For there, crouched in a corner of the window-sill, was a tiny furry ball.

Old Mrs. Berry put a shaking hand over her mouth to quell any scream that might escape her unawares. Motionless, she gazed at the mouse. Motionless, the mouse gazed back. Thus transfixed, they remained. Only the old lady's heavy breathing broke the silence that engulfed them.

After some minutes, the mouse lifted its head and snuffed the air. Mrs. Berry caught her breath. It was so like Stephen Amonetti, as he had sprawled in the armchair, head back, with his pointed pink nose in the air. She watched the mouse, fascinated. It seemed oblivious of danger and sat up on its haunches to wash its face.

Its bright eyes, as dark and lustrous as Stephen's, moved restlessly as it went about its toilet. Its minute pink paws reminded Mrs. Berry of the tiny pink shells she had treasured as a child after a Sunday-school outing to the sea. It was incredible to think that something so small could lead such a full busy life, foraging, making a home, keeping itself and its family fed and cleaned.

And that was the life it must return to, thought Mrs. Berry firmly. It must go back, as surely as Stephen had, to resume its proper existence. Strange that two creatures, so alike in looks, should flee their homes and take refuge on the same night, uninvited, under her roof!

The best way to send this little scrap on its homeward journey would be to open the window and hope that it would negotiate the frail stairway of the rosebush trained against the wall, and so return to earth. But the thought of reaching over the mouse to struggle with the window catch needed all the courage that the old lady could muster, and she sat on the bed summoning her strength.

The longer she watched, the less frightened she became. It was almost like watching Stephen Amonetti all over again — a fugitive, defenseless, young, and infinitely pathetic. They both needed help and guidance to get them home.

She took a deep breath and stood up. The bedsprings squeaked, but the mouse did not take flight. It stopped washing its whiskers and gazed warily about it. Mrs. Berry, gritting her teeth, approached slowly.

The mouse shrank down into a little furry ball, reminding Mrs. Berry of a fur button on a jacket of her mother's. Quietly, she leaned over the sill and lifted the window catch. The mouse remained motionless.

The cold air blew in, stirring the curtain and bringing a breath of rain-washed leaves and damp earth.

Mrs. Berry retreated to the bed again to watch developments. She sat there for a full minute before her captive made a move.

It raised its quivering pink nose and then, in one bound, darted over the window frame, dragging its pink tail behind it. As it vanished, Mrs. Berry hurried to the window to watch its departure.

It was light enough to see its tiny shape undulating down the crisscross of thorny rose stems. But when it finally reached the bare earth, it was invisible to the old lady's eyes.

She closed the window carefully, sighed with

relief and exhaustion, and clambered, once more, into bed.

Her two unbidden visitors — her Christmas mice — had gone! Now, at long last, she could rest.

Behind the row of wallflower plants, close to the bricks of the cottage, scurried the mouse, nose twitching. It ran across the garden path, dived under the cotoneaster bush, scrambled up the mossy step by the disused well, turned sharp right through the jungle of dried grass beside the garden shed, and streaked, unerringly, to the third hawthorn bush in the hedge.

There, at the foot, screened by ground ivy, was its hole. It dived down into the loose sandy earth, snuffling the dear frowsty smell of mouse family and mouse food.

Home at last!

At much the same time, Stephen Amonetti lowered himself carefully through the pantry window.

The house was as silent as the grave, and dark inside, after the pallid glimmer of the moon's rays.

With infinite caution he undid the pantry door, and closed it behind him. For greater quietness, he removed his wet shoes and, carrying them in one hand, he ascended the staircase.

The smells of home were all about him. There was a faint whiff of the mince pies Mrs. Rose had made on Christmas Eve mingled, from the open door of the bathroom, with the sharp clean smell of Lifebuoy soap.

Noiselessly, he turned the handle of the bedroom door. Now there was a stronger scent — of the liniment that Jim used after football, boasting, as he rubbed, of his swelling muscles. The older boy lay curled on his side of the bed, dead to the world. It would take more than Stephen's entry into the room to wake him.

Peeling off his clothes, Stephen longed for bed, for sleep, for forgetfulness. Within three minutes, he was lying beside the sleeping boy, his head a jumble of cake tins, fierce old ladies, stormy weather, sore feet.

And somewhere, beyond the muddle, a hazy remembrance of a promise to keep.

Chapter Ten

Christians awake, salute the happy morn!
—*John Byrom*

IT WAS LIGHT when Mrs. Berry awoke. She lay
inert in the warm bed, relishing its comfort, as
her bemused mind struggled with memories of the
night.

The mouse and Stephen! What a double visi-
tation, to be sure! No wonder she was tired this
morning and had slept late. It must be almost eight
o'clock — Christmas morning too! Where were
the children? Where was Mary? The house was
uncommonly quiet. She must get up and investigate.

At that moment, she heard footsteps outside in
the road, and the sound of people greeting each
other. Simultaneously, the church bell began to
ring. Yes, it must be nearly eight o'clock, and those
good parishioners were off to early service!

Well, thought Mrs. Berry philosophically, she
would not be among the congregation. She rarely
missed the eight o'clock service, but after such

a night she would be thankful to go later, at eleven, taking the two little girls with her.

She struggled up in bed and gazed at the sky. It was a glory of gray and gold: streamers of ragged clouds, gilded at their edges, filled the world with a luminous radiance, against which the bare twigs of the plum tree spread their black lace.

She opened the window, remembering with a shudder the last time she had done so. Now the air, fresh and cool, lifted her hair. The bells sounded clearly, as the neighbors' footsteps died away into the distance.

"Awake then?" said Mary, opening the door. "Happy Christmas!"

She bore a cup of tea, the steam blowing towards her in the draft from the window.

"You spoil me," said Mrs. Berry. "I ought to be up. Proper old sleepyhead I am today. Where are the children?"

"Downstairs, having breakfast. Not that they want much. They've been stuffing sweets and the tangerines from their stockings since six!"

She put the cup on the bedside table and closed the window.

"They wanted to burst in here, but I persuaded them to let you sleep on. What happened to the mouse? Is it still about? I see the trap's sprung."

"I let it out of the window," said Mrs. Berry. She could not keep a touch of pride from her voice.

"You never! You brave old dear! Where was it then?"

"On the sill. I got so tired by about three, I risked it and came up. I don't mind admitting I fair hated reaching over the little creature to get at the latch, but it made off in no time, so that was all right."

"That took some pluck," said Mary, her voice warm with admiration. "Can I let those rascals come up now, to show you their presents?"

"Yes, please," said Mrs. Berry, reaching for her cup. "Then I'll get up, and give you a hand."

Mary called down the staircase, and there was a thumping of feet and squeals and shouts as the two excited children struggled upstairs with their loot.

"Look, Grandma," shouted Frances, "I've put on my slippers!"

"Look, Grandma," shouted Jane, "Father Christmas brought me a dear little doll!"

They flung themselves upon the bed, Mary watching them with amusement.

"Mind Gran's tea," she warned.

"Leave them be," said her mother lovingly. "This is how Christmas morning should begin!"

Smiling, Mary left the three of them and went downstairs.

On the door mat lay an envelope. Mary's heart sank, as she bent to pick it up. Not another person they'd forgotten to send to? Not another case of Mrs. Burton all over again? Anyway, it was too

175

late now to run about returning Christmas cards. Whoever had sent it must just be thanked when they met.

She took it into the living room and stood with her back to the fire, studying the face of the envelope with some bewilderment. Most of the cards were addressed to "Mrs. Berry and Family," or to "Mrs. Berry and Mrs. Fuller," but this was to "Mrs. Bertie Fuller" alone, and written in a firm hand.

Wonderingly, Mary drew out the card. It was a fine reproduction of "The Nativity" by G. van Honthorst, and inside, beneath the printed Christmas greetings, was the signature of Ray Bullen. A small piece of writing paper fluttered to the floor, as Mary, flushing with pleasure, studied the card.

She stooped to retrieve it. The message it contained was simple and to the point.

I have two tickets for the New Year's Eve concert at the Corn Exchange. Can you come with me? Do hope so!

RAY

Mary sat down with a thud on the chair recently vacated by young Jane. Automatically, she began stacking the girls' bowls sticky with cornflakes and milk. Her hands were shaking, she noticed, and she felt shame mingling with her happiness.

"Like some stupid girl," she scolded herself, "instead of a widow with two girls."

176

She left the crockery alone, and took up the note again. It was kind of him — typical of his thoughtfulness. Somehow, he had managed to write the card after seeing her yesterday, and had found someone in the village who would drop it through her letterbox on the way to early service. It must have taken some organizing, thought Mary, much touched. He was a good sort of man. Bertie had always said so, and this proved it.

As for the invitation, that was a wonderful thing to have. She would love to go and knew that her mother would willingly look after the children. But would she approve? Would she think she was being disloyal to Bertie's memory to accept an invitation from another man?

Fiddlesticks! thought Mary robustly, dismissing such mawkish sentiments. Here was an old friend offering to take her to a concert — that was all. It was a kindness that would be churlish to rebuff. Of course she would go, and it would be a rare treat too!

Calmer, she rose and began to take the dishes into the kitchen, her mind fluttering about the age-old problem of what to wear on such a momentous occasion. There was her black, but it was too funereal, too widowlike. Suddenly she wanted to look gay, young, happy — to show that she appreciated the invitation, she told herself hastily.

There was the yellow frock she had bought impulsively one summer day, excusing her extravagance by persuading herself that it was just the thing for the Women's Institute outing to the theater. But when the evening had arrived she had begun to have doubts. Was it, perhaps, too gay for a widow? Would the tongues wag? Would they say she was "after" someone? Mutton dressed as lamb?

She had put it back in the cupboard, and dressed herself in the black one. Better be on the safe side, she had told herself dejectedly, and had felt miserable the whole evening.

Yes, the yellow frock should have an airing, and her bronze evening shoes an extra shine. Ray Bullen should have no cause to regret his invitation.

She turned on the tap, as the children came rushing into the room.

"Why, Mummy," exclaimed Frances, wide eyed with amazement, "you're *singing!*"

Upstairs Mrs. Berry put on her gray woolen jumper and straightened the Welsh tweed skirt. This was her working outfit. Later in the morning she would change into more elegant attire, suitable for church-going, but there was housework to be done in the next hour or two. Last of all, she tied a blue and white spotted apron round her waist, and was ready to face the day.

Once more, she opened the window. The small birds chirped and chatted below, awaiting their morning crumbs. A gray and white wagtail teetered back and forth across a puddle, looking for all the world like a miniature curate, with his white collar and dove gray garments. The yellow winter jasmine starred the wall below, forerunner of the aconites and snowdrops soon to come. There was a hopeful feeling of spring in the air, decided Mrs. Berry, gazing at the sky. How different from yesterday's gloom!

The children's happiness was infectious. Their delight in the simple presents warmed the old lady's heart and set her thinking of that other child, less fortunate, who had no real family of his own and who had wept because of it.

How was he faring? Had he, after all, found a watch among his parcels? Mrs. Berry doubted it. The Roses had spoken truly when they told the child that a watch was too much to expect at Christmas. No doubt, lesser presents would make him happy, assuaging to some extent that fierce longing to have a watch like Patsy's and Jim's. A passionate child, thought Mrs. Berry, shaking her head sadly. Pepe all over again! It made life hard for the boy, and harder still for those who had to look after him. Would he ever remember any of the good advice she had tried to offer? Knowing the ways of children, she suspected that most of her admonitions had gone in one ear and out of the other.

Ah well! One could only hope, she thought, descending the staircase.

Mary had set a tray at the end of the table for her mother. Beyond it stood the pink cyclamen and a pile of parcels. The two children, hopping

179

from leg to leg with excitement, hovered on each side of the chair.

"Come on, Gran! Come and see what you've got. Mum gave you the plant!"

"Mary," exclaimed Mrs. Berry, hands in the air with astonishment, "you shouldn't have spent so much money on me! What a beauty! And so many buds to come out too. Well, I don't know when I've seen a finer cyclamen, and that's a fact."

She kissed her daughter warmly. Why, the girl seemed aglow! Christmas was a comforting time, for old and young, thought Mrs. Berry, reaching out for the parcels.

"Open mine first," demanded Frances.

"No, mine," said Jane. "I'm the oldest."

"I'll open them together," said the old lady, taking one in each hand. "See, I'll tear this bit off this one, then this bit off that one —"

She tugged at the wrappings gently.

"No, no!" cried Jane, unable to bear the delay. "Do one first — don't matter which — then the other. But read the tags. We wrote 'em ourselves."

Mrs. Berry held the two tags at arm's length. Her spectacles were mislaid amidst the Christmas debris.

" 'Darling Grandma, with love from Jane,' " she read aloud. She shook the parcel, then smelled it, then held it to her ear. The children hugged each other in rapture.

"Why do you listen to it?" queried Frances. "Do you think there's a bird in it?"

"A watch perhaps," said Mrs. Berry, surprised by her own words.

"*A watch?*" screamed the girls. "But you've got a watch!"

"So I have," said Mrs. Berry calmly. "Well, let's see what's in here."

Wrapped in four thicknesses of tissue paper was a little eggtimer.

"Now, *that*," cried the old lady, "is *exactly* what I wanted. Clever Jane!"

She kissed the child's soft cheek.

"Now mine!" begged Frances. "Quick! Undo it *quick*, Gran."

"I must read the tag. 'Dear Gran, Happy Christmas, Frances.' Very nice."

"*Undo it!*" said the child.

Obediently, the old lady undid the paper. Inside was a box of peppermint creams.

"My favorite sweets!" said Mrs. Berry. "What a kind child you are! Would you like one now?"

"Yes please," both said in unison.

"I hoped you'd give us one," said Frances, beaming. "Isn't it lucky we like them too?"

"Very lucky," agreed their grandmother, proffering the box.

"Let Gran have her breakfast, do," Mary said, appearing from the kitchen.

"But she's got lots more parcels to open!"

"I shall have a cup of tea first," said the old lady, "and then undo them."

Sighing at such maddening adult behavior, the two children retired to the other end of the table where they had set out a tiny metal tea set of willow pattern in blue and white.

"This is my favorite present," announced Frances, "and the teapot pours. See?"

Mary and her mother exchanged amused glances. The set had been one of several small toys they had bought together in Caxley to fill up the stockings. The chief present for each girl had been a doll, beautifully dressed in handmade clothes worked on secretly when the girls were in bed. It was typical of children the world over that some trifle of no real value should give them more immediate pleasure than the larger gifts.

At last, all the presents were unwrapped. Bath cubes, stockings, handkerchiefs, sweets, a tin of biscuits, another of tea, and a tablecloth embroidered by Mary — all were displayed and admired. Mary's presents had to be brought from the sideboard and shown to her mother, to please the two children, despite the fact that Mrs. Berry had seen most of them before.

"Now, what's to do in the kitchen?" asked Mrs. Berry, rising from the table.

"Nothing. The pudding's in, and the bird is ready, and the vegetables."

"Then I'll dust and tidy up," declared Mrs. Berry. "Upstairs first. I can guess what the girls' room looks like!"

"At least there are no mice!" laughed Mary.

The children looked up, alert.

"No mice? Was there a mouse? Where is it now?"

Their grandmother told them about the intruder, and how she had settled by the fire, but at last gone up to bed and had let the mouse out of the window.

What would they have said, she wondered, as she told her tale, if she had told them the whole story? How their eyes would have widened at the thought of a boy — a *big* boy of nine — breaking into their home and trying to steal their grandmother's Madeira cake! As it was, the story of the real mouse stirred their imagination.

"I expect it was hungry," said Jane with pity. "I expect it smelled all the nice Christmas food and came in to have a little bit."

"It had plenty of its own sort of food outdoors," Mrs. Berry retorted tartly.

"Perhaps it just wanted to see inside a house," suggested Frances reasonably. "You shouldn't have frightened it away, Gran."

"It frightened *me* away," said the old lady.

"Perhaps it will come back," said Jane hopefully.

"That," said her grandmother forcefully, "I sincerely hope it will not do."

And she went upstairs to her duties.

When the children and her mother had departed to church, the house was blessedly quiet. Mary, basting the turkey and turning potatoes in the baking dish, had time to ponder her invitation. As soon as the children were safely out of the way she would have a word with her mother, then reply.

But where should she send it? There had been no address on the note, and although she knew the part of Caxley in which Ray lived, she could not recall the name of the road, and certainly had no idea of the number. Perhaps the best thing would be to send it to the office of *The Caxley Chronicle*, where he worked. He would be going into work, no doubt, on the day after Boxing Day. Plenty of time to spare before New Year's Eve.

Now that the first initial surprise of the invitation was over, Mary found herself growing more and more delighted at the thought of the evening outing. Caxley had produced a New Year's Eve concert as long as she could remember, and she and Bertie had attended several of them.

The Corn Exchange was always full. It was something of an occasion. The mayor came, all the local gentry sat in the front rows, and everyone knew that the music provided would be good rousing stuff by Handel and Bach and Mozart, with maybe a light sprinkling of Gilbert and Sullivan, or Edward German, or Lionel Monckton, as a garnish.

It was definitely a social affair, when one wore one's best, and hoped to see one's friends and be seen by them. It would be good, thought Mary, to have a personable man as an escort instead of attending a function on her own.

Kind Ray! Good Quaker Ray! How did that passage go in the library book — "Very thoughtful and wealthy and good"? She could vouch for two of those virtues anyway!

She slammed the oven door shut and laughed aloud.

At one o'clock the Christmas dinner — everything done to a turn — was set upon the table, and the two little girls attacked their plates with enviable appetite. Their elders ate more circumspectly.

Nevertheless, at two o'clock it was the children who played energetically on the floor with their new toys, whilst Mary and her mother lay back in their armchairs and succumbed to that torpor induced by unaccustomed rich food.

"We must take a turn in the fresh air before it gets dark." Mrs. Berry yawned; Mary nodded agreement drowsily.

They woke at three, much refreshed, donned their coats and gloves, and set off. The bright clouds of morning had gone; a gentle gray light veiled the distant scene.

The four of them walked towards the slope where young Stephen had walked scarcely twelve hours earlier. Mrs. Berry's mind was full of memories of her Christmas visitor. She strode along, dwelling on the oddity of events that had brought one of the Amonetti family into her life once more.

Ahead of her, holding a child by each hand, Mary was running a few steps, then stopping suddenly to bring the two children face to face in an ecstatic embrace. It was a game they had loved as toddlers, but it was years, thought Mrs. Berry,

since Mary had played it with them.

Their delighted screams matched the calling of the flight of rooks above, slowly winging homewards against the evening sky.

Now they had reached the top of the slope, and Mary, breathless, stopped to wait for her mother.

They stood together looking across the shallow valley, already filling with the pale mist of winter.

"That's Tupps Hill over there, isn't it?" said Mary. Her mother nodded.

"D' you remember the Roses?"

"Vaguely," said Mary. "Why?"

There was an intensity about her mother's gaze that made Mary curious.

The old lady did not answer for a moment, her

186

eyes remained fixed upon the shadowy hill beyond the rising mist.

"I might call on them one day," she said, at last. "Not yet awhile. But some day — some day, perhaps." She turned suddenly. "Let's get home, Mary dear. There's no place like it — and it's getting cold."

Chapter Eleven

Dulce Domum

IT WAS HARDLY SURPRISING, at teatime, to find that the family's appetite was small, despite the afternoon walk.

"I'll just bring in the Christmas cake," said Mary, "and the tea tray. Though I expect you'd like a slice of your Madeira, wouldn't you?"

"No, thank you," replied Mrs. Berry hastily. "Nothing, dear, for me."

She pondered on the fate of the Madeira cake as Mary clattered china in the kitchen. It certainly seemed a terrible waste of sugar and butter and eggs, not to mention the beautiful curl of angelica that cost dear knows how much these days. But there it was. The thought of those pink paws touching it was enough to put anyone off the food.

Perhaps she could cut off the outside, and slice the rest for a trifle? Waste was something that Mrs. Berry abhorred. But at once she dismissed the idea. It was no good. The cake must go. No doubt the birds would relish it, but she must find an opportunity for disposing of it when Mary was absent from the scene. Explanations would be difficult, under the circumstances.

Mary returned with the tray. To the accompaniment of cries of appreciation from the children the candles were lighted on the Christmas tree and at each end of the mantelpiece.

Outside, the early dusk had fallen, and the shadowy room, lit by a score of flickering candle flames and the glow from the fire, had never looked so snug and magical, thought Mrs. Berry. If only their menfolk could have been with them . . .

She shook away melancholy as she had done so often. The time for grieving was over. There was much to be thankful for. She looked at Mary, intent upon cutting the snowy cake, and the rosy children, their eyes reflecting the light from the candles, and she was content.

And that child at Tupps Hill? Was he as happy as her own? She had a feeling that he might be — that perhaps he had been able to let the Christmas spirit soothe his anxious heart.

Jane's Christmas cracker had yielded a tiny spinning top that had numbers printed on it. When it came to rest, after being twirled on the table, the number that was uppermost gave the spinner his score. This simple toy provided part of the evening's play time, and all four played.

Later, Mrs. Berry played Ludo with the children

— a new game found in Frances' pillow slip —
while Mary wrote some thank-you letters. By
seven o'clock both children were yawning, although they did their best to hide this weakness
from the grown ups. It would be terrible to miss
anything on this finest day of the year.

"Bed," said Mary firmly, and as the wails
greeted her dictum, she relented enough to say:
"You can take your toys upstairs and play with
them for a little while."

Within half an hour, they were safely in bed,
and Mary and her mother sat down to enjoy the
respite from the children's clamor.

"Why, there's a new Christmas card!" exclaimed
Mrs. Berry, her eye lighting on Mary's from Ray.

Mary rose to fetch it from the mantelpiece and

handed it to her mother.

"Someone dropped it through the letterbox first thing this morning. I bumped into Ray yesterday when we were shopping and he helped us onto the bus with our parcels."

"Typical of the Bullens," commented Mrs. Berry, studying the card with approval. "I knew his mother when she was young. A nice girl."

Mary took a breath. This seemed as propitious a time as any other to mention the invitation.

"There is a note somewhere. He has asked me to go to the New Year's Eve concert. Would you mind? Looking after the girls, I mean?"

"Good heavens, no! I'm glad to think of you getting out a little. You'll enjoy an evening with Ray Bullen," said her mother easily.

Mrs. Berry leaned back in the chair and closed her eyes. It had been a long day, and she was near to sleep. A jumble of impressions, bright fragments of the last twenty-four hours, jostled together in her tired mind like the tiny pieces of colored glass in a child's kaleidoscope.

Stephen's mousey face, his pink hand spread like a starfish upon his knee, with a shining tear upon it. Her own shadow, poker in hand, monstrously large on the passage wall as she approached the unknown intruder. The furry scrap crouched on the windowsill with the wild weather beyond. Stephen's resolute back, vanishing round the bend of the lane as he marched home. The reflection of the candles in her grandchildren's eyes. The candles in the church — dozens of them today

— and the sweet clear voices of the choir boys.

She woke with a jerk. The clock showed that she had slept for ten minutes. Her last impression still filled her mind.

"It was lovely in church this morning," she said to Mary. "Flowers and candles, and the boys singing so sweetly. You should have come."

"I will next Sunday," Mary promised. "A New Year's resolution, Mum."

There was a quiet happiness about Mary that did not escape Mrs. Berry's eyes, but in her wisdom she said nothing.

Things, she knew in her bones, were falling, delicately and rightly, into place.

"I'll go and tuck up the girls," said Mrs. Berry, struggling from her chair, "and switch off their light."

She mounted the stairs and was surprised to see that both children were in her own room. They were kneeling on her bed, very busy with something on the windowsill.

They turned at her approach.

"We're just putting out a little supper for the Christmas mouse," explained Jane.

On the ledge was one of the doll's tin willow pattern plates. Upon it were a few crumbs of Christmas cake and one or two holly berries.

"They're apples for him," said Frances. "When people call you should always offer them refreshment, Mummy says."

Mrs. Berry remembered the steaming bowl of

bread and milk clutched against a duffel coat.

"She's quite right," she said, smiling at them. "But somehow I don't think that mouse will come back."

Stephen's dwindling figure, striding away, came before her eyes. The children looked at her, suddenly forlorn. She offered swift comfort.

"But I'm sure of one thing. That Christmas mouse will remember his visit here for the rest of his life."

The rising moon silvered the roofs at Shepherds Cross and turned the puddles into mirrors. The sky was cloudless. Soon the frost would come, furring the grass and hedges, glazing the cattle troughs and water butts.

Dick Rose, at Tupps Hill, was glad to get back to the fireside after shutting up the hens for the night.

The table had been pushed back against the wall, and the three children were crawling about the floor, engrossed in a clockwork train that rattled merrily around a maze of lines set all over the floor. Betty sat watching them, as delighted as they were with its bustling maneuvers.

"It's only fell off once," said Stephen proudly, looking up at his foster father's entrance.

"Good," said Dick. He never wasted words.

"Are you sad Father Christmas never brought you a watch?" asked Patsy of Stephen. Dick's eyes met his wife's.

Patsy was still young enough to believe in the

myth, and the boys had nobly resisted enlightening her.

Stephen turned dark eyes upon her.

"Never thought about it," he lied bravely. "I've got all this, haven't I?"

He picked up the little train, and held it, whirring, close to his face. He turned and smiled — the radiant warm smile of his lost father — upon his foster parents.

"You're a good kid," said Dick gruffly. "And your birthday ain't far off."

For the first time since Stephen's tempestuous arrival, he thought suddenly, the boy seemed part of the family.

There was a stirring beneath the third bush in the hawthorn hedge. A sharp nose pushed aside the ground-ivy leaves, and the mouse emerged into the moonlight.

It paused, sniffing the chill air, then ran through the dry grass by the shed, negotiated the mossy step by the wellhead, and stopped to nibble a dried seed pod.

On it ran again, parting the crisp grass with its sinuous body, diving down ruts, scrambling up slopes, until it gained the wet earth behind the wallflower plants.

Between the plants and the brick wall of the cottage it scampered, until it reached the foot of the rosebush, where it stopped abruptly. Far, far above it, lights glowed from the windows.

A tremor shook its tiny frame. Its nose and

whiskers quivered at the sense of danger, and it turned to double back on its tracks, away from the half-remembered terrors of an alien world.

It hurried out into the moonlight and made for the open field beyond the hawthorn hedge. There among the rimy grass and the sweet familiar scents, its panic subsided.

Nibbling busily, safely within darting distance of its hole, the Christmas mouse was at peace with its little world.